THE CHAINS OF HEAVEN

THE CHAINS OF HEAVEN

An Ethiopian Romance

PHILIP MARSDEN

HarperCollins*Publishers*

HarperCollins*Publishers*
77–85 Fulham Palace Road,
Hammersmith, London W6 8JB
www.harpercollins.co.uk

Published by HarperCollins*Publishers* 2005

3

A catalogue record for this book is
available from the British Library

ISBN-10 0 00 717347 4
ISBN-13 978 0 00 717347 1

Set in Linotype Granjon by
Rowland Phototypesetting Ltd, Bury St Edmunds, Suffolk

Printed and bound in Great Britain by Clays Ltd, St Ives plc

For my parents,
with love and gratitude

CONTENTS

ILLUSTRATIONS

All photographs © the author

GLOSSARY

Agawigna – language of the Agaw people

amba – flat-topped mountain, often used for monasteries, and in former times as prisons for the rebellious offspring of rulers

Amharic – first language of Ethiopia, language of the Amhara people

askari – Eritrean fighter; those who fought for the Italians

ayzore – 'be strong', expression of encouragement

azmari – traditional singer, often itinerant, performs *samenna worq* (q.v.)

bahtawi – hermit

belg – season of 'small' rains, March and April

berberi – dried and powdered red chilli pepper

bet – house

bilowa – butchery knife

birr – Ethiopian currency

bokra – large lemon-like fruit

buda – spirit capable of bodily possession

chai – tea

debenya – speckled pigeon (*Columba guinea*)

debtara – non-ordained church official, responsible for music and dancing, often expert in herbal lore

dejazmach – lit. 'guardian of the main gate', a traditional title of the nobility. Sometimes shortened to *dejach* or *dejmach*.

dula – stick carried by travelling highlanders

Derg – lit. 'committee', governed Ethiopia 1974–91, formerly the AFCC

ELF – Eritrean Liberation Front

EPDM – Ethiopian People's Democratic Movement

EPLF – Eritrean People's Liberation Front

EPRDF – Ethiopian People's Revolutionary Democratic Front (coalition of rebel movements that overthrew the Derg in 1991)

farenj – foreigner

fidal – syllabary of 252 characters used to write Amharic, Ge'ez and Tigrinya

fitawrari – pre-revolutionary military rank, roughly equivalent to colonel

gabbi – thick blanket of woven cotton, usually white, worn over the shoulders

Ge'ez – also known as Ethiopic, a Semitic language, the root of both Amharic and Tigrinya. Survives as the liturgical language of the Ethiopian Church

Gondarene – of the Gondar dynasty (sixteenth to eighteenth centuries)

gwaro – fields or tilled land close to the homestead

hejira – 'flight', exile of early Muslims

hidmo – homestead

hudadie – the fifty-six-day fast that precedes Easter

injera – flat bread made from *teff* (q.v.) flour

kebelle – administrative district

kebbero – large church drum, made from olive-wood with goatskin tympanum

keremt – the season of 'big' rains, roughly late June to early September

Kidane Mehret – 'covenant of mercy', Mary's agreement with God to offer redemption to sinners

kidassie – *hudadie* prayers, conducted in the hours after midday

kobe – skullcap of monks, nuns and priests

kolo – roasted corn

kuta – a double-layered dress worn on holy days

lamd – uncured skin used for sitting on rock

leiba shai – thief-seeker

maqdas – sanctuary of church in which the *tabot* (q.v.) is housed

masenqo – single-stringed instrument played with a bow, usually by *azmari* (q.v.)

memhir – abbot, head of Ethiopian monastery

MEISON – anti-Derg movement

migib – food

mihrab – niche in mosques indicating the direction of Mecca

nagarit – silver drum used by Ethiopian nobility

negus – Ethiopian king

qamis – monastic or eremitic robe

qene – church devotional poetry

qene mahalet – outer section of an Ethiopian church, for the laity

qola – lowlands

ras – high Ethiopian noble, roughly equivalent to prince

Sadqan – the Nine Saints, a group of fifth-century evangelists to Ethiopia credited with establishing monasticism in the country

samenna worq – lit. 'wax and gold', sung verses which rely for their effect on complex double meaning and layered references

shamma – loosely woven cotton shawl

Sheol – the underworld

shifta – bandit

shurro – a sauce of crushed beans, eaten on fasting days

sistra – (sing. *sistrum*) hand-held musical instrument of wood and brass. Makes a tinkling noise when shaken

tabot – sacred object at the centre of all churches, each a representation of the main *tabot* in Aksum, itself believed to be the Ark of the Covenant

teff – *Eragrostis abyssinia*, indigenous Ethiopian wheat, staple of the highlands

tella – beer brewed with barley and sometimes sorghum

Tigrinya – language of the Tigrayans, descended like Amharic from the Semitic Ge'ez

timat – a measurement of land area: the area that two oxen can plough in a day

tirumba – funereal horn

TLF – Tigrayan Liberation Front

TPLF – Tigrayan People's Liberation Front

tselot zezewota – daily prayer

usshi – a ubiquitous expression, meaning OK

washint – flute-like wooden pipe, played by shepherds

woreda – administrative district

wot – spicy sauce

Zagwe – dynasty of Ethiopian rulers (1137–1270)

zemecha – campaign conducted by the Derg immediately after the fall of Haile Selassie in which students and high-school pupils were sent to the villages to help organise the revolution

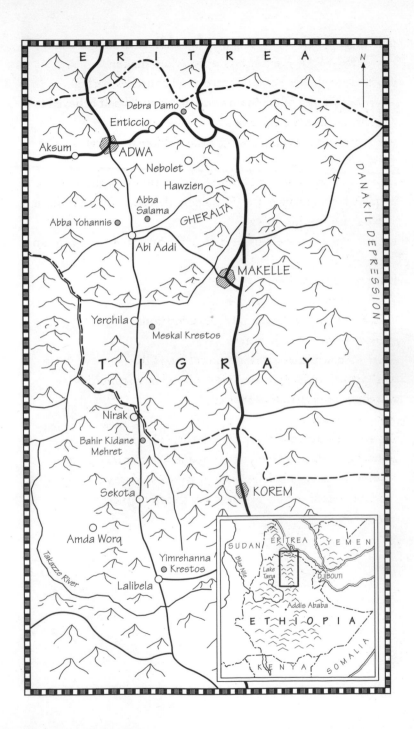

A Short History of Ethiopia

Aksumawi was the son of Ethiopis and the great-grandson of Noah. He established the kingdom of Aksum which is itself the ancestor of modern Ethiopia. Unfortunately a snake took power in Aksum and ruled for four hundred years. The snake was 170 cubits in length, had teeth a whole cubit long, and the people of Aksum had constantly to supply it with milk and virgins. One day a stranger came and slaughtered the snake. The stranger was called Angabo and he in turn became ruler of Aksum.

Angabo married the Queen of Sheba, and after he died she left the city of Aksum with 797 camels to visit Solomon in Jerusalem. There, with Solomonic guile, he seduced her. Back in Aksum she gave birth to a boy named Menelik, and when he came of age he journeyed to Jerusalem to see his father. When he left Jerusalem he had the Ark of the Covenant. With the Ark the blessing of the Lord was transferred from Jerusalem to Aksum, from the people of Israel to the people of Ethiopia. Menelik was the first of Ethiopia's line of Solomonic rulers.

1

The land around Aksum was very fertile and it came to be known among the world's peoples as a place of wondrous plenty. Every rock on its open plains was a loaf of bread. Once for eight days showers of gold and pearls and silver fell on its hills and filled the rivers with riches. Palaces and temples swelled the bounds of the city. The graves of its kings were marked by standing stones and with each passing king the stones grew higher until they scraped the underside of the sky.

In 1974, Ethiopia was still ruled by the 225th member of the Solomonic line. Emperor Haile Selassie was then an old man. On the morning of 12 September, Ethiopian New Year, some junior officers of the Derg came to his palace, read out a deposition order and took him away in the back of a Volkswagen.

Derg means 'committee' in Amharic. It was established as a small concession to the armed forces and ended up taking over the whole country. With the emperor gone, the Derg ruled from his palace. In the cellar below the throne room, they imprisoned about 150 men. They were members of the emperor's family, his generals, his government ministers and senior clerics. They were kept there for eight years. When the Derg met in the throne room, the prisoners below could look up from their dungeon and through gaps in the floorboards see the feet of the new rulers pacing back and forth.

1

When I was twenty-one, I went to Ethiopia for the first time. I had never been outside Europe, had never in fact been any further south or east than the top of Italy. Ethiopia amazed me. It shocked me, revolted me, awed and terrified me. It reawakened in me the childlike sense that the world was a vast, diverse and wonderful place – a sense that has remained ever since.

It was the early 1980s, and it was the rainy season. Billows of cloud half-covered the Entoto hills. From the airport the road entered Revolution Square beneath a triumphal arch which read, in English and Amharic: LONG LIVE PROLETAR-IAN INTERNATIONALISM! Marx, Lenin and Engels gazed out from a giant hoarding beside it, and I crossed beneath them. In a small Soviet-style block beyond the square, I reached the rain-streaked, plate-glass front of Wonderland Tours.

The door squeaked open on a darkened office. Sun-faded tourist posters were taped to the wall. A man in a goatskin chair stirred from his sleep, leapt up, gripped my hand in both of his, and grinned – as if the sight of a stranger in Wonderland Tours was itself a great joke.

Teklu was a Tigrayan. I had never come across anyone quite like him. He was no older than me but had the advantage of not having just spent his adolescence in a petulant daze. From the age of fourteen he had fought for the Tigrayan rebels. He had lived in caves, conducted night assaults, sprung ambushes. He had been captured, tortured and escaped. He then walked to Addis where another Tigrayan, Dr Mengesha, gave him a job and anonymity. Dr Mengesha owned Wonderland Tours. He was also an enthusiast, a lovely, grinning man in a dark suit who came jogging down the stairs from his office to greet me. 'Congratulations,' he said. 'Congratulations for coming to Ethiopia!' He sent me off with Teklu to find a hotel.

That afternoon in a flophouse near Giorgis cathedral Teklu and I lay on the twin beds and, while rain fell like gravel on the corrugated iron roof, I let him conjure up another country. He spoke of rock-cut churches among fairytale peaks, monasteries accessible only by rope or chain, treasures hidden in caves of gold and holy men who would vanish even as you talked to them. He spoke of his native Tigray and his own local town of Aksum where miracles happened every day and a caste of mute monks guarded the true Ark of the Covenant.

'If you try and get close,' he laughed, 'they kill you!'

'Can we go to Tigray?' I asked.

He politely shook his head.

The few expats in Addis were less forgiving: 'You're a damned idiot, boy – you come here expecting a nice little holiday. This country is a *living hell*!'

Over the coming days, it became obvious even to me. Addis Ababa was paralysed with fear. Not all the figures lying on the edge of the road were sleeping. The Red Terror, when thousands of counter-revolutionaries were shot, was over – but the disappearances and killings continued. Rumours of patrols swept through the shanty like the afternoon rains sending everyone scurrying for shelter. And over it all presided the man who gazed down from the wall of every office – Colonel Mengistu Haile-Mariam.

For days, Teklu and I did the rounds of ministries trying to get permission to travel. We met only the mumbles and head-shakes of frightened officials. After a week, I decided to cut my losses and return home. I went back to Wonderland Tours. Dr Mengesha was there. He heard out my story and saw my frustration.

'Ethiopia *is* a wonderful country, you know.'

I shrugged. I was in no mood to agree.

He tapped a pencil on his desk and said, 'Come back this afternoon at four.'

I still don't know what he did, nor why he chose to stick his neck out for a useless and ignorant *farenj*. But later that day he handed me an envelope and again said: 'Congratulations!' In it were all the right papers with all the right stamps. He spread out a map and explained our route. He took Teklu and me to the store and handed us a tent, a stove – and lifejackets. He was sending us to Lake Tana. Teklu grinned at me and winked. In that cowed city, Mengesha and Teklu seemed the only people who were truly alive.

So we did go north. We spent days on the lake, walking its bouldery shores, paddling from island to island on papyrus rafts, visiting monasteries. We watched the islanders spear catfish in the shallows. We asked when the last foreigners were there and they said: 'Never.' We almost drowned when a sudden storm caught us on the lake. 'It is a beautiful adventure!' Teklu was a man whose enjoyment grew in proportion to the level of danger.

Teklu and I exchanged letters for months afterwards. 'Dr Mengesha says hello and do not forget us.' How could I? Ethiopia had gripped me by the shoulders and shaken me awake. 'Not too many tourists these days,' Teklu wrote, without irony. He told me he had taken some Soviet bigwigs down the Omo river. A hippo overturned their boat. 'We had a beautiful adventure!' Then the letters stopped.

At the time few people were going to Ethiopia and I was able to indulge the illusion that I was something of an expert. I wrote about it, lectured about it, bored anyone who cared to listen. Ethiopia was my country. It was the central column of a shaky structure – life in my early and mid-twenties.

I went back a few years later. It was the rainy season again; torrents of water sluiced down Africa Avenue and into Revolution Square. LONG LIVE PROLETARIAN INTERNATIONALISM! was still there, as was the triumvirate of beards. I found myself again outside Wonderland Tours.

This time the plate-glass was daubed with swirls of white paint; traces of the name could just be read on the signboard. A paper seal covered the door and the jamb, with a purple ministry stamp. Wonderland Tours had gone. No one could tell me what had happened to Dr Mengesha or to Teklu.

After another three years I returned. I travelled in the south and east. I revisited Lake Tana and Gondar. But no arm-twisting, no amount of lobbying could yield permission to see Lalibela or Aksum or Tigray, to reach the mountaintop monasteries of the north, the rebel heart of the old country. Nor was anyone forthcoming about Dr Mengesha and Teklu. The country was still in Colonel Mengistu's grip, and I developed a perverse obsession with him. I listened to the whispered atrocities of war in Tigray and Eritrea, of the meetings when Mengistu himself would shoot his failing generals. I sought out dissidents, heard hinted fantasies of coup and assassination. But it was wishful thinking. I left Ethiopia sickened by its cruelty and torpor, convinced that Mengistu and the Derg would be in power for a generation or more.

For ten years I travelled. I roamed the Middle East and the regions of the old Soviet bloc. I never spent more than a few months in the same place. I found myself drawn to remote and restive minorities, to the passionate fringes of religious belief. I am convinced now that if I had not chosen Ethiopia, if I had not met Teklu, if Dr Mengesha had not procured the papers that afternoon in 1982, I would not have lived the life I have, would not have travelled quite so obsessively, and would never have begun to write.

All writing careers begin with a single sentence. Mine was: *Teklu was a Tigrayan.* (Actually it was *Telku waS a Tigtayam*, but a little Tipp-Ex remedied that.) I read it aloud – *Teklu was a Tigrayan* ... It had a natural rhythm. It had alliteration, a declarative simplicity. I pictured prizes, heard plaudits, projected the entire range of human experience flowing through my fingertips. It was a long time before I wrote another sentence. When after five years the sentence was finally published, Mengistu was still in power and it read, for Teklu's safety: *Yared was a Tigrayan.* The book that contained it was not a great success.

One spring I was in Armenia. Snow shone on the peaks of Zangezur, walnut trees were bursting into life and Grad missiles were falling on the town of Goris. The first of the post-Soviet wars was beginning – just as another was ending in the Horn of Africa. Mengistu's military machine had been propped up for years by the Soviet Union, but now his brand of hard-line Leninism was out of fashion. The removal of Moscow's support tipped the balance in the rebels' favour. In that crumbling southern corner of the Soviet Union I crouched in the doorways of makeshift shelters listening to their progress on a short-wave radio. The TPLF and its allies were fighting along the shores of Lake Tana, at Bahir Dar. They were marching on Addis Ababa. Their tanks were entering Revolution Square. Then they were firing on the Ghibbi, the palace where the Derg was making a final stand. Mengistu had fled.

Twelve years passed. I was involved in other places, pursuing other ideas. But Ethiopia was where it all began – and it was unfinished business. At the age of forty-two, I went back.

The arch had gone. Above the entrance to Revolution Square there was no more LONG LIVE PROLETARIAN INTERNATIONALISM! The hoarding of Marx, Lenin and Engels had been replaced by one which warned of the dangers of HIV/Aids. Stencilled on the plate-glass front of Wonderland Tours was the silhouette of a woman's head and: LUCY UNISEX HAIR SALON. The door opened on a late-afternoon hubbub of coiffurerie. The air was steamy with hair-washing. Along one wall ran a line of space-helmet driers; two or three white-coated women were giving manicures. But yes, this was the place – there was the mezzanine where Dr Mengesha had had his office; and that was where his wife Almaz sat doing the accounts. The back room had been the equipment store, where Mengesha had handed Teklu and me the equipment for Lake Tana. Now it was the Gentleman Salon.

'Sir, please. Haircut?' a man in a barber's coat asked.

'Thank you, I'm just looking.'

Under the stairs, in half-darkness, was the cashier's desk. A woman was sitting there. I could see her now more clearly. It was Almaz.

My heart was racing. 'You won't remember me, but I came here twenty-one years ago – when it was Wonderland Tours.'

She smiled. She didn't have a clue who I was.

But we went through to the Gentleman Salon and sat on a two-seater sofa. Almaz was wearing a sky-blue jacket. She placed her long fingers against her cheek. Before she married Mengesha she'd been an air hostess; it had been her face that had gazed out from posters of Ethiopian Airlines. The years had done little to her beauty.

I asked about Dr Mengesha.

'Mengesha? They came one night and took him.'

'Did they give a reason?'

'They did not need a reason.' Her voice was detached, distant. 'Just "against the revolution" – that was all they needed to say.'

A man brought us tea on a stainless steel tray.

Slowly Almaz sipped from her cup, then replaced it in the saucer. She eased into speaking. 'After Mengesha was taken, our son became very agitated. His school said to me, He is daydreaming, he cannot concentrate. So I thought if we could just see his father, it would be better. I went to the *kebelle*. I told them, Please, let me see my husband, you must let me see my husband . . .'

Her voice drifted off. She looked out through the open door.

'Did they let you?'

'We went to see him.'

'How was he?'

'The same old Mengesha! Joking and laughing. He was

telling me, Don't worry, Almaz, they are going to let me out very soon! He was so optimistic, always optimistic.

'After that my son was better. But I was still worrying. I was imagining all the time, what will happen to Mengesha? And I was becoming very afraid for my son. Most mothers are pleased when they see their sons growing. But I just thought, they will take him to the army or to prison. In the end, I had to send him away. I said he was my servant's son. They allowed him to go to the United States. It was many years before I saw him again.'

'What about Mengesha?'

'They moved him to another prison outside Addis. It took a long time before I could find out where it was. I used to go there with food – but I was not allowed to see him.'

A fat man in a suit came in, followed by the barber. The man took off his jacket and hung it on the coat rack. Braces swelled over his bell-shaped belly. The barber flicked open the folds of a towel and tied it around the man's neck. He leaned back in the chair and fell asleep.

'Then someone told me he was dead. But someone else said no, he was alive. I couldn't imagine Mengesha dead so I convinced myself he was coming back. When the house needed redecorating, I did it in the colours he liked. He loved his books, and I took each one of them and cleaned them. After the Derg went, they opened up the prisons. I waited at home for him to come.'

We could hear the scrape of the razor on the man's cheek. He was still sleeping.

'One day on television there was a list of names. They said they had found papers saying Dr Mengesha Gabre-Hiwot had been killed in prison. That was how I discovered, like that.'

She was silent for a moment. 'He loved this country. He

was so proud of Ethiopia. He just wanted people to see it – "wonderland", that's what he thought it was.'

Reminiscence had made her fluent. 'When I think of Mengesha now, I think of him always as an optimist. It made me afraid sometimes. It didn't matter under the emperor. But in the Derg time, well, it was dangerous. I told him, It's changed now, Mengesha, you cannot do that, not now. He just said, You must not worry, Almaz! He was always such an open man, so generous . . .

'You know, before we were married, and he was away in Europe or America, he would telephone me every day. I would tell him it was expensive – he should not telephone. All right, Almaz, he laughed – and then the next day he would telephone me again. That was how he was.'

'I know. What he did for me – it changed my life.'

We stood. We made our way to the front of the shop. As we

said goodbye, she cocked her head. 'I remember you now – you went on a bus, didn't you?'

'That's right. To Lake Tana.'

'Of course. No foreigners went on buses. I said to Mengesha, This is not safe. There will be trouble. He just told me not to worry!'

'What about Teklu, Almaz?'

'Teklu?'

'Teklu Abraham.'

'He escaped to Kenya,' she said. 'Walking.'

'Is he still there?'

'No, no. He went to America – I hear he has a liquor store in Denver, Colorado.'

2

Addis Ababa was always a dog city. You'd hear them at night, after curfew, ranging the empty streets in yelping packs. Sometimes there would be the sound of a military Jeep and the stutter of gunfire, but once it had gone, it left just the sound of the running dogs. It was said they were the guard dogs and pedigree pets of the old nobility – those families whom the revolution had chased abroad or imprisoned or shot. It was also said that during the Red Terror they had developed a taste for human flesh.

There were still stray dogs. But the years in between had levelled the pedigrees to a sort of uni-dog. The sounds of the night now were more varied – screeching cats, night traffic, and at dawn the sound of a dozen muezzin echoing through the city. The churches' amplified prayers began a little later.

One morning I revisited the Institute of Ethiopian Studies. I used to spend days up in the empty reading room, countering the fear and reticence of Addis with the enthusiasm of previous generations of travellers, historians and archaeologists. The institute was housed in the emperor's first palace. Under the Derg, Haile Selassie's private quarters were closed off, but now, at the end of a corridor behind the museum, I found myself in the empress's bedroom. Across the hall were the emperor's own rooms, and in his bathroom I met a man who for thirty years had worked as his valet.

Our voices echoed off the marble surfaces. Through the window, students went to and fro beneath the date palms. Mammo Haile had chaotic teeth, a hangdog expression, and an undimmed devotion to his master.

'Day and night His Majesty thought only about his people. He was always thinking how to develop them. I have such a deep emotion when I think of him.' Mammo Haile looked away. 'His Majesty had a special way with dogs. If we were travelling and he saw some stray dogs he would say, Mammo Haile, please round up those dogs! I want to give them breads. His Majesty's favourite dog was Lulu.'

I had seen a picture of Lulu sitting in the emperor's lap while he stroked her with his small, feminine hands. She was a tiny, frog-eyed Chihuahua.

'If there was a reception Lulu would go round among the legs of the officials. If one of them was holding a bad feeling about His Majesty, Lulu would touch the man's foot and that was how His Majesty knew. One minister was very popular but Lulu touched his foot and after that no one trusted that man again. Lulu was a very brilliant dog.'

'What happened to her?'

'Paul killed her.'

'Paul?'

'Big palace dog. Like a big fighter, like a wrestling man. He took Lulu by the neck and shook her and shook her. She was only a tiny dog – and *finito*! Lulu *finito*. Such a tiny little

14

dog.' He looked down, toeing the ground with his shoe. I thought he would cry.

'It was only a year or two after that when they took His Majesty away.'

During that first week back in Addis someone gave me the name of Dejazmach Zewde Gabre-Selassie, who had been a minister under both the imperial regime and the Derg. He was the great-grandson of Emperor Yohannis IV, and was now living with a friend while he tried to get his own house back. 'Wretched Derg confiscated it.'

Dejazmach Zewde was a charming, egg-shaped man with a marcel wave in his hair and a patrician manner. He had spent years as an academic in Oxford – 'I think my happiest years' – but a few months before the revolution, Haile Selassie had called him back to be Minister of the Interior.

'It was my job to deal with the Derg. At that time I have to say they were really pretty amateurish. Used to park a tank outside the ministry for meetings, that sort of thing. Once they came to me and demanded the release of political prisoners. I said to them, Do you mean a complete amnesty, or some sort of selective policy? And they said, We don't know.' The *dejazmach* laughed. 'They didn't know! Well, come back when you do, I told them, and they just sat there. Well? I said. We can't go back to barracks empty-handed. So I decided to call their bluff. Why not demand constitutional reform? Two weeks later they came back and said, We demand constitutional reform! So we appointed another committee to look at reform. Thought it might check the Derg's power. Trouble is, the Derg started to arrest that committee.'

'Did you know Mengistu?'

He nodded. 'First time I met Mengistu was at a big meeting I called with the Derg. He was just a low officer then. Fifty members came and the senior ones were sitting and the rest were standing. One of those standing held up his hand. Minister, please, what do you think of socialism? he says. Well, I told him, there are different shades of socialism. In England there is Fabian socialism and then you have Swedish-style socialism and at the other end Albanian socialism. So if you mean policies aimed at achieving equality, I would say yes – but in general I am not for socialism.'

'And that was Mengistu?'

'That was him, yes.'

'So what about the emperor?' I asked. 'Did you admire him?'

The *dejazmach* did not answer at once. He gazed up at the ceiling with such trance-like neutrality that I thought he hadn't heard.

'Earlier on, he was an astonishing figure. Decisive, effective, punctual. His greatest weakness was that he could not share power. I think that was it ... Yet right at the end he had an amazing calm. Everyone else was nervous and jumpy, but he was calm. Just before he fell, I went to see him. The Derg were pretty much in control by then. They'd shown the Jonathan Dimbleby film exposing the famine, and said on television that no one should go to the palace, none of the workers or retainers. I was really very upset by the film – on the emperor's behalf. So I went to see him. He was alone. The palace was completely empty. Just the two of us. He wanted to talk about foreign matters. I had just been in Iran and he said: So tell me, how *is* the shah? Two days later they took him away. They asked me to be foreign minister. I still thought it would all turn out all right, so I accepted. But then came Black Saturday.'

'What was that?'

'Hauled sixty of those out of the cellar beneath the throne room and shot them. I was in New York when I heard. Resigned at once.'

Two days later, through a coffee merchant, I was introduced to the emperor's grandson. Prince Ba'eda Maryam Makonnen had a business importing coffee machines. He was an ordinary-looking Ethiopian in a zip-up cardigan – but on his index finger he wore a signet ring with a gold relief of a lion and staff, the Conquering Lion of the King of Judah.

Ba'eda was the son of Haile Selassie's favourite child, the Duke of Harar, who had been killed in a car crash when Ba'eda was only fourteen days old. With his brothers and sisters he had then gone to live with his grandfather in the Jubilee Palace. Later he was one of those imprisoned in the Ghibbi, the Grand Palace.

'When we were in prison Mengistu came to see us. He was always very polite. He called my grandfather Getay – master – and always made sure to salute him.'

In the end Ba'eda was moved to the cellar beneath the throne room. He passed me on to another of its inmates. I went to see Teshome Gabre-Maryam on a warm, sunny afternoon. He had served in the emperor's government and was now a prosperous lawyer. He worked in an office in the leafy compound of his home. When I arrived he was with another man, General Negussie Wolde-Mikhael.

Thirty years of power shifts had seesawed the lives of these two men. They had both begun their careers under the

17

emperor. They were both high-fliers: Teshome had helped draft the constitution, General Negussie was chief of police in Addis. But when the Derg came, it had imprisoned one and promoted the other. While Teshome counted off the months and years in the palace cellar, General Negussie was made Chief Justice of the Martial Court.

'One day, they took me for trial,' explained Teshome. He reached out and, with a smile, took the general's hand. 'Who was there presiding in the court?' He raised the general's hand. 'He could have had me executed!'

'Why did you let him off?' I asked, smiling.

The general glanced at Teshome. 'He was a lawyer. He stood up in the court and convinced me.'

'That he was innocent?'

'No – that the court had no validity.'

Teshome laughed. He was still holding the general's hand.

Teshome was released, and when the Derg fell General Negussie himself was imprisoned. He had only just been released. Now Teshome was helping him; he had given him a car.

'Did you approve of the Derg?' I turned to General Negussie.

'To begin with, I was very happy with the ideology. We really believed it would help Ethiopia. But for me it changed completely when they executed my uncle. I was so filled with anger – I wanted to kill every one of those Derg men. My colleagues suggested I apply for a transfer. They probably saved my life. For six and a half years I was administrator of Hararge region. Then in 1982 the Derg asked me to become a minister – Minister without Portfolio.'

'Did you accept?'

He shrugged. 'I had ten children.'

'What do you remember of Mengistu?'

'Very moody. Very violent. My office was just above his and I could always hear his shouting. The only quality I know he had was that he loved his country. Also he was not corrupted at all. He was very honest with money. And he was very good at listening. He always knew exactly what the important point was.'

'Did you admire him?'

He looked at me. Prison had greyed his hair; his face was soft and troubled. 'Every day I was with Mengistu, I was thinking: how can I kill this man? We were always searched before going to our office. But when I was alone with him I would watch him and think how could I do it – he was a small one and I am a judo expert. I travelled with him to different provinces and I sat behind him on the plane looking at the back of his head and he had one little scar just here –' the general leaned forward and tapped the top of his neck '– and I was thinking, that would be the place, that would do it. A bullet just there . . .'

General Negussie stood and said goodbye. He walked stiffly to the door. For a moment after he had gone, Teshome and I were silent. A yellow weaver bird was pecking at the window-pane – *tap-tap . . . tap-tap-tap*.

Teshome and I carried on talking. I told him about my first trip to Lake Tana, about Wonderland Tours and Teklu and Dr Mengesha.

'Mengesha Gabre-Hiwot?'

'Yes.'

'I was brought up with him! We were classmates at Tafari Makonnen school. He helped me. He gave me money when I came out of prison in September 1982.'

'That was a few weeks after I was here.'

The weaver bird was again tapping at the window –

sparring with an aggressor that matched him blow for blow.

Teshome pursed his lips and let out a long, frustrated '*Dhaaaaa* . . .' for all the shattered years, the Derg's brutalities, the squandered hopes of his own generation.

'Do you know what happened to him, Teshome, why he was detained?'

'Do I know?' He looked at me blankly, then nodded. 'They said he read and distributed some anti-Derg literature.'

'Did he?'

'Actually he did, yes. In fact he showed it to me and I was very nearly imprisoned again as a result. It was also a time that the TPLF was advancing – so of course Tigrayans were not that popular.'

The weaver bird was still attacking its glass opponent – *tap-tap* . . . *tap-tap-tap* . . .

'What happened in the end?'

'They tortured him. He got gangrene in his leg – they had to amputate it. The gangrene was also in the other leg, and they had to amputate that one too. In fact, he was given permission to go home. But someone apparently said: What will people say when they see him with no legs? Much easier to kill him. They took him to a place on the edge of Addis known as "Bermuda" – the Bermuda Triangle. When people went there they never came back. They killed him there.

'Mengesha was one of the best, one of the most decent indi-viduals you could ever imagine.' Teshome pressed his fists hard on the desk. For a moment he looked overwhelmed by his own anger. 'That was the worst of it. They took men like that and destroyed them. Those *animals*.'

*   *   *

I had kept an image in my mind all those years, an everyday Ethiopian image glanced from a bus window. It was of a farmer, bare-legged, his *dula* flexed across his shoulders, setting off on a narrow path across the plateau.

Ethiopia taught me many things. As a naïve twenty-one-year-old, with years of flunked schooling behind me, I was ready for the simplest of lessons. Instead I was presented with paradoxes. I learnt of the cruelty that could be perpetrated in the name of a good idea. I saw how a people hurtling towards catastrophe, hungry, with population growth out of control, could go on living day to day with such astonishing grace. I saw how those apparently ignored by divine goodness could still apply their greatest energy to worship. I learnt that the human spirit is more robust than life itself.

Ethiopia opened my eyes to the earth's limitless range. I pictured the country's startling scenes and stories multiplied across the globe, then factored up by the past. It made the notion of 'a small world', 'a shrinking world', look absurd, and it made me restless.

Ethiopia instilled in me the habit of a lifetime, the habit of travel. It revealed the rewards that can be had simply from being footloose among strangers, from taking remote and narrow paths with bare-legged farmers. It bred in me the conviction that if there is any purpose to our time on this earth, it is to understand it, to seek out its diversity, to celebrate its heroes and its wonders – in short, to *witness* it.

There is a saying in Ethiopia: '*Kes be kes incular bekuro yihedal*' ('Step by step the egg starts walking'). My Amharic teacher would use it whenever I showed signs of frustration. I was a hopeless pupil; he used the expression very often. But now, after twenty-one years, the egg was hatching. I would go north into the roadless heart of the country, set off across the plateau. I would go to the places first conjured up by Teklu that afternoon in Mengistu's stifled city, with the rain hammering on the tin roof. I would go to Lalibela, to the sacred city of Aksum, and I would walk between them.

'Walk?' spluttered an Ethiopian friend. 'You can't *walk*! Foreigners don't *walk*.'

Walking was what villagers did. They walked and walked, to find grazing, to church, to market, to clinics. Until the nineteenth century wheels were unknown in the highlands. They still are in most places – no barrows, no carts; just legs and shoulders and mule-backs and the glimpse of a government or NGO's 4×4 as it races by, leaving you coughing in its dust-wake.

I made plans. I began the Ethiopian game in which information, misinformation and pure fantasy are all cunningly dressed up as each other. With such distances, I asked, might it be better to ride? Yes, ride, ride – on a horse! No (there are no horses, not up to the terrain). Should I go alone? Yes, yes – all alone! No (suspicious villagers would march you straight into the first town). Is it safe? (Very safe, no bandits/you will need one unit of armed guards). Is there food? (No food/lots of food). The truth was that no one knew anything other than a couple of the towns on my route.

I found a tent, bought a kerosene stove and stocked up with packet soup and sardines. I tracked down a Tigrinya-speaking guide named Hiluf in Aksum; I asked him to take a bus and meet me in Lalibela. I prised a map from the appropriate government agency.

One morning, I climbed the hill to Giorgis cathedral. It was not yet eight. The crowds were flooding up past the equestrian statue of Emperor Menelik. We were pressed closer and closer together, swept forward on an unstoppable tide. The octagonal church rose from a mass of white *gabbis*. All around me people were in various states of rapture. Some men were dancing. Others bowed their heads. Women stood in tears. From the steps, a flop-haired hermit delivered a eulogy to the dual virginity of Mary: *'There is nothing that equals her glory. She is higher than all creatures, men as well as angels! Her dress is the sun with the moon beneath her feet ...'* Amputees dragged themselves among the worshippers' legs. A group of boys had climbed into the trees to watch. It could have been the fifteenth century, or any century.

Giorgis cathedral was the first place I ever saw the spectacle of Ethiopian worship. I had come here with Teklu on my second day in Addis. After a lifetime of sober grey churches and bloodless rite, I was astonished. Christianity to me was something dusty and ossified, but not here. Over the years, the Ethiopian Church came to distil for me all that was extraordinary and ageless about the country. After my first visit, I thought you only had to step out over the threshold of Europe to be faced with such a sight. Now I know that that is only partly true. There is nowhere else on earth quite like Ethiopia.

The next morning, with 130 pounds of equipment and food, I flew to Lalibela.

3

An hour before dawn and Lalibela's rock-cut trenches are dark as oil. Their high sides rise to a narrow strip of stars. Underfoot the tufa is rough and pitted. I steady myself with a hand on the cold walls. The night air is sharp against my nostrils. Along the tunnel from the church of Debra Sina comes the nasal sound of chanting. Each phrase lasts a minute. Then – *boooom*! – the first beat of the *kebbero*. It is a sound like no other. It strikes you somewhere deep in the thorax. Another beat, and I quicken my pace.

Far below ground level, the base of the church rises from its own plinth of bedrock. Sandals are heaped by the door. Light glows from keel-arch windows. Inside is warmth, the smell of an all-night presence. Dozens of people are wrapped in white *gabbis*. Some are no more than shapes on the floor; others are standing heron-still around the central bay. On sturdy columns can be seen the chisel-cuts in the rock. The columns rise to shallow cupolas. Far beneath them two drummers squat beside their *kebberos*. Slowly, alternately, with the flat of their hands, they are beating the goatskin tympana.

The *debtara* are standing over them. They are elongated figures in white turbans and hanging white shawls. They are chanting. The drums beat, the *debtara* drop their wrists and their handheld sistra rattle like coins.

One of the drummers gives a quick, double *bo-boom*! The other follows. The tempo increases. One by one the shapes rise from the floor. In two lines the *debtara* shuffle towards each other. Their prayer sticks cluster above them. At the exact moment they begin the dance, a blind cantor steps to the front, his mouth open in song. He is wearing a pair of women's dark glasses. The drummers are standing now. Each *kebbero* hangs from a shoulder-strap. They circle each other. They give two more double beats. Rhythmic clapping spreads through the church. One of the drummers leans to the right, the other to the left. Now they are spinning. They are crouching, rising. Their faces glow with abandon. The people press closer around them. The cupolas fill with ululations. The drummers' eyes flash in the half-light. The *debtara* are swinging the prayer sticks now, surrounding the drummers in their ecstasy of beating. A young boy joins their line, his head level with the men's hips. He is imitating their movements.

Out of nowhere, a man leaps into the midst. His matted hair swings from side to side. He dips his cross-staff above his head. His movements are fluent and precise. A grin splits his skull-like face. The boy has stopped dancing. He is standing still, buffeted and jostled by those around him. He is staring at the man, and his eyes are wide with fear and amazement.

No force on earth could stop this. The man is revolving around the drummers. Sweat flicks from his hair. Deep below

the ground, the hollowed-out chapel is filled with drumming, filled with clapping, filled with ululating, and it all merges in a fever of sound and movement and devotion.

Then it is over. The drummers are lifting the *kebberos* over their heads. The *debtaras'* sistra tinkle as they set them down. Two priests are involved in a hissed argument, flicking through a psalter. The shapes on the floor are re-forming themselves. The man with matted locks has disappeared.

Outside again, dawn is a pale loom above the trench. It is still cold. From the distance comes the sound of a *tirumba*, the funereal horn – and a cry: '*Citizens of Lalibela! Come out – come out! Come and help bury the body of Colonel Melaku. Citizens of Lalibela, come out, come out!*'

Lalibela is a town to die in. The tunnels that once linked the complex of churches are clogged with centuries of corpses.

To make a pilgrimage to Lalibela eases your later passage to heaven – but to die here is much better. The soil itself is sacred, and those who take the journey are buried in shallow graves.

The site has never been conclusively dug by archaeologists. Scholars know by heart the handful of significant written references to it. It is easier to list what is not known about Lalibela than what is. It is not known precisely when the churches were carved, whether they were started during the thirteenth-century reign of King Lalibela or much earlier. Nor is it known where all the excavated rock was deposited, nor if any outside expertise was responsible. Nor why, deep in the mountains of Lasta, the Herculean task of chipping out these eleven churches and their labyrinth of link trenches was undertaken. Like Ethiopia itself, it is a timeless place, veiled by layer upon layer of mythologies.

The town's earlier name of Roha is linked perhaps to al-Ruha, Arabic for the holy city of Edessa which was lost to the Christians just before the reign of King Lalibela. Then again it was the heir of the holy city of Aksum, believed by Ethiopians (never shy in their myth-making) to be Zion itself. So Lalibela took on something of the aura of Aksum and Zion, and thereby of the holiest of all earthly places, Jerusalem. King Lalibela himself was taken on a dream-tour of Jerusalem by the Angel Gabriel and was able to replicate its sites. Pilgrims therefore needed to go no further than Lalibela to earn God's favour.

The yearning for Jerusalem has haunted generations of Ethiopians – a yearning amplified by its extreme risks. Wild animals, pirates and Muslims have combined in the imagination of Ethiopian Christians to create an *über*-threat for all those daring to leave the mountains. In the eighteenth century Queen Mentuab wailed to James Bruce that, after thirty years on the throne, she would give up everything if only she 'could be conveyed to the church of the Holy Sepulchre in Jerusalem, and beg alms for my subsistence all my life after'. Jerusalem was where it all began for Ethiopian kingship, where the union of Solomon and Sheba took place and from where Menelik I acquired the Ark of the Covenant, dancing before it like King David.

So Lalibela became a Biblical Land in miniature. Here is Golgotha, Cana and Nazareth. Beneath Calvary is the Tomb of Adam. I had skirted the slopes of Mount Tabor, Mount Sinai, crossed the River Jordan and climbed the Mount of Olives. In the compound of Beta Maryam, I had bent to smell the single rosebush from the Garden of Eden. Beside the church of Beta Giorgis is a slope of un-dug rock which is Mount Ararat.

Lalibela carries with it a weighty cargo of symbolism – not a place for the literal-minded. It made me think of Robert Southey's comment after once visiting William Blake: 'Blake showed me a perfectly mad poem called *Jerusalem*,' he reported. 'Jerusalem is in Oxford street!'

It was a lovely morning. A few high clouds drifted in a clear blue sky. I passed the fresh grave of Colonel Melaku, where a mound of stones covered his body. An olive-wood cross rose at one end, and on it was nailed a crude plaque: *Colonel Melaku Fetem born 1935 EC died at 61*. The wreath of marigolds and mimosa was already wilting in the heat.

I was on my way to see a *bahtawi*. A churchman in Addis had given me the name of Abba Gabre-Meskal. 'He may be there or –' the churchman dropped his voice – 'he may have already *vanished*.'

I was in luck. I found him up a dusty alley, sitting outside his own lean-to. He was stitching a patch into his *qamis*, his anchorite's shawl, dyed yellow (the Ethiopian monks use for this yellow the native plant *Carthamus tinctorius*, or 'bastard saffron'). I sat on a stool opposite him and, as I tried to read the wrinkles of his cheek, asked if he knew anything about the dead colonel.

'Colonel Melaku? He was my neighbour. Very religious man. He came to Lalibela for his death. He was a Derg colonel.'

'But the Derg were against the Church?'

'The Derg were devils! Some of the top ones, they just kept it hidden – they prayed *in private*.'

Abba Gabre-Meskal was pleased by the thought, and a smile spread across his weathered face. The smile became a chuckle, and the chuckle became a cough – and the cough bent him in two. During the last rains, pneumonia had forced him down from the mossy cave where he had lived for ten years. I offered him water. He drank it in short sips. I didn't want him vanishing on me.

He was a tall man. He had deep-set eyes and skin like oxhide. His expression swung between comic innocence and holy rage. He raised the yellow *qamis* to his face to examine his stitching.

'You a Christian?'

'Of sorts,' I said.

'Protestant?'

I nodded.

'Luther, Luther!' He was sewing with quick, even stitches, even though he could hardly see. 'Tourist?'

'Yes. I'm going to Aksum. On foot,' I added, for effect.

He wasn't impressed. 'Tell me, have you ever heard of a place called Jerusalem?'

I told him I had lived for a time in a monastery in the Old City.

Leaning down to gnaw through the thread, he looked at me properly for the first time. He folded the *qamis* and put it to one side. He laid his hands together in his lap, drew a big breath and, for an hour or more, captured me with a long and beautiful story about his own attempt to reach Jerusalem.

Abba Gabre-Meskal had begun his career at a religious school in the Gondar region. One day a fellow student died. The *memhir* called everyone together and said: 'One of our brothers has died suddenly. Something is not right.'

They agreed that it was a punishment from God. It made them uneasy because they did not know what they had done wrong, and they couldn't tell what would happen next.

'We must make a pilgrimage,' the *memhir* said. 'Someone must go to Jerusalem, without shoes.'

A senior monk was chosen as leader and two others appointed to go with him. Young Abba Gabre-Meskal was one of them. They took with them the Psalms of David, a Book of Hours and gourds for water.

'We set off with our faith. We put our trust in the will of God.'

They had no shoes.

In Tigray they came to the palace of Ras Seyoum. At the gates were many people – the sick, the poor and the needy. But the pilgrims' leader was a well-known monk and Ras Seyoum himself came down to see him.

'What are you doing?' he asked.

'We are going on a pilgrimage. One of our brothers died.'

The *ras* asked the monks to say a prayer for him at the church of the Holy Sepulchre. He gave them thirteen silver Maria Teresa thalers. The monks went on their way. They reached the border to the Sudan, and on the other side, the soldiers arrested them.

'You are spies!' they said.

'We are not spies,' explained the monks. 'We are pilgrims on our way to Jerusalem. Look, we have no shoes.'

But the soldiers put them in the prison. They stayed there for a month and then the monks heard the soldiers say: 'Perhaps these men are not spies. They have no shoes.'

So the monks were released. They carried on through the desert. It was a very difficult time. They found only salty water and the ground was hard and stony. One day a stranger came up to them and said: 'Why do you walk without shoes?'

'We are pilgrims. We are going to Jerusalem.'

'Look,' he said, pointing to the distance. 'There is a train. I can ask it to stop and then you can travel easily to your destination.'

They looked at the train. They saw the long line of carriages and the white trail of smoke above it. They saw its round spinning feet and they realised the man beside them was Satan, sent to tempt them.

'Go away!' they shouted, and he disappeared.

Sometimes they followed the Nile and sometimes they were in the desert. They reached the border to Egypt and on the other side of the border the soldiers arrested them.

'You are spies,' they said.

'We are not. We are holy men. We have no shoes.'

The soldiers saw that it was true. But then one of the soldiers said: 'Be careful – they may be extreme believers!'

So the soldiers put them in prison for being extreme believers. They spent months in that Egyptian prison. Abba Gabre-Meskal said the prison wasn't too bad. It reminded him of the monastery. He did not mind being locked up, the poor food, the crowding. What he did not like were the rats. In the end the Egyptians released them and they carried on. They came to a famous place. It was, said Abba Gabre-Meskal, a great piece of water between Egypt and Lebanon. They stood by the water and they realised they could not cross it. They were very sad, but thought: It is not the will of God that we reach Jerusalem.

'Our leader said he would stay. He would wait to try and cross the water. But we decided to go home. It was the end of the journey.'

Abba Gabre-Meskal rose to his feet. He fetched a bowl of *kolo*, roasted corn.

'There is one more interesting thing.' He stood high above me, the sun behind his head and one finger pointing at the sky.

On the way home, he said, the two of them reached a place where they'd been warned there was a great variety of wild animals. They decided they must sleep in the trees. They tied themselves to the trees so that they wouldn't fall out, and in the night the wild animals came. First, he said, were the ones with horns, although in fact some of the ones with horns did not have horns. He and the other novice could see them down below in the moonlight. Suddenly the ones with horns began a great battle with the ones who did not have horns. There was such a noise and such fighting that the two young monks became afraid. But all at once the animals left – as if a lion or a tiger had come to the area. In fact, a lion had come to the area and beneath the tree there were suddenly many lions. Then there were also tigers. They had to beat metal objects together to stop the animals climbing the tree. Then the lions and the tigers started to fight and there was a terrifying noise as they fought.

But then they too ran away. 'That was when we began to hear another noise. It was the biggest noise you can hear in the forest. The lions and the tigers stopped fighting and they were afraid. They ran away.'

'What was the noise?'

'A great big one!'

'An elephant?'

'Bigger than an elephant. I don't know its name. We did not see it. We only heard its noise. Like a, like a . . . *thing*.' He failed to find anything worthy of comparison. 'Everyone knows it. It is a hundred devils in one!'

For the rest of the night they prayed and they heard the noise of the big thing moving among the trees. But as it became light, the noise stopped. Merchants came with camels and they came down out of the tree and the merchants gave them food. The two of them went on their way.

In Tigray they wanted to see Ras Seyoum to tell him they could not reach Jerusalem. They wanted to give him back his thalers. But their leader was not with them and they were just ordinary churchmen and so they waited, standing at the gates for a long time. Then they gave the money to a guard.

'We returned to Gojjam after many difficulties. But we also met good people on the way.'

'So, did you reach Jerusalem later?'

'I went to Addis Ababa. I became known there. Did you hear the name of Empress Menen?'

'The wife of Haile Selassie?'

'She said she wanted me to go. She was going to arrange it. "Abba, you must go to Jerusalem!" But she died.'

He let out a long sigh. 'I went to see the emperor's daughter, Tenagne Worq. She asked her father. He said to me, Abba, where is your file? Where is my file? I didn't have a file! But by

God's will they found my file. His Majesty held the file and said, You can go.

'So I did go to Jerusalem. I went to the Holy Sepulchre, I went to Deir es Sultan, to Addis Alem monastery. I went to Bethlehem. But I was not as strong then as now. If I had gone now, I would have studied *great books* – they have books in Jerusalem that are as big as doors! But I was young then. I was not prepared.'

Hiluf was on a bus from Aksum. He would be in Lalibela in a few days. I meanwhile was staying at the Jerusalem Guest House, trying to prepare for the coming walk. Information was still patchy. Even the mysteries of the rock-cut churches were easier to pin down. *There'll be plenty of food in the markets . . . no food in the markets . . . you will need one mule . . . three mules . . . a car . . . no idea . . . militia . . . very hot . . . very cold . . . very steep . . . no food . . .*

I had a problem with Ethiopian food. When I first arrived in 1982, I loved its spicy sauces, its spongy *injera* bread. But then on the second journey I picked up a stomach infection of such virulence that for a decade or more I lost a day or two each month to it. I assumed the years had sorted it out; but a meal in an Addis restaurant a week earlier had proved me wrong.

So I went to Lalibela's weekly market. I found shallots and garlic and chilli peppers. I found rice and pulses and tomatoes. I bought screwtop containers. I bought biscuits and sugar and a block of sawn-up salt from the Danakil desert. I lined all the food up in my room. I had the tinned fish from Addis, and the sachets of soup. I packed it all very diligently into a canvas bag. I spread out the maps from Ethiopia's Mapping Agency.

I sliced off the unnecessary parts – the desert to the east, the Takazze lowlands to the west. I taped the folds. I sliced the Maudes' translation of *Anna Karenina* into three pocket-sized sections and taped the spine (I kept the five-thousand-rouble note I had used as a bookmark when I'd first read it, ten years earlier, in Lithuania).

With the help of the Jerusalem's proprietor, I settled on two mules and two muleteers – by the name of Bisrat and Makonnen. Bisrat was gentle and subservient, Makonnen canny and wiry. The mules looked healthy enough. They would come with us as far as the town of Sekota.

The days slipped by. I jostled with pilgrims and travellers at the sacred sites. I tried to ignore the immensity of the backdrop mountains, the heat that clambered up through the hours of each morning, my own breathlessness. In the evening, I sat on the terrace outside my room and read. A breeze would come up from the south and a thousand eucalyptus leaves brush together with a long watery *shhhh*. I was filled with expectation. Each morning I lay in bed and watched daylight leak into the eastern sky. Each morning I heard a blast of the *tirumba*: '*Citizens of Lalibela – come out, come out! Come out for the burial . . . come out, come out!*'

One evening I returned to the guest house and there was Hiluf sitting on a wall. A small bag lay beside him, a water bottle and three tied-together batons of sugarcane. He had the thick-lashed eyes and easy smile of the Tigrayans. He jumped down and we embraced. I liked him at once.

In my room, I showed him the neatly-packed bag of supplies. At once he set about repacking it, with the reverence for food of those who have lived with real hunger. We looked at the maps. I ran my fingers up across the dense contours of Wag and Lasta, into Tigray, Tembien and Gheralta.

'Do you know any of this?'

He shook his head.

I glanced at his feet. 'Hiluf, your shoes!'

He bent down and poked his finger through the sole. 'It's all right – they are quite good shoes.'

He looked up at me. He began to laugh, and I couldn't help laughing with him.

'We'll have to get you new ones.'

Hiluf bent down and took a needle and thread from his bag.

In the morning Bisrat and Makonnen were at the gate. They held a mule each. The sun was a pale glow behind Mount Eshetan. We loaded the mules and set off. It was a feast day at Beta Giorgis. I let the others go on and went down to join the ring of worshippers on the edge of the pit. Another crowd filled the shadowy space below. The fat cruciform block of the

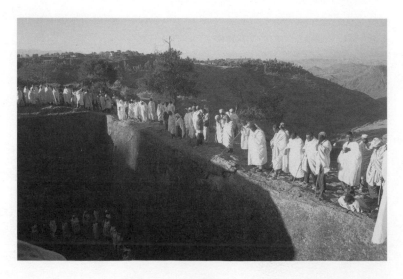

church rose high above their heads. The *debtara* were dancing. The beat of a *kebbero* sounded from among them.

The sun reached me with a warning flash in the corner of my eye; in a few hours it would be hot. I turned to leave and wound up through the gathering crowds. I stopped a woman with a flat-pan basket on her head and bought six bananas. They were stumpy and very sweet. The woman had a burn-mark covering one cheek. 'Pay me what you like,' she said.

As I caught up with the others, there was a distant cry: '*Citizens of Lalibela! Come out! Help bury Girma Gabre-Selassie! Citizens of Lalibela, come out, come out!*'

4

The path north from Lalibela cut down the mountainside in short zigzags. Pilgrim heads bobbed up it. They were blowing horns. They were shaded by umbrellas. They were leading sheep. They were carrying rust-coloured cockerels suspended from sticks. They were all heading for the feast of Giorgis.

I stood aside to let them pass and looked down beyond them to the valley floor and the grey riverbed. On the opposite side the path began to rise. I followed its course with my gaze, through a series of fields bordered by rocky outcrops, up to where the rise steepened to cliffs. There the path reverted to zigzags before reaching the flat ridge-line of the plateau. It left a hollow feeling in my stomach.

It was mid-morning by the time we started to climb. Hiluf and the mules went ahead. Their pace was easy, untroubled. I felt the hot sun on my back. For months I had been preparing for this. But now, in the first hours, I was fading. The path steepened. I gulped at the thin air. Flies buzzed into my panting mouth. Each step became a mountain in itself.

Stumbling the last few yards, I cleared the ridge and joined the others under a lone olive tree. It was a false summit. The path continued up.

A man sauntered down it. 'Peace be on you!'

'And on you . . .'

He put a foot up on a rock and looked at me flopped on the ground. The sun was behind his head; as he moved it flickered on and off. He wore a bath-cap of yellow towelling.

'Has the *farenj*'s car broken?' he laughed.

By mid-afternoon we were following a broad shelf around the northern slopes of Abune Jozef. The concentric lines of terraces bordered the fields. There were homesteads and small villages and stock grazing. The path was flat. The walking was easy. Then the terraces stopped. They gave way to a pair of gate-like rocks. The ground dropped at our feet. The sight ahead was so vast, so overwhelming that we all stopped.

'*Whweeeee!*' hissed Makonnen.

Between the rocks, row upon row of ridges stretched out into the distance. Their grey flanks were dappled with cloud shadows. The horizon was a graph of hazy peaks and saddles. The line of our path followed the mountainside, shrunk to a thread by the vastness all around it. I could see beyond it to the next spine of rock rising from a hidden valley, and beyond that another and another. I forgot the morning's labour and felt a sudden surge of exhilaration. It was the reckless confidence that comes at the beginning of a journey, and I longed to be in each one of those valleys, each little smear of a village, each hut.

Makonnen grinned at me. In a wave-like motion he raised and lowered his hand over imaginary hills. He was looking forward to watching the *farenj* deal with it all.

'Which way is Sekota?' I asked.

With his *dula*, he pointed north. The sides of a large mountain shouldered the sky.

'Behind, behind! That road we call "the breaker of knees".'

But we were not going to Sekota, not directly anyway. I wanted to try to reach the rebel town of Amda Worq.

'And Amda Worq?'

He swung his *dula* to the west. Partly in shadow, the ridgeline was more distant. Makonnen raised his voice to an excited falsetto. 'Way, waa-ay over!'

'And what is that road like?'

He shook his head. He had never been there. 'They say it's the devil's own.'

We carried on. The path continued as a narrow ledge. When the mules stumbled, rocks slid out from under their feet and rolled down the scrub, gathering pace until they were bouncing off the mountain and plunging into the emptiness.

We dropped into a small juniper forest. The boughs of the juniper were hung with lichen. It was late afternoon. Makonnen put his *dula* across his shoulders and began to sing: '*Aya alemayehu igray derso!* May my foot reach the place I want!'

That evening we put up our tent in a village above the monastery of Yimrehanna Krestos. I cooked a meal over the kerosene stove. Hiluf and I sat outside the tent spooning up rice from plastic bowls. I felt a little life flowing back into my limbs. The stars above were pinpricks in the darkening blue.

Hiluf was twenty-six. He had been born in the mountains of south-eastern Tigray, a region famous for its frequent rebellions. His father was a priest and his mother was just thirteen when he was born. Hiluf was her third child.

In 1984 the great famine came, and Hiluf's father left for the west of Tigray to try to find farm work. The clay vats of grain ran down. The cattle grew weaker. Their neighbours left the land to look for food. His mother said: 'We will stay, your father will soon be back.' But in the end they too were forced to leave. They walked two days north to a feeding camp.

Hiluf wrapped his hands round a mug of tea. 'My mother left behind my brother to look after my little sister and the animals. All the time she was just sobbing.'

One day Hiluf was in the camp, on his way to collect their ration of flour and milk powder. Suddenly he saw his father.

'At once he started crying,' said Hiluf, ' "Why did you leave our land?" '

Hiluf explained and his father embraced him. He had money from the west; now he could take them home!

So the two of them went to the distribution point. They sat and waited with hundreds of others. But before they could collect the food a man came with a long stick. He was tapping people on the shoulder with his stick.

'Stand up, you . . . and you . . .'

He picked Hiluf's father. They took him to a lorry. Hiluf ran to fetch his mother and sisters and they managed to get on the lorry too. They were taken to a place near Makelle airport. Thousands of people were there, in the open. Hiluf's father put his head in his hands and wailed: '*Wai-amlaki, wai-wai-wai* . . .' He knew what was coming.

Resettlement was the Derg's chosen solution to the famine. Shift tens of thousands to the fertile prairies of the south and there would be no more hunger (and no more rebels). The family were separated. Hiluf and his father were flown to Addis Ababa in the hold of an Antonov. By bus they continued south. They were left in the forest. Local villagers brought them food. Every morning and every evening, Hiluf's father would stand outside and pray to find his family. One day, Hiluf's uncle came. He had been looking for them for months. He took them to his village, and there were Hiluf's mother and all his brothers and sisters. 'Oh – what a happy moment!'

For many years they lived in the south of Ethiopia.

'But it wasn't a good place,' said Hiluf. 'It was a very bad place they sent us to.'

It was the lowlands. To the Amhara and the Tigrayan highlanders nothing is as intrinsically bad as *qola*, the lowlands. It is the place of insects and diseases, big animals, dangerous Muslims and *budas*.

'In the day the monkeys took the maize, at night the fox, porcupine, wild cat and wild pigs. We children became ill.

A *buda* came to my sister and my brother. The *buda* was talking and shouting through them. They fell on the floor. They would have died but someone went into the forest and collected the right roots and ground them up and burned them. The *budas* screamed, they shouted – but the smoke drove them away.'

Those who were caught trying to return to the north were killed by the Derg. In 1991, Hiluf's family heard that Mengistu had fled the country and the EPRDF were in power. They made their way back to Tigray. Their house was destroyed, but his father kissed the soil and soon they had built another.

'All my brothers and sisters are still there, on the land,' he said, with a hint of sadness.

'How is it that you're not a farmer, Hiluf?'

'I was always too lazy to do farm work! I said I wanted to go to school instead. I liked to learn. I would always get more than 90 per cent. So I went to university.'

It was late. The moon had broken free of the ridge-line and was roaming the open country above. Bisrat and Makonnen were asleep, their heads propped on the packsaddles. The priests and monks were making their way down to church, a row of ghostly figures moving through the trees.

'Shall we join them?' asked Hiluf.

'Let's sleep.' I rolled out my sleeping bag. I was exhausted. 'We can go to the church in the morning.'

I'd been waiting for years to see the church of Yimrehanna Krestos. My hankering for the forbidden north of Ethiopia had been offset in part by frequent thumbing of Georg Gerster's illustrated *Churches in Rock*. Gerster had travelled in the north during the last years of the emperor. It was largely his work that revealed Lalibela to the world. But for me his pictures of Yimrehanna Krestos were somehow more striking. Whereas Lalibela's churches were a feat, dug out of the rock, King Yimrehanna Krestos had in the twelfth century built this edifice *inside* an existing natural feature. The juxtaposition was a stroke of genius. With its neat striped walls pinched between rough floor and rough ceiling, it spoke of man's frailty in the natural world. But it was also faintly comic – a piece of confectionery popped into the cave-mouth.

At dawn, we stumbled down through the trees. Prayer hummed from the cave entrance. Straw covered the bare rock floor and one or two carpets lay over it. From under one of the carpets wriggled a priest.

'You! You!' he shouted. 'Who are you? What do you want?'

'We want to look at the church.'

His aggression dissolved as he woke. He yawned and picked the straw from his hair. Then he put on his turban. He led us into the treasury where the other priests and *debtara* sat dazed after the night's worship. The church itself, a cave within a cave, was crusted with centuries of devotion. The walls were dark and tallow-stained. Its trussed wooden roof suggested an upturned boat and generations of hopeful souls sheltering beneath it. Geometric inlay covered much of the walls and ceilings. Set into it was a mysterious cast of heraldic beasts – peacocks, double-headed eagles, men with wings, men with scorpions, vulture-headed men and a large number of elephants.

Beside the church was the tomb of Yimrehanna Krestos himself, a dwarf cottage hung with drapes. Two women circled it with rocks on their shoulders. From time to time they would lean over, press their hands on the drapes and kiss them. They were muttering, as if purging some deep-held trauma. When I looked more closely one of their rocks turned out to be a baby.

The priest was also watching them. He was still picking pieces of straw from his beard. He had been earnest in the treasury, earnest in the church, and was very earnest here at the royal tomb. But at the back of the cave his mood lightened: 'Look – dead people!'

The light of my torch lit up a sea of bodies. They stretched far back into the darkness. In places a thigh bone or forearm raised itself from waves of skeletons and tattered cloth. At my feet was a dug-out coffin and a body squeezed into it. There was skin still on the cheek.

'The followers of Yimrehanna Krestos. They came from Jerusalem.'

There was a squeaking from the back of the cave and a stream of bats whistled out over our heads. I ducked. The priest ignored them.

With a grand sweep of his hand he took in the entire range of the bodies. 'Five thousand seven hundred and forty! The king told them when they finished work, Go back to your own country. But they said, No, your majesty, we want to stay here. With you! Think of that – they could have lived out their days in the holy city, but they chose to stay here.'

Just as Ethiopians have idealised far-off Jerusalem, so their own isolation has created in their name a glorious gallery of mythical figures. The most potent of all emerged at about the time of Yimrehanna Krestos. It was then that news reached the rest of Christendom of a powerful ruler beyond the Islamic cordon. Originally he was believed to reign over both Asia and Ethiopia, but as Asia opened up and there was no sign of him, so Ethiopia became the only possible site for his kingdom.

Prester John changed the shape of the known world and haunted the European imagination for centuries to come.

Around the year 1165 a letter was sent, addressed to the Byzantine emperor Manuel Comnenus I:

> I, Prester John, by the Grace of God and the strength of our Lord Jesus Christ, king of kings and lord of lords, to his friend Manuel, Governor of the Byzantines, greetings, wishing him health and the continued enjoyment of the divine blessing ... I have determined to visit the sepulchre of our Lord with a very large army, in accordance with the glory of our majesty to humble and chastise the enemies of the cross of Christ and to exalt his blessed name.

The Christian rulers were in desperate need of strong, unifying allies. Torn apart by their own feuds, they were also losing ground in the east. The fall of Edessa in 1144 was followed fifty years later by the Crusaders' loss of Jerusalem. But Prester John's letter brought with it the breath of salvation and, in describing his realm, conjured up the bliss that was possible on this earth for good, victorious Christians.

When he went to war, Prester John explained, fourteen crosses were carried before him. The crosses were made of gold. They were studded with jewels. Behind each cross was a corps of ten thousand cavalry and behind them one hundred thousand footsoldiers. In Prester John's provinces were no venomous snakes, no scorpions and no loud frogs. The riverbeds were covered in emeralds and sapphires, topaz and onyx.

One river only flowed for three days in the week, allowing it to be crossed on the remaining four. Into another river, which rose in Paradise, plunged great flying dragons with carbuncles in their foreheads; after seventy days the people could go and pluck out the jewels. There was also a great plain, and a stone in the middle, and in the stone a cavity in which water collected that could cure every known ailment (as long as the patient was a sincere follower of Christ). Prester John's robes were spun from gold by salamanders that lived on a mountain of fire. In his lands, all strangers and travellers were welcome. There were no poor and no thieves. Adultery and greed were unknown. Liars were ostracised. There was no flattery.

Seventy vassals paid Prester John tribute. Yet he also knew humility. He was waited on by kings, but he himself took the title merely of 'Prester', or priest. When he rode out, a page carried before him a plain wooden cross to represent Christ's Passion and a vase of soil to remind of his own mortality. His palace was roofed in ebony with windows of crystal. Each day, thirty thousand people sat to eat at tables of gold. The tables were supported on amethyst columns which could prevent drunkenness. In front of his palace was suspended a vast mirror in which the great and magnanimous ruler was able to see at once all that was happening in his kingdom.

Copies of Prester John's letter were soon circulating the courts of Europe. Scores of translations were made. Manuscripts exist in Anglo-Norman, French, Serbian and Hebrew; five versions have been found in High German. A Welsh translation survives, one in Scots dialect and two different versions in Irish. The Russian translation stirred the thoughts of many a steppe adventurer, and the letter has left echoes in the *bylina* or folk ballad, *Diuk Stepanovich*. Prester John enters the Grail myth: as priest-king he was equated with the guardian of the Grail. Sir John Mandeville lifted details of his kingdom for the fictitious account of his own travels. The letter's images of faith, power and wealth fill the verses of the Renaissance poet Ludovico Ariosto – he describes a mythical flight beyond the Muslim world to the glittering palace of Prester John. With the development of printing, the letter found an even wider public. In France it was in such demand that it went to fourteen editions.

For hundreds of years, Prester John and his kingdom occupied that now-vanished region where the known world recedes and the imaginary one begins. Early mappers like Cosmas Indicopleustes dealt with such places by imposing a satisfying symmetry: the fringes of his map are full of straight lines and right-angles. But in medieval Europe they knew better. The questing spirit of the age placed wonders beyond the horizon – utopias, lost countries, strange creatures, sacred mountains, paradisial kingdoms.

The letter of Prester John is a glorious fake. It is the work, in all likelihood, of a German monk. Like James Macpherson's Ossian, it achieved popularity by fleshing out a collective fantasy – proof that literature is as adept at wishful thinking as it is at truth. Even as late as the sixteenth century, maps show the area of Ethiopia as the land of Prester John. Once placed in those imaginary regions, it is hard to return to earth.

The lure of Prester John was partly responsible for one of Europe's most ambitious enterprises. When Henry the Navigator sent his *fidalgos* down the coast of Africa, he was hoping for an alliance with the great ruler. The Portuguese popular imagination had already been fed by the chapbook *Libro del Infante Pedro de Portugal*, which included a mythical visit to Prester John by the brother of Henry the Navigator.

The Portuguese weren't the only ones hunting for Prester

IOANES·PRESBR·MAX·DE·IDIA·ET·ETHIOPIA·

PRESTO·GIOVANNI·DE·INDIA·ET·ETMIO

John. A merchant from Ragusa or Dubrovnik, Vincenzo Matteo, was reported to be on his trail. The Dutch thought the Zambezi a possible route to the kingdom, and called it Prester John's river. But it was the Portuguese who were the most dogged. In 1487 King John II despatched an envoy from Lisbon overland to find Prester John. He reached the Ethiopian court, the first recorded European to do so, but he never returned.

It is another Portuguese, Francisco Alvares, who gives us the earliest report of Prester John. In 1520 he and his party arrived in Ethiopia from Goa. After months of travelling they came to the king's camp. They had to wait days for an audience. At last the summons came. They were shown in behind a set of curtains. Beyond these curtains were others, made of even finer cloth. Behind them was a room laid with beautiful carpets and a dais which was concealed behind a further set of curtains. When these were drawn back, there he was – King Lebna Dengel. On his head was a great crown of gold and silver, and in his hand was a silver cross. A veil of blue taffeta covered his mouth and beard, and his robes were of gold brocade.

Even so, Lebna Dengel and his mountain kingdom were something of a disappointment. The Ethiopians were clearly in no position to launch a crusade; they themselves were too busy trying to keep the khanates of the plains from invading. This Prester John was certainly Christian, but he was no saviour, and his people were frankly pretty poor.

The world lost a little of its colour. In Portugal, millennial enthusiasts transferred their hopes to Sebastianism, the cult of the conquering ascetic, the martyr-king Sebastian I who succeeded in returning from the dead on four separate occasions.

Not for the first time, nor the last, Ethiopia had helped give solid form to rumour. The Ethiopians themselves were as baffled then by this 'Prester John' as they have been more recently by the Rastafarians' elevation of Haile Selassie. In 1441, an Ethiopian delegation to Rome became quite irritated with their interviewers: 'We are from Ethiopia. Our king is Zara Yaqob. Why do you call him Prester John?'

Before leaving the monastery of Yimrehanna Krestos we called in on Abba Gobeze – 'herbalist, wise teacher, old man', according to the priest.

His hut was dark and hot. He was lying on his bed. He was gazing up into the corrugated iron roof. From a crossbeam of eucalyptus hung his clothes. He was in a good mood. His brother had come to see him from Lalibela and brought news and some medicine. His brother was not a monk but a priest, and he sat on a stool by his bed.

First on one elbow, then another, Abba Gobeze raised himself up. He glanced at me; he had wonderfully hooded eyes which, once seen, made you want to hear his every word. He stretched up his hand and from the beam above drew down a shirt.

'Yimrehanna Krestos, he is a saint and a king, and also a priest.' He spoke faintly. 'Ethiopia is always the representative of God . . . Foreigners are now coming to Lalibela to learn . . . the whole world will learn from Ethiopia . . .'

He paused to arrange the shirt on his lap, and laughed at himself: 'We monks, we are dead people. We have no physical life.'

His brother nodded proudly as if to say: He is a *monk*, you understand, a hero of the war between world and spirit.

Abba Gobeze put his hand-cross on the blanket. 'Yes, we just hold our lives in our hand. Death is always close beside us.'

Death certainly did not seem far away for old Abba Gobeze. His body had little flesh on it. After doing up each button he paused to catch his breath. His shoulders rose with the effort. Once the shirt was on, he took down another. This one went on more quickly. He swung his legs down. They didn't quite reach the floor, and he spent a moment looking at his toes.

'Our bodies are nothing!'

Then he pulled down a jersey. He pulled down a pair of trousers and a belt. With each layer his strength increased. He ran his hand playfully through the remaining clothes. Most were rags, strips of torn green serge, corners of brown homespun. He took another pair of trousers and pulled them on over the first. He began to sing. '*Yejamarish inje yecharesech . . . dum-da-yesh . . . da-yesh . . . er . . .*'

His brother said, in a stage whisper: 'He has been very unwell.'

Abba Gobeze couldn't remember the rest of the song. 'My brothers taught it to me. They went to the coronation of His Imperial Majesty. It was in Addis. I was too young to go.'

'We were both too young to go,' echoed his brother. 'In fact, I wasn't born.'

'Are your family from this region?' I asked.

'Always from here!' boomed Abba Gobeze. 'Father was a priest, grandfather was a priest. All priests –'

'They were all priests. Always priests!'

Abba Gobeze scowled at his brother. 'My children are not priests. Not one.'

'Children, Abba?' I asked. 'But you're a monk?'

'I became a monk when my wife died. My children are in Addis now. They are teachers, lawyers, people like that.'

'One of them's a doctor!' beamed his brother.

'Would you rather they had been priests?'

'Yes, of course,' the Abba's brother nodded.

'No,' countered Abba Gobeze. 'Look at us – we're just ignorant. When we were young we were only looking after cattle and sheep. But *they* are educated.'

He looked up. From the cross-beam he took down the final piece of his dress – a cotton scarf of such age that it had reverted to the colour of the earth itself. Bandaging it around his head, he began again to sing.

He was still singing when we left. His brother saw us to the door and out into the midday sun. He pointed out the road ahead and we followed it down into the valley, rising and falling with it over a series of rounded hills.

5

It was late in the afternoon when we reached the rock-hewn church of Bilbala Giorgis.

'Very holy place!' With his *dula*, Makonnen pointed to the traffic of bees around a blind window. 'Their honey – you must take it for illness of legs, for illness of the stomach, and –' he tapped his temple '– illness of the head.'

A man sat alone in front of the church. He was pestling the red tufa to granules.

'What is that used for?' I asked him.

He looked at our mules and our baggage. 'Men take this one to prevent journey-accident.'

'*Usshi, usshi,*' I conceded, smiling.

I bought a cup of the powder and put it in water. I stirred it with a pencil, drank it and passed the cup to Hiluf. It tasted of, well, ground-up rock.

'Do you think that will see us to Aksum?'

'Aksum?' The man frowned and shook his head. 'You'll need more.' He watched me fill a film canister with the dust.

'The people who took it to fight the Italians or the rebels – those who took the soil always came back. Always.'

Below the church was Bilbala itself. It was a brown and dusty town. The buildings were brown and dusty, the road that split the buildings was brown and dusty, and the children who played in it were brown and dusty. The only colour was the orange and green of plastic bottles hanging outside a store.

We pitched our tent in the grounds of the town's clinic. A sign outside, in Amharic and English, urged RESPONSIBLE REPRODUCTIVE BEHAVIOUR.

Darkness fell upon Bilbala with a series of shouts, ox-bellows and baby-wails. We sat with the clinic guard. He was an elderly man and had fought for the rebels.

'We killed many Derg soldiers, many,' he recalled. 'Some of them were even my neighbours.' He had a warm and friendly face.

I spread out the maps on the clinic's concrete verandah. The light from my head-lamp picked out Bilbala and Amda Worq, and between them several inches of alarming gradients. Tigray and Aksum were a whole yard away in the darkness – and Lalibela just a thumbnail south of Bilbala. For all the aches and sweat, we'd done *nothing*. Folding away the map, I let the word 'bus' seep into my forward planning.

At dawn two sets of headlights raked across the scrub beyond Bilbala and bumped away to the south. In single file we climbed the low embankment and crunched across the gravel of the main road. The mules slid down the other side, and trotted ahead with a jangle of cooking pots. The air was crisp. Behind us, the fingers of the sun stretched high above the ridge of

Abune Josef. We headed north-west into the hills. The path was a shadow of a path. It followed a series of gentle valleys. Sometimes it disappeared altogether.

Bisrat hummed quietly as he walked. He was taller than Makonnen and had a very gentle manner. He walked with soft slow steps but covered the ground at a great pace.

Soon after midday we reached a shallow gorge. It was too hot to carry on; in the shade of some ironwood trees I called a halt.

Makonnen unloaded the mules. He fell asleep against the bags. I lay back and enjoyed one of walking's simple rewards: gazing up at the sky. It glowed deep blue between the leaves. A bird was going *puk-puk-puk* ... *puk-puk-puk* ... It took a while before I spotted its blood-red throat: double-toothed barbet, according to my *Birds of Eastern Africa*. I dozed off.

Bisrat was busy prodding at the ground with a stick when I woke. He had an expression of childlike innocence. I found myself hoping that everything was OK for him. As I watched, a faint smile spread across his face.

'What are you thinking, Bisrat?'

'It's all right. I'm not thinking anything.'

He carried on with his prodding.

'Were you born in Lalibela?'

'I was born there, yes.'

'Do you have family?'

'I have five children. Three brothers, two girls. My wife is dead.'

'What land do you have?'

'Three *timat*. But it's not good land. It's stony.'

'What can you grow?'

'Only barley and *teff*.'

'Is it steep?'

'It's half steep and half flat.'

'Enough for consumption?'

He shook his head. 'I collect relief food for two months.'

'And is this mule yours?'

'No.'

Bisrat had no livestock at all. Until recently he had had no land either. He had always worked for others. But when the Derg fell he was given land – three *timat* of land that no one else wanted.

He gave me a look of genuine gratitude. 'My life is better now, thanks to God.'

Some way further on, we spotted the round roof of a church. Its compound was bordered by euphorbia – not the candelabra euphorbia but the *ḳ'inch'ib* tree – *Euphorbia tirucallii* – known as 'finger cactus' for its fat succulent leaves.

A couple of priests were reclining in its shade; they were an elderly priest and a young priest. Two laymen reclined with them, and one of the laymen, it turned out, was having a little trouble with his daughter.

'I have found someone for her. He comes from Tara. But she will not have him.'

'Why not?'

'She wants to go to Bilbala to work.'

'She is throwing her life away!' said the young priest; he was very interested in two pebbles by his feet.

'I told her, I told her.'

'That is good.'

The men were all agreed that the girl needed correcting,

and in their agreement they lapsed into a satisfied silence.

'What is happening? In the old days girls were afraid.'

'They won't do grinding now.'

'The government tells us a girl cannot marry until she is eighteen.'

'You cannot expect a girl to keep her virginity until then.'

'Now if you show her your back for one minute,' said the old priest, 'a girl will throw away her virginity.'

'It is better if they marry young.'

'Eleven is the best age.'

They lapsed into another satisfied silence. Across the valley, a man was driving two oxen to plough.

I asked the men: 'Do foreigners ever come here?'

'Foreigners?'

'Foreigners have never been here.'

'I saw foreigners once,' said the elderly priest. 'In Lalibela. They looked very worried.'

'They were probably ill,' concluded the man with the troublesome daughter.

The young priest nodded. 'Ill,' he muttered. He showed no interest at all in his first foreigner. He was trying to arrange the pebbles on a flat stone, but they kept slipping off.

The way to Amda Worq took us to the edge of another gorge, much deeper than the first. The path narrowed and we were dropping down through rock-chutes, then along the cliff in a steep diagonal. We could see the same line in the path on the opposite side. Far below was a corridor of pale shingle. Loose stones chinked like broken china at our feet. The rock was cut back in places where the water cascaded down the cliff. But there was no water now. We jumped the last few feet onto pebbles and the mules were pressing their nostrils to the green trickle which was all that remained of the river.

We had a problem climbing out of the gorge. The mules reached a slope of bare rock. Their hooves splayed when they tried it. They slid back. Bisrat and Makonnen freed them of their loads. I looked at the angle of the rock face and thought: this is impossible. Hiluf shook his head. So what now? This was the only path. There were no bridges – the Sekota road was a day's walk in the wrong direction. In the rains the entire area was cut off.

The first mule tried again – and slipped back. Bisrat put a rope around her halter and tugged. Makonnen pushed from below. Three, four steps up. She sidestepped, away from Makonnen. Then they were both sliding. Below them was a gully which dropped sheer to the river below. Makonnen cried out. Bisrat yanked. The mule stretched her chin but her legs were floundering. Makonnen was on his knees, on the very edge of the gully. Bisrat pulled again. '*Ayzore! Ayzore!*' One of her sliding feet gained purchase. Then the others. The second mule followed more easily.

Makonnen was grinning as he reloaded. Relief drove a monologue, delivered in an intermittent falsetto. 'Oh be praised, Mother of God . . . keep us safe from danger and bless this road which is so steep . . . which is so difficult . . . oh Lord, this terrible road, it is too steep.' His hands were shaking.

Above the cliff, the path levelled out. It crossed an area of terraced plots; we were joined by a man with a mattock over his shoulder. He saw the sweat covering my face and neck.

'We were born to suffer on these roads. But why the *farenj*?'

His village was a speckle of brown huts high above us. Twenty or thirty people gathered as we stepped between brush fences. A young woman served us *tella* from a cool earthenware jug. She had a certain way of holding the jug and half-hiding her face. Makonnen held out his mug to refill; he was still animated from earlier, and he gave her a conquering smile.

It was already evening when we cleared the ridge. A cold wind swept up to meet us. A whole new world opened at our feet – grey cliffs and islands of yellowy fields wherever the ground was level enough. To the west, cloud hid the late sun. The strip of sky beneath was a fierce liquid orange.

'*Hard* land,' mused Bisrat, letting out a low whistle. 'Hard land.'

Just below was a lone pair of huts. Above the wind, I said: 'What about there, Hiluf?'

'We'll send the others ahead.'

'They might object to me?'

'Also me!'

Bisrat and Makonnen came back flanking a wiry old man called Teshome. It was all fine. We led the mules through a gap in the fence. We bought feed from Teshome and put up the tent.

I sat and loosened my boots. This was a lot tougher than I'd expected. The relentless up and down: up, when each step was an effort; and down, when your knees were constantly flexed and you had to watch every footfall on the bare rock, or on the loose sliding stones.

I took a long swig of water. Today's intake: three and a half litres. And to eat: a few biscuits at midday; in the morning, half a bowl of last night's spaghetti; now some packet soup and a tin of sardines. I could feel the dizziness from too much sun. I unpacked the stove and again the subversive thought came: buses – rattling boneshakers, rolling kilns on wheels, happily pushing back the miles towards Aksum!

Later, after the sun and the temperature had dropped, we sat with Teshome in the moonlight. Two families lived up here – two old men, two elderly women, two young women and a very large number of children. The young men, said Teshome, had taken the livestock to the lowlands.

In 1984, when the BBC first aired footage of the Korem feeding camp, many of those staring faces came from this area. The Derg had lost the entire region to the rebels. But the rebels could not cope with the famine. I asked Teshome about that time. In the Ethiopian calendar it was 1977.

'*Sabat-sabat?*' He stared at me without expression. 'You must not even talk of it.'

'How was last year's harvest?'

'The crop was destroyed by hail.'

He looked away. In the pale light, his profile was impassive. 'My God,' he hissed, 'save us, have mercy upon us.'

The next morning we left early. Teshome walked with us. The descent continued in a series of giant steps. A troupe of gelada baboons was feeding below. Teshome picked up a handful of rocks and we all joined him, pitching the rocks and shouting. The baboons loped off across the stubble.

We said goodbye to Teshome.

'You will reach Arzilo tomorrow,' he said. 'Amda Worq is not half a day from there.'

We dropped to the next layer of terraces. When I looked up Teshome was still there above the cliff, watching us go. The baboons were waiting in the trees.

We were resting at the top of a pass. The mules were nosing the dust for food when we heard whistling from below. It was a man with a goat. Over his back was a *masenqo*, a single-stringed fiddle and bow.

He joined us in the shade and, placing the *masenqo* between his knees, looked at each one of us. Then he started to play.

'People travelled far like the clouds
but could not find the way back to their home.
Wherever we may wander
Please God make sure we find our way home
So that we may not perish in the desert.'

He was an *azmari*, one of a caste of wandering musicians. He had been playing at a three-day wedding; the goat was his payment. Now he was on his way to another wedding near Bilbala.

'The best sorghum can be found
in the region of Yejju.
A man with a good baby
will forever be remembered by that child.'

He gave an ambiguous grin. Ambiguity is the *azmaris*' stock in trade, the basis of their verses. It is also what makes the *azmaris* the most revealing aspect of all Ethiopian secular culture. Some of their verses are traditional, some direct, some spontaneous compositions about those present. But the most popular carry in them a heavy load of meanings, puns and allusions – and the heavier the better. 'Weighty verses,' goes the Amharic saying, 'warm the insides like warm clothing.'

This style of figurative song has its own figurative name – *samenna worq* ('wax and gold'). To sculpt a gold figure, a clay cast is formed around a wax representation. The cast is heated, the wax pours out and the gold is poured in; once cooled, the cast is broken and the gold figure uncovered. Likewise *azmaris* compose verses that have an initial 'wax' meaning, and a more hidden 'gold' meaning. (For those who find 'wax and gold' too simple, there is an even trickier form known as *wasta wayra* – 'inside the olive tree', olive bark being a very different colour to the wood.)

The anthropologist Donald Levine named his classic Amhara ethnography simply *Wax and Gold*. Working in pre-revolutionary Ethiopia, he saw the verses as central to an appreciation of an entire way of thinking. 'Wax and gold represents more than a principle of poetic composition and a method of spiritual gymnastics ... *Samenna worq* colours the entire fabric of traditional Amhara life'.

He quotes an example:

> *'Etsa balas balto addam kanfareshe*
> *Madhene alam lebe tasaqala-leshe.'*
> (Since Adam – your lip did eat of that tree
> The Saviour – my heart has been hung up for thee.)

This is pure wax and gold, in which the two meanings sit one above the other – Adam/lip and Saviour/heart. The wax meaning is: Because Adam ate of the Tree of Knowledge/The Saviour of the World has been crucified for you. The gold meaning shimmers beneath. It depends on the verb *tasaqala* being a synonym for 'was crucified' and 'is anxious to be near'. So listeners would smirk when behind this piety they heard: 'Because of your [tempting] lips/My heart is anxious to be near you.'

While celebrating its complexity, Levine saw *qene* and *samenna worq* as an obstacle to progress in Ethiopia: 'nothing could be more at odds with the ethos of modernisation than a cult of ambiguity ... modern Western culture rests on a commitment to unambiguous communication'. At the time of his work, in the 1960s, ethnography was relying more and more on linguistics. And the most unambiguous language of all was about to come into its own: binary, the language of computers. In Ethiopia, the revolution was only a decade away.

The *azmari* pressed his ear to the sound box. He retuned the horsehair string.

> 'The home of the beauty of Rayanz is at the banks of the
>   Abbay river
> His chest burns like the cooking-pan . . .'

The next verse was a little more direct:

> 'Death is a horse always riding towards us
> Let's eat and drink and keep that horse away.'

So we ate – I produced bread and biscuits, and water. I also fished out some money.

> 'Whisky refreshes – beer cleans the blood
> It's very good to play to Father Farenj!
> May God bless this green place where I met Father Farenj!'

The *azmari* untied the goat, put the *masenqo* over his back and set off southwards. We had walked on some way before Makonnen let out a sudden squeal of pleasure.

'Father Farenj! Father Farenj!' he mocked. 'You – Father Farenj! With your pocket full of money!'

*   *   *

We dropped down into a third gorge. As we crossed the river and climbed up the first steep section we came across a boy half-sitting and half-lying beneath a bush. It was very hot. The sweat glistened on his cheek. Two flies were angled at the caruncle of one eye. He had malaria.

'Leave me.'

'You can't stay down here,' urged Hiluf. 'Night is coming.'

'Leave me . . .'

His chin dropped to his chest. We gave him water. We took him by the arms. Once on his feet he was able to walk.

'Eat.' Hiluf pressed biscuits on him. 'You don't feel hungry but you must eat.' He was in no doubt that the boy would die if left in the gorge.

He was young – in his late teens – and his story was this. He and a few others had been taking grain to the mill. It was a good half-day walk. They were on their way back when the fever set in. He had dropped behind. Those with him wanted to get out of the gorge before dark. They drove on the donkeys and were soon out of sight.

He was now delirious. It was dusk by the time we reached his village. We saw him off to his hut and arranged to stay the night in another compound. It turned out to belong to one of those who had gone to the mill.

'Why didn't you go back for him?' I asked. 'He had no water, no food.'

'It's all right. We spoke to his relations. They were about to go back and collect him.'

In the morning we went to see him. He was still feverish. He was shy and grateful. But it turned out he was a hired hand. His own family, with not enough land to support him, lived two days' walk away. There were no relations to go back. He was simply abandoned.

*　　*　　*

The next day we reached the bottom of the deepest gorge. Bisrat and Makonnen watered the mules and I lay on a slab of flood-smoothed granite. We were in shadow. High above me I could see sunlight catching tufts of clifftop grass.

The air was still. Heat pressed down into the narrow space between the cliffs. It was a heavy heat, not the familiar thin heat of the highlands. These chasms were like another element. Beneath them is a region known as *maq* where the bodies of sinners fall after burial (in Ge'ez, the Hebrew equivalent '*Sheol*' is also used). Down there too is *weqniyanos*, the vast primal ocean into which flow all the rivers of the world. There was a time, according to the Ethiopians, when the earth itself was entirely smooth – but then came the flood, and in its wake it left the broken terrain that man struggles to live in now.

Thomas Burnet's *The Sacred Theory of the Earth* puts forward a similar notion. I had stumbled on this wonderful piece of seventeenth-century literature years earlier in the British Library. I was chasing a reference to something called 'the Abyssinian Philosophy' – which turned out not to be a piece of forgotten Ethiopian wisdom but a description of Burnet's theory, turning as it did on the role of the 'abyss'.

Several things convinced me to carry on with Burnet. Could a notion of the 'abyss' have crept into the perception and spelling of Abyssinia, the name used for Ethiopia for many centuries? Was this another instance of Ethiopia representing an idea as much as a place? I was also hooked by Burnet's extravagant imagery, his prose, and a sense of that heady freedom of thought possible in the early years of the Enlightenment when the world was still waiting to reveal its secrets.

In 1711 Joseph Addison discovered Burnet's writings, and he too was ecstatic. In the *Spectator* he wrote of the pleasure of reading 'sublime thoughts communicated to us by men of great genius and eloquence'.

Burnet's theory is a hymn to the natural world. 'Since I was first inclined to the Contemplation of Nature,' he begins, 'I had always, me-thought, a particular Curiosity to look back into the Sources and Original of Things.' On a walking tour of the

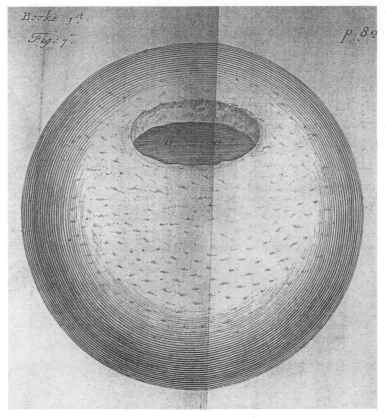

Thomas Burnet's smooth Convex of the Earth, showing an Aperture (a–a) to reveal the great watery Abyss beneath

Alps it occurred to him that there was a problem with the story of the Biblical flood. Looking at the soaring peaks, he realised that there couldn't possibly be enough water on earth to swamp them all. Borrowing a few elements from Descartes' *Principia Philosophiae* he suggested therefore that the earth's surface must originally have been smooth, like an egg. It was also a perfect world. Covered in a coating of moist and fertile soil, 'it had the Beauty of Youth and blooming Nature, fresh and fruitful, and not a Wrinkle, Scar or Fracture in all its Body'. But such was man's wickedness that the shell cracked, the waters burst out and our broken world with its jagged coasts and great mountains was formed.

Burnet's theory in its time was of great significance. It sparked a long series of debates at the Royal Society, but it was by no means universally accepted. While broadly supportive, Isaac Newton could not condone the way Burnet challenged the truth of Genesis. And that was the stumbling block for poor old Burnet: it was all very well to try to understand the laws of the Cosmos, but step beyond the eternal verities of the Bible and you entered the realm of the absurd. At one point Burnet even went so far as to parody the story of Eve. The wags of the day taunted him for maintaining

That all the books of Moses
Were nothing but supposes

and:

That as for father Adam
With Mrs Eve his madam
And what the serpent spoke, Sir
'Twas nothing but a joke, Sir,
And well-invented flam.

Burnet spent a good deal of time trying to defend his theory. At one point he cited the evidence of an 'Aethiopian philosopher' who had recently visited Spain. This philosopher explained the Ethiopian view of the primeval earth – a view which not only concurred with what is now known of Amhara cosmology, but tied in exactly with Burnet's own vision:

> [The Ethiopians] say the first Earth ... was smooth and regular in its surface, without mountains or Vallies, but hollow within: and was spontaneously fruitful, without plowing or sowing. This was its first State: but when Mankind became degenerate and outragious with Pride and Violence, the angry Gods, as they say, by Earthquakes and Concussions, broke the habitable Orb of the Earth, and thereupon the subterraneous Waters gushing out, drown'd it in a deluge, and destroy'd Mankind.

Burnet also answered those critics who wondered why there remained so little in the way of accounts of his First World. Either destroyed, he claimed, like the great libraries of Alexandria and Constantinople, or like those at Buda or Fez 'in the hands of Mohametans'. But in an ancient Abyssinian library, he claimed, could be found both the source of his theory and the evidence to back it up. No foreigner at the time could get into the country without being killed. As nothing could be verified, all manner of wonder was possible.

But in fact, early in the seventeenth century Samuel Purchas in *His Pilgrimage* had already talked of a great library on a mountain in Ethiopia – three great halls, each two hundred paces long. With a bibliophile's glee he described some of its contents: the volumes of science and cosmography, philosophy, the lost Book of Enoch, the writings of Abraham, and of Job

when he had recovered his wealth. The works of Aquinas and
Augustine were there, and those of the Jews exiled from Spain.
And here too was gold 'as the sands of the Sea and the stars in
the sky'. It was also to that mountain, he recorded, that all the
royal princes were sent at the age of eight and imprisoned.

All these, explains Purchas, could be found on the Ethiopian
mountaintop of the Holy Cross. This identifies it as Amba
Gishen, to the south of Lalibela. (I had spent a night up at
Amba Gishen monastery in 1988 – a very extraordinary flat-top
peak, shaped like a cross, no princes, many monks, no sign of a
great library.) Purchas calls the mountain Mount Amara. When
Coleridge fell asleep and 'dreamed' his poem 'Kubla Khan', one
of Purchas's volumes lay open on his lap: 'It was an Abyssinian
Maid/And on her dulcimer she play'd/Singing of Mount
Abora.'

In those days it was possible to step out of the Reading Room
of the British Library and straight into the British Museum.
There I found Coleridge's original manuscript in a display

cabinet. The manuscript shows clearly that he did not write the 'Mount Abora' that now appears in the standard edition of the poem, but 'Mount Amara' – site of Purchas's great library.

Coleridge had a high regard for Burnet, and quotes from his work for the long epigraph to *The Rime of the Ancient Mariner*. He also had a plan to convert Burnet's *The Sacred Theory of the Earth* into a great epic of free verse. For each of these men – Purchas, Coleridge and Burnet – Abyssinia was a place of the imagination, an unattainable and ancient store-house of wisdom and wonder.

As for tracing the 'abyss' in Abyssinia, my efforts became ever more open-ended. Abyssinia is usually believed to have come from 'al-Habasha', the Arabic name for the country. From that to 'Abyssinia' has always seemed to me quite a leap. I spent many hours scouring indexes, examining the dates of variant spellings, feeling tangible evidence slip in and out of my grasp.

These digressions taught me a couple of lessons. 1. How much pleasure can be had in copyright libraries flitting from book to book, touring centuries less world-knowing than our own. 2. How you can drive yourself half-mad trying to find proof in such places.

Sliding off my rock, I dropped onto the shingle. The mules were already halfway up the opposite cliff. I could see them, neck-dipping and scrambling up another difficult path. I crossed the river. The clear water welled at my boots.

We were entering Agaw country. The river marked the border of the province of Wag. The Agaw were among the original inhabitants of northern Ethiopia. Waves of migration from across the Red Sea brought the Semitic ancestors of the Amhara and the Tigrayans. Over time it was these groups and these languages which achieved dominance. But in this region many Agaw still speak Agawigna, a Kushitic language known as 'the language of the birds' by other Ethiopians, who make no attempt to understand it.

In the mid-morning we reached the town of Arzilo. On the edge was a fence around two hand-pumps. A plate on their standpipes said: MADE IN INDIA, *December 2001*. One of them was broken; at the other was a woman with couple of jerry-cans. She filled our water bottles.

'Is there fruit in the town?' We had run out of fresh food two days ago.

'Fruit?'

'Bananas, papaya –'

'No fruit.'

'Tomatoes, onions?'

She gave me a stony look.

The market square was empty. There was little but grain and soap in the stores. We asked for Amda Worq and they pointed us to the north-west and a rocky path across bare fields. A little way outside the town, Bisrat and Makonnen spotted the white gable of a tent.

'We will catch you up!' they called.

'What is it?' I asked Hiluf.

'A wedding.'

'Let's all go!'

'Not you.' Hiluf shook his head. 'You would distract them.'

For Bisrat and Makonnen the tent was good news. It signalled a big wedding, and a big wedding meant *tella* for all comers.

But all did not go well for Bisrat and Makonnen. It was

certainly a big wedding. There was plenty of *tella*, and the two of them tied up the mules outside and were happily drinking in a corner when three armed militiamen came over.

'Those your mules?'

'Yes.'

'The bags on them?'

'Yes, it's all right. They're a foreigner's. We're with a foreigner.'

'You're lying. There are no foreigners here.'

The militiamen said they were thieves. They said they must be thieves because of the stuff on the mules and because they were not from round there.

'We are arresting you!'

Makonnen persuaded them to come and find Hiluf and me. The first we knew of it was seeing the two of them and the mules cresting the ridge with an armed guard. Then they wanted to know what I was doing. Hiluf smoothed things over, and they pointed out the way ahead.

'Amda Worq? Across here, over that hill, down, then up, up, up!'

The path dropped through shelves of pale tufa. Makonnen was angry, and in his anger he hurried. Watching him below, leading the mules down into another gorge, I heard him singing:

'Why do you boast and for whom is the fame?
It is usual for the poor to beg at the threshing-place.'

From which I understood: there's no need for those with power to swagger around reminding the poor that they must beg even for *tella*.

We rested beside a dry river. In places spring-water rose

and trickled among the rocks before sinking away. Makonnen unloaded the mules. He was soon asleep.

He woke in a better mood. As we climbed back up to the first terraces and the first huts, as he and Bisrat drove the tired mules, he punctuated his shouts with sung couplets:

'Wag is the best land
Where the ox and cattle spend all day together . . .
Meat cannot be eaten without pounding it.
Is that how Wag remains the country of youth?'

In the late afternoon we came across an elderly man sitting outside a hut. He had lived most of his life in the town of Amda Worq, but had come here recently to stay with his daughter. He was called Berhan and he stalled us with the story of the founding of Amda Worq. It was a favourite story, combining as it did the beautiful truths of the past with the perennial treachery of women.

It happened during the Gondarene period. A man named Za-Selassie came and stood on top of the cliffs. He looked around him and saw that all was good – the very narrow approach, the view of all directions. 'This is the place for a town!' he thought.

Za-Selassie at the time was married to the daughter of the emperor, the great Fasilades. One day the couple had a quarrel. Unknown to Za-Selassie, his wife went to her father and told him of the quarrel. So Emperor Fasilades summoned Za-Selassie to Gondar and asked: 'So, how is my daughter?' 'She is well,' said Za-Selassie. Fasilades killed him at once.

Then the region around Amda Worq fell into chaos. Four local chiefs went to the emperor in Gondar. Below the palace they saw a servant washing clothes in the river. It was Demo –

the child of Za-Selassie by another woman. In the palace they stood before the emperor and said, 'We have no chief and we are living in chaos. Please appoint a chief; anyone is good enough – even a man like Demo who is only a servant but is one of ours.' So the emperor appointed Demo.

'That was how the town of Amda Worq received its first chief, its first *shum*.' Berhan looked out over the hills and nodded as if to say: That is the way of the world.

He directed us on round the side of a conical peak, and with the sun raking across the stony ground we joined the main road into town. The road had been hard-won. Outcrops of basalt had been blasted in two. The carcasses of bulldozers lay abandoned where they had broken.

It had been market day in Amda Worq and villagers were returning home in their thousands. We weaved our way through them – whole families, large high-spirited groups. One or two elderly men rode on mules. Others carried dirty blocks of Danakil salt on their shoulders. Donkeys were light-footed with empty panniers or slow with swollen bags of grain. Women walked barefoot beside their sandalled husbands. Priests sat laughing in roadside *tella bets*.

We rounded a bluff and there was the town. Silvery roofs shone out among the hanging eucalyptus. Beneath them, the sheer rock glowed yellow in the evening sun – that was the *amda worq*, the 'pillar of gold'. A dotted line of people ran out on the far side, following another cliff-cut path. Amda Worq was sited at the very rim of the sky. It was a natural fortress.

The Glorious Victories of Amda Seyon

King Amda Seyon ruled Ethiopia in the fourteenth century. His reign was a troubled one. There was an occasion when ten Muslim kings attacked his narrow strip of highlands all at the same time. But fortunately Amda Seyon, whose name means 'pillar of Zion', had God on his side. The earliest piece of literature in the Amharic vernacular is *The Glorious Victories of Amda Seyon*, and during his time there were many glorious days to record, like this one:

Amda Seyon king of Ethiopia killed ten thousand and thousands with the help of God. Men's blood flowed like water, and bodies lay like grass on the earth. On that day the king himself killed with his own hand those who had swords, bows, javelins of wood, and spears of iron and were exceedingly brave. If I were to tell you the number of those killed by the king that day, you would believe it was a lie and say, 'In truth this is impossible.'

Amda Seyon is regarded as the father of the modern Ethiopian state, yet his chronicle records that, like Prester John, he displayed great humility: 'King Amda Seyon, gentle and humble like Moses and David; discerning, merciful, and patient; caring for the aged like his father, the poor like his mother, and priests and monks like his Lord. Though king, he humbled himself before all like a poor man.'

Amda Seyon married his father's concubine and slept with one of his own sisters, and maybe two of them. When a delegation of priests came to admonish him for it, he brought on the royal lions to bare their teeth at the priests and then had them flogged until their blood flowed. The strange thing was that in the place where the priests were punished, a fire broke out. The fire spread to the king's door and he diverted a river to extinguish it. But the fire spread further. Then a plague of white flies came and bit the king's horses and mules and they all died.

6

We spent a couple of days in Amda Worq. Bisrat and Makonnen drank a lot of *tella*, the mules ate a lot of hay, Hiluf had his shoes fixed and I found some bananas. We all relaxed in our own way. And from the height of Amda Worq, with the peaks and ridges spread out below, with my legs a little stronger, the path to Aksum appeared suddenly more manageable.

Look in the index of Ethiopian histories and you will find *Amba Alagi, battle of*; *Amda Seyon, King (1314–44), glorious victories of*; amda worq *(part of a church)*; and *American Peace Corps, Amhara, Amharic* and *Amharisation*. But no *Amda Worq, town of*.

For centuries Amda Worq, in the Ethiopian way, has gone about its business in splendid isolation. Rulers have sometimes managed to place a garrison up here, but never for very long. The people have always been wild and independent, quick to arms, knowing that the world is a distant place they could resist with impunity. They have also been very devout.

This rocky region helps to solve the riddle at the heart of Ethiopia's history: how has it sustained its sovereignty? Why did it not, like its neighbours, become Muslim? Why was it the only African country to resist the European colonial adventure? The glib answer is mountains – and perhaps it really is as simple as that. Landscape has translated its spirit to produce a deeply religious and bellicose people. Its sons have veered towards being either monks or warriors, proving that in this case spiritual devotion and militancy are just two cuts of the same cloth. Each sacrifices his physical life for an abstract cause. The rebel is as opposed to foreign or central rule as the contemplative is to the material world. Each has helped make Ethiopia what it is.

Perhaps it is no coincidence then that the most successful of all the anti-Derg rebel movements, the one that currently rules Ethiopia, was also the one that was most ascetic in its discipline and its ideology. The TPLF made its fighters, men and women, take a strict vow of celibacy, and anyone caught breaking it was killed.

On our first morning, Hiluf and I went to call on an old man named Ababew Tesema. In his yard, a boy was watching a loose-legged calf stumble over some rocks.

'Ababew? He is my grandfather.'

Ababew himself was inside, facing the wall of his room and praying. In his dirty grey undershirt, he stood with head bowed and hands clasped together in front of his waist. A shotgun hung on the wall above him.

We waited. The fly-buzz of his prayers droned around the room. They rose in volume. They flew back and forth among the rafters. They became a half-shout. 'Mother of God, you say let them insult us, you say it increases our account in heaven but if they go on insulting us FOREVER, what then?

Should we not rid the world of such DEVILS? Mary, Mother of Light, grant your blessing.'

He coughed. He yawned and rubbed his beard.

'Grandfather –'

'Yes?'

'A foreigner has come to see you.'

'A foreigner?' Ababew unhooked the shotgun. 'Where is he?'

The barrel swung round with him. The boy reached out and pushed it up to point at the roof.

'Where is he!'

Ababew's eyes glowed like pale moons. He had advanced trachoma. I leaned forward and gripped his elbow. 'I'm here.'

He blinked at my touch. His face opened in a wide smile. 'I wasn't going to shoot, signor! We don't shoot foreigners, not any more. Look – I bought this gun from a *dejmach*. It's Italian.'

He took my arm and we all went outside. The early sun was not yet hot. Ababew sat straight-backed on a stool, talking of his life in a strong, mellifluous voice. The gun stood between his knees while he tinkered with a cartridge belt.

In his seventy-eight years, Ababew had seen it all. As a boy he had stood by the road and watched the Italians march into Amda Worq; he had watched them being driven out a few weeks later; he had watched them return, then run away again. He had watched the Derg march in, seen them driven out, come back, leave, come back and leave for good.

Ababew loved all things Italian – even though the Italians had come to Amda Worq and occupied it by force, even though it was for an Eritrean working for the Italians that his mother abandoned him when he was just two years old. 'Those cursed *farenji*!'

'Ababew,' I said, 'you've seen all these different people coming to Amda Worq. Who is best?'

He fingered the barrel of his gun. His lips quivered. Behind his sightless gaze paraded a lifetime of governors, occupiers, liberators, ideologues and rebels.

'None of them is good, signor. They all insult us, those devils – and we chase them out.'

'What about the Wagshum?'

'The Washkum?'

'Yes – the Wagshum.'

'Well, he was like a king! When he rode through the countryside everyone threw down their tools and ran along behind him.'

From somewhere deep in Ababew's chest rose a volcanic eruption of laughter, but whether it was mocking or respectful, I doubt even he knew.

For centuries this province of Wag was ruled by hereditary Wagshums (*shum* being 'chief' in Amharic). Claiming direct descent from the Zagwe rulers, the Wagshums represented – in their own eyes at least – a kind of parallel Ethiopian royal family. Whenever they visited court, they exercised rights denied to the other nobility. They approached the emperor without rolling their robes from their chest; they washed in the same gold basin as him, were seated at table before the food was served and sat in a chair beside the imperial throne. They were also allowed to beat their *nagarits*, the silver drums of rank, right up to the palace gates.

In Addis Ababa a few weeks earlier, I had been given the name of Tafari Wossen. He lived in a house wrapped in imperial-purple bougainvillea. He ran a media company called Waag Communications, had been educated at a British private school and spoke English with a certain fruity charm. Tafari's father had been the last Wagshum.

'Yes, he was the last one. But he didn't spend a lot of time in Wag. The emperor made him ambassador in Greece.'

Tafari had been born in a small village somewhere near Amda Worq. When I asked him where, he said: 'To tell you the truth, I'm not really sure. It was during the Italian occupation and we were constantly moving. Everything was a little bit chaotic.'

The Italians were not keen on Tafari's family, and in particular his great-uncle, the famous resistance leader Dejazmach

Hailu Kebede. Tafari had a photograph of him in the hall. He was an impressive figure. He had a squarish face, both authoritative and humorous, and a distinctive moustache.

'The Italians did rather go after him,' said Tafari proudly.

In Italy, the humiliation of the 1896 battle of Adwa proved momentous. Early in 1935, with the other European powers basking in their African dominions, Mussolini stood before the crowd in the Piazza Venezia. 'We have been patient for forty years,' he boomed. 'Now we too want our place in the sun!'

His forces marched into Ethiopia. For a week they met no resistance. The first setback was Makelle. The Tigrayan capital was, thanks to a duplicitous governor, supposed to fall into their hands without a fight. But before the Italians arrived, seven thousand Wag men sacked Makelle and sent the traitor fleeing to the Italian lines. The men were under the command of Tafari's uncle, Dejazmach Hailu Kebede.

Largely brought up by his own uncle, the hero of Adwa, Wagshum Gwangul, Hailu had learned the traditional skills of fighting and command. His men were driven by the zeal of mountain-dwellers – a zeal that helps blur the distinction between the love of freedom and the love of killing outsiders. But in 1935 they discovered that warfare had moved on a little since the battle of Adwa.

The Italo–Abyssinian war of the mid-1930s was a clash of two divergent worlds. It was a conflict in which tanks were swarmed over by Ethiopians, who beheaded the crews with home-forged swords; in which twenty-five thousand high-landers could march six hundred miles in a matter of weeks, only to be scattered in minutes by a few planes dropping canisters of mustard gas. In his palace in Addis Ababa, Emperor Haile Selassie hosted feasts for several thousand warriors in lion skins, feeding them entire herds of raw beef, while recommending (for their own security) that all foreigners in the city decamp to its fringes.

Dejazmach Hailu and his army did not hold Makelle. He was forced to retreat to Tembien. Near Abi Addi, he managed a successful counter-attack. He and his men were poised to break through the Italian lines. In doing so, they would leave the whole of Tigray exposed. But the order came to halt. The Italians reinforced and the moment was lost. Soon the army from Wag, depleted by the day, was falling back towards Sekota.

Dejazmach Hailu sensed then that the conventional war was lost. When a last rallying call came from the emperor, he sent only a deputy. But word spread that Haile Selassie himself, the Conquering Lion of Judah, Elect of God, had come to the front to take command. Even for the men of Wag, that made it less a case of loyalty to the crown than a matter of divine obligation. They flocked to the south-east to join him. Hailu was forced to lead them.

Haile Selassie was always adept at exploiting the theatre of his office. Surrounded by his nobility, he took up position in a large cave. On a throne of skins and rugs, he looked out over the plain of Lake Ashangi, across to the Italian lines. Morale in the Ethiopian camp was high – parallels with Adwa were too many to suggest that God had chosen anything other than triumph for Ethiopia. The day for the attack too was auspicious – the feast of Ethiopia's patron saint, Giorgis. Victory was written in the sky.

The memory of Adwa had also shaped Italian preparations. Their lines were well-built, protected by the natural barbed wire of thorn. All day the Ethiopians charged it, but they failed to break through. Dejazmach Hailu was badly wounded. He was carried back by his men into the mountains of Wag.

The emperor retreated. He did the natural thing. He went to Lalibela for three days and sat in prayer and contemplation. But within a month the Italians were in Addis. Haile Selassie had fled the country, leaving the fight to guerrilla leaders like Dejazmach Hailu.

'So that was Hailu,' mused Tafari.

'What happened to him?'

'In the end?'

'Yes.'

'Not very nice,' he sighed. 'Why don't we go and talk to my aunt. After all, she's his daughter.'

It was a lovely, fresh Addis afternoon. Scribbles of high cloud were etched above the Entoto hills. Woyzero Tsehayenesh Hailu lived in the Kechene district, on a large triangle of ground once granted to the Wagshum by the emperor. Her spare rooms were always free to citizens from Wag. If they needed food or the fare home she would dip into her own purse. But her largesse now outstripped her means. Shanties pressed at the fences of her compound and her own quarters showed the signs of penniless nobility.

Like that of any elderly widow, Woyzero Tsehayenesh's living room was a gallery of family portraits. Beside framed pictures of her daughter, son and grandchildren was one of her father, Dejazmach Hailu. It was the same photo that had hung in Tafari's hall.

'And that also is him.'

She pointed over my shoulder. I turned. It was a photograph of three Italian soldiers. They wore well-pressed uniforms, their shirtsleeves neatly rolled above the elbow. On one pale forearm was a wristwatch. One of the men was holding a severed head by the hair. The eyes were closed, but it was the same moustache.

By the rainy season of 1937, the Italians had consolidated their territory. The emperor was in exile in Bath and his people were becoming used to the occupation. Resistance had been reduced to small areas, mere tickles on the leathery hide of Il Duce's *Africa Orientale Italiana*. But then, in the Ethiopian new year, a sudden series of attacks reminded the Italians that even 650,000 European troops could not control such a barbarous country.

In retaliation they set out after the one leader whose name they knew, who had harried them since the first days of the invasion. The order went out to hunt down Dejazmach Hailu.

'They came after us first,' Woyzero Tsehayenesh began quite matter-of-factly. 'I was with my mother and sister in a village near Amda Worq. They sent one hundred soldiers to get us. But the people of the town were good to us. They killed all but ten.'

As soon as her father heard he came up from his camp near the Meri river. He destroyed the Italian garrison at Amda Worq, then took to the bush to continue his guerrilla campaign. For some time he moved around Wag, engaging with the Italians, retreating, travelling on. But the forces against him were growing. The Italians recruited men from the Galla tribes. At about five one afternoon, some way to the east of Sekota, Dejazmach Hailu was pressed to the edge of a cliff and surrounded.

Woyzero Tsehayenesh paused. 'It was a Thursday. They burned the church. When it became dark my father hid among the trees. His men slept while he prayed . . .'

Her voice fell away. In the dim light I could see tears on

her cheeks. The story was showing strange parallels with the Passion.

'At daybreak on the Friday they came for him again. At ten he was hit and he fell . . .'

Dejazmach Hailu lay dying. He called a priest to his side. 'Abba, I have no visible sin. I have been loyal to my wife. I have killed only in battle.'

At midday the Italians found his corpse. They cut off the head and threw the body over the cliff.

'It landed near the village of Kulamat. The people there knew whose it was. They covered it with a *gabbi* and hid it until the evening. Then they buried it.'

Woyzero Tsehayenesh took a handkerchief from under her *shamma*. 'He was always a wonderful father.' She dried her eyes. She blew her nose. 'When I think of his death, it is as though it was yesterday. It never grows any further away.'

A woman brought in a tray of coffee. Woyzero Tsehayenesh drank it quickly. She looked again at the picture.

'They weren't sure it was him at first. But some people came and when they saw the head they burst into tears. Then the Italians knew it was him.

'They killed those people. Then they put wire round my father's head. On Saturday they took it to Alamata and displayed it in the marketplace. On Monday they took it to K'obo and displayed it.' With each day, with each place, she struck the table in front of her with the flat of her hand. 'On Thursday they displayed it in Korem. On the next Monday they displayed it in Makelle . . . and from there to Asmara.'

'What happened to you?' I asked.

'We were still children. My mother looked after us. She took over my father's command until the emperor came back.' She smiled. A sheen of tears still covered her cheeks. 'The Italians came to Amda Worq looking for us, so we were sent down to the Takazze. Terrible place – lowlands! I got malaria.'

In Amda Worq we met a man who, for several years during the Derg period, had been the town's administrator. Amsalu was an affable giant with an attractive line in self-deprecating humour. We sat on the edge of the cliff. It was evening. We looked down over the tangle of hills and ridges towards the Takazze river. The low sun dissolved everything in its dusty yellow light.

'You worked for the Derg, Amsalu?'

He nodded.

'Did you approve of them?'

'I was stupid. I saw just in front of my face.' He waved one hand before his nose.

'When I worked for the emperor's people, I found them corrupt. The Derg came and said: Now everyone will be equal. And I thought: that sounds a good idea. So I worked with the Derg for a few years. But one day they captured eighty rebels. They chained them together and shot them. So when the EPDM took the town and said everyone should elect their own leaders, I thought: that sounds a good idea, I'll go with you.' Amsalu chuckled at his own capriciousness.

When someone stops believing in God, it is said, he will believe in anything; and when a people ditch an absolute ruler, they will follow anyone.

So with the fall of Haile Selassie, factions multiplied. Even within the Derg there were factions but Mengistu made sure he killed his rivals so those around him could focus on the job in hand. Elsewhere, the country became a jumble of liberation fronts, revolutionary parties, democratic unions, people's revolutionary parties, democratic liberation fronts and revolutionary people's liberation unions.

First were the Eritreans, already veterans of a long struggle against the emperor. But they were divided. There was the largely Muslim ELF and the newer, Christian EPLF. The ELF and the EPLF frequently fought each other. When the Derg came to power, replacing the AFCC with the PMAC, the ELF encouraged Tigrayan dissent through the TLF, but the TLF had to contend too with the TPLF which had grown out of the TNO which set them against the TLF because of the TLF's sympathies with the reactionary EDU. The TPLF were Marxists, even though like the EDU they drew much of their leadership from offspring of the nobility. But after the TPLF had executed the TLF leader, the TPLF incorporated the TLF and its members. But because of the ELF's alliance with the now defunct TLF, the TPLF used the ELF's rivals the EPLF to marginalise the ELF. Meanwhile the EPRP had taken a battering from the Derg during the Red Terror, itself a campaign against the counter-revolutionary forces not only of the EPRP, but also the EDU, MEISON, the OLF and the Ogadenis. The EPRP had fallen out with the TPLF and the EDU and themselves fractured into three groups, one of which, with TPLF support, became the EPDM. The rump EPRP continued to fight the TPLF. The TPLF continued to fight the ELF and the EDU. And all of them, whenever they could spare the time, fought against the Derg.

That was in the late 1970s. A decade later, with the Derg still in power, a meeting took place near Amda Worq. By then most of the capital letters had been scattered like so many pebbles in the riverbed. The rebel movements had consolidated into the TPLF, the EPDM and the EPLF. The meeting was held in the badlands around the Takazze river, in a big cave.

Amsalu was at that meeting.

'What did we talk about first at this great democratic meeting? We talked about flags. Outside the cave hung the TPLF flag next to the Amhara flag. The TPLF flag was higher because they were stronger and the Amhara said, That is not right! So someone went and dropped the TPLF flag to the same level. But the Tigrayans said, No that is still not right. So he raised them both to the original level and everyone agreed that that was how the flags should be.'

Then they found other things to argue about. The arguments went on for days until someone said: Unity is strength! That was the first point everyone could agree on. And the strange thing was that they then found they could agree on other points too. Eritrea should have independence from Ethiopia. The other parties should unite. They would divide command, combine operations, pool resources. They would take over the rest of the country!

'The meeting took two months. Afterwards there was a big feast. We killed twelve cows.'

From then on, the fall of the Derg was simply a matter of time.

7

We left Amda Worq on a crisp mountain morning. We turned off the main road and skirted round one of the sugarloaf peaks. From the clifftop I looked north. Every crease and contour, every flat-topped summit, every distant line of rucked-up rock was picked out in the early brightness. We were heading for Sekota, fifty miles or so to the north-east.

Five hours later we were all lying under a tree. The buzz of flies filled the canopy above. The cuckoo-hoot of a *debenya* sounded from another tree. We were drowsy.

Over the brow of the road came a man – first his head, wrapped against the sun in a green woollen turban, then his stick and his torso, finally his bare legs and sandalled feet.

He had been selling eggs in Chila. He stood and looked down at us, then sat on a root.

'How is life in these parts?' I asked.

'It is beautiful.'

His clothes were rags, not beggars' rags but farmers' rags, worn by work. His jacket and the seat of his shorts were patched; the patches themselves now needed patching. He had an ageless face; he could have been forty or he could have been sixty.

'Do you remember the time of the emperor?'

'Who?'

'Janhoy.'

'No.'

'The Derg?'

'I don't remember.'

We lapsed into silence. The *debenya* resumed its hooting.

He nodded towards the far hills. 'The rebels used to attack from there, suddenly, at night. The Derg didn't know what to do. They left. They went to Lalibela. They told us to attack the rebels.'

'Did you?'

'That was a bad time. I cannot remember it well.' He straightened his turban. 'I used an Italian rifle. It's at my home now. Do you want to see it?'

I shook my head. 'Do you remember the famine?'

'I don't know when it was.'

'But you remember it?'

He thought for a moment. 'The Derg sent people to the south. We were about to go. Then some foreigners came. They had food. That's what happened.'

'And now, is the new government better?'

He stood and picked up his stick. 'If someone kills a man now, you cannot put him in prison. You have to have evidence.' He narrowed his eyes at the glare of the road and concluded: 'No, you cannot say it is better.'

* * *

In the town of Chila we sat in a sunken room and drank *tella* from gourds. Low mud benches ran around the wall. Road-workers, farmers and ox-traders sat with us. Ploughing was the main theme in that *tella bet*.

'I have almost finished my *gwaro*–'

'My ox is lame. All year grazing and he goes lame when I need him.'

A man among them was embroidering. He had a little coil of yellow thread in his lap and another one of mauve. He was decorating the hem of a woman's dress.

'It is the first year my son is ploughing,' said one of the farmers. 'He has good control but does not possess enough strength.'

The seamster held up his work to the light. 'God will give him strength,' he said. 'God will provide.'

Outside Chila, we headed up towards the pass. The sun was at its hottest. For two hours we sat beneath an *imbis* tree. Free of their loads, the mules picked their way through the stubble, nibbling at broken barley-stalks.

From above us came shouting. Someone was pleading, using all his powers of persuasion. I scrabbled up the bank and found a man driving two oxen around a pitch of terraced ground.

'Be straight, Berhan, PLEASE be straight! Jimba, go on – GO ON!'

A green and red cloth was wound around his head. In one hand he held a long whip – a *giraf*. With the other he was pressing at the tilt, keeping the share dug in.

'Straight! Berhan, pull . . . Jimba, to the left, please!'

Berhan and Jimba strained at the yoke. Their names meant 'light' and 'sunset'.

'To your place, Berhan – YOUR PLACE! Ohhhh . . . ohhh . . .' The farmer had an actor's vocal range. Begging, he kept them in line. Coaxing, he urged one of them to stall. Commanding, he drove the other round.

As they turned, he raised the flashing blade from the soil. Fine red tilth poured from the mould-boards.

'No! No, Jimba – stay – sta-aay!'

When they were in position he dropped the share and the two beasts began to heave again. Their legs drove into the earth. Ridges of muscle striped their haunches. The share hardly moved. The farmer leaned forward; all his weight was keeping down the blade. Berhan raised a foreleg and stepped forward. Jimba lurched to the right.

'No, Jimba – GO STRAIGHT!' The whip broke the stillness of the afternoon. Its rifle-shot echoed off the cliffs above. The oxen rolled like tugboats. They pulled. The whip cracked again. 'Be straight now . . . straight – STRAIGHT!' The blade began to cleave the furrow, throwing out a bow-wave of dark soil. They slowed towards the edge of the terrace, and the farmer prepared to turn them.

It was still hot when we reloaded the mules and started to climb towards the pass.

That night we pitched our tent in the threshing circle of a homestead. An enormous man named Solomon lived there with his family. When a group of militia came to inspect my papers, Solomon stood behind them. He towered over their heads and they handed back my papers without question and disappeared into the darkness.

We squatted on stones. The night cooled fast. The moon rose behind the mountains and Solomon's gravelly voice rolled around us. He had once been a rebel in the army of Gugsa Amdaw.

'I saw him on the road there. Hundreds of men were with him. So I joined.'

It was 1977. First he saw the Derg troops on the road, survivors fleeing the Amda Worq garrison. They were in olive-green uniforms and forage caps. They were carrying their wounded. Gugsa's men came some time later. They had no uniforms. They had a few guns but those without guns carried sticks. They had captured a vehicle and were in high spirits. 'I just walked up the path onto the road.'

Gugsa Amdaw came from a family of minor landowners. Under Haile Selassie he had been the administrator of Amda Worq. When the Derg came to power in 1974, the region was too remote to install their own man. They kept him on. Gugsa used his autonomy to build a peasant army and in 1977, as Mengistu eliminated his rivals in the politburo, Gugsa and his men destroyed the Derg garrison at Amda Worq.

They marched to Sekota. There too they drove out the Derg. Gugsa rallied his men: they had succeeded in occupying the capital of Wag – now they would drive the Derg beyond the ancient borders! They set off towards Korem. The dizzying scent of victory drew in more followers. Thousands of Wag men, remembering the victories of Dejazmach Hailu!

At Korem they met the fate of all such peasant armies. The Derg's tanks and machine guns wiped them out. Gugsa escaped, back to Sekota, back to Amda Worq, then into the rebel-held areas of the Simien mountains.

Solomon escaped with him. But in truth he had lost faith. 'They were already looting other peasants. Gugsa was a brave man but he lacked discipline.'

In the Simiens, Gugsa continued the fight. He retained a handful of men. He attached himself as best he could to the fringes of anti-Derg operations. But his mind deteriorated. He was said to have been half-crazed when one of his men shot him.

I was woken long before dawn by the sound of mechanical grinding. It went on for two hours, regular and ceaseless. When I rose, I found two women crushing beans by hand, grinding together quern-stones of rough granite.

Solomon was driving out the stock as we left. '*Wuch-wuch – Zabia! Hab-hab!*' His broad torso and Greek head rose high above the cattle-backs. He raised his stick and waved us off into the morning.

We had stopped in a shallow canyon. Makonnen watered the mules. Bisrat watched the stream. I sat on a neighbouring rock and washed. The stone was warm beneath me. I let the warmth rise through my thighs, then splashed my face. Just upstream there was a sudden flash of black and white. A pied kingfisher swooped over the water. It landed on one of the boulders. Its tail twitched as it secured its perch. It had a long beak and flecked scapulars. I watched it until a sudden fall of sand and pebbles frightened it off.

Bisrat and I both looked up. A herd of goats was making its way down the cliff. When they reached the water they spread their feet apart and drank. The kids were the first to bounce back up the path. One of them placed its front legs at the foot of a sheer cliff. It looked up. It gave a little leap and its hooves found a ledge, but it slipped back again. It lurched up, slipped, recovered and reached the ledge. Within two minutes it was up at the top, its coppery coat shining in the sun, its long legs shaking.

'Tell me, Bisrat, have you ever seen one of those young ones fall?'

'I've seen them fall, yes. But I've never seen one hurt.'

The kingfisher was back. It was hovering over a pool. Its wings were a blur, its beak pointing downwards. When it dived, it was in and out of the water in an instant. It landed on a boulder and the water shone on its feathers. From its outsize beak stuck the head of a small fish.

Bisrat was watching the bird, smiling his gentle smile.

Shortly before Sekota, we fell into step with an elderly couple returning from the mill. She was a slight woman with a sack of milled grain over her shoulder. He carried only a stick and, in imperial times, had been a member of the minor nobility. His name was Gabre-Selassie.

'This was the land given by God' – he swept his stick towards the parched and treeless slopes – 'in the years past.'

'Under the emperor?'

'The emperor? Ffah! Under the Wagshum.'

As we walked, he told the story of how Wagshum Gwangul saved Ethiopia and died for his trouble, victim of the southern usurpers of the ancient kingdom.

'It was after Adwa.'

When in the 1880s Italians began sniffing around Ethiopia's northern territories, Wagshum Berru saw in them a way to undermine Menelik and make his own claim to the throne. Menelik suspected his duplicity, and threw him in jail. His son Gwangul took over as Wagshum. In March 1896 the two armies, Italian and Ethiopian, met on the slopes above Adwa. Wagshum Gwangul and the men of Wag, united against a common enemy, proved both loyal and highly effective.

A couplet celebrates the Wagshum's part in the Ethiopian victory:

The Janterar of Ambassal, the Wagshum and the Fitawrari
of Adwa –
Who else would dare to wear your trousers!*

But in the byzantine world of the Ethiopian court, there were
no constants. Wagshum Gwangul's allegiances wavered. With
his father still imprisoned, his resentment towards Emperor
Menelik grew. The emperor summoned him to Addis Ababa.
The Wagshum travelled down from Wag with a guard of
Adwa heroes. But Menelik at once placed him under house
arrest. Within a short time he was found dead. His father,
Wagshum Berru, also died mysteriously. It was said that news
of his son's death killed him. But two dead Wagshums in the
emperor's custody looked more than careless. The people of
Wag were left without a *shum*, abandoned to their traditional
lot of isolation, hardship and famine.

'Wait, wait.' Gabre-Selassie paused on the road while he
tried to recall another couplet from that time. 'Yes –

'I cannot buy food since the *birr* is in Shoa
I cannot trade, since the ship is broken.'†

Gabre-Selassie raised his stick again and directed us towards
the church of Wukro Meskal Krestos, the old burial site of the
Wagshums.

We left the road and followed a path over a low hill. A valley
spread out below and on the other side was a cluster of juniper

* Trousers are the traditional symbol of a man's courage.
† The *birr*, the Ethiopian unit of currency, is a play on the name of
Wagshum Berru; Shoa is the province of which Addis Ababa was the
capital, while the Amharic for ship, *markab*, was the name of Wagshum
Gwangul's horse, itself used as a *nom de guerre*.

and mimosa. A foal was on the grass outside the church's rubble perimeter. Its chestnut coat gleamed in the sunlight and it was leaping for the fun of leaping, kicking out its hind legs and leaping again. Inside young deacons were standing in the grass, clutching leatherbound psalters, muttering prayers. The senior priest shuffled out of a hut. Beneath a sand-coloured *gabbi* his hands fiddled, and he threw one edge of the cloth over his shoulder.

'You want to see the burials?'

The royal vault was cut into the cliff. I ducked through an arch and entered a low chamber. This was all that remained of the centuries of autonomous rule for the kingdom of Wag – this and the photo of Hailu Kebede's severed head. Broken rocks covered the floor and around the edge were a number of coffins. Some of them had collapsed to reveal lumps of bone and broken skin.

'Wagshums,' explained the priest. He was standing behind me in the tunnel.

The air smelt of dry rot and old meat. It was full of tiny flies. I covered my nose.

'That is Woyzero Laqech,' said the priest. 'Go forward – look! There – Wagshum Kinfu.'

'And that?' I pointed at a collapsed cask. I could hardly breathe.

'That one? That one, I do not know. Look, over there – more Wagshums. Look, look – Wagshum.'

I could bear it no longer.

'*Bakka*,' I said, hurrying out. 'Enough Wagshums.'

We left the tunnel and caught our breath in the fresh air. Beyond the wall the chestnut foal was still jumping. The priest watched us with a detached curiosity.

'Where have you come from?'

'Amda Worq,' said Hiluf. 'We're going to Sekota.'

The priest nodded.

'And before that Lalibela,' I added. Hiluf was far too modest. 'And we are walking to Aksum.'

The priest looked at us. He re-threw the edge of the *gabbi* over his shoulder. 'Come.'

We followed him down another trench. The cliff closed over our heads. A rock-cut ambulatory ran around the back of the main church. Inside the church it was dark. The light from my torch lit up columns pocked with chisel marks. The *maqdas* was hidden behind a rope-hung blanket. In front of it, lying on the bedrock floor, was a row of olive-wood boards. The priest squatted down and raised them one by one. His bare feet curled over the lip of a large tunnel.

'This way goes to Lalibela.'

'It must be a long tunnel,' I said.

'Of course it is. The saints dug it.'

His finger jabbed into the darkness. 'And this one leads to Zion.'

'Zion?'

He looked up at me. 'Aksum.'

8

We approached the town of Sekota from above. It stood in a bowl of dry brown slopes – a dense concentration of green eucalyptus and acacia, and low crammed-together buildings. A minaret stuck up from the rooftops like a child's hand in class.

Days of walking had created in me a blunt sense of desire – thirst, hunger, fatigue, all rolled into one. In Sekota's narrow main street I stumbled into a shop and drank half a litre of Highland mineral water in one go. The shop was little bigger than a cupboard. As I raised the bottle again, I spotted on the top shelf, among the soap bars and candles, a tin of fruit.

'Please?'

The trader stretched up and blew the dust from the tin. It read TELEPHONE BRAND FRUITS COCKTAIL, and featured a tempting bowl of fruit pieces beneath the logo of a telephone. On the side a very long postal address ended in Kuala Lumpur, Malaysia.

'How many do you have?'

'Four.'

'I'll have them all.'

With four tins of TELEPHONE BRAND FRUITS COCKTAIL, I caught up with the others. We entered the yard of the Tadessa Hotel. Bisrat and Makonnen unloaded the mules for the last time.

'Won't you wait?' I didn't want them to go. I already felt a nostalgia for the roads of Wag and Lasta. 'Here – have some fruit cocktail.'

Makonnen shook his head. Bisrat smiled. I paid them and we shook hands. Was that it? I walked with them to the gate and watched them weave back through the evening crowds, past a spreading sycamore and up towards the main road. Bisrat turned and waved. Makonnen was looking ahead; he was already thinking of Lalibela.

Back in the hotel yard, Hiluf and I made quick work of the first tin of TELEPHONE BRAND FRUITS COCK-TAIL.

'What do you think, Hiluf? Another?'

'You have it.'

He was unlacing his shoe. It had fallen apart again.

I gripped his arm. 'Hiluf, we'll find you the finest boots in all of Sekota!' The cubes of Telephone pineapple and Telephone papaya were starting to work.

Then we heard the far-off sound of motorcycles.

First they were a grunt. The grunt grew louder. It dropped to a purr outside the steel gate of the Tadessa Hotel. The gate clanged open and two KTM 640 trail bikes thundered into the yard. The drivers heeled down the side-stands. They cut the engines, slid off their helmets. They were Poles; the plates had PL in a ring of yellow EU stars.

Witek had long fair hair and Bartek had none; the back of his neck was bright pink. Their boots had no articulation at the ankle and they walked stiff-legged across the yard. A few generations ago, I thought, they would have been Uhlans in Piłsudski's cavalry, charging down the Reds of Budyonny, slicing a new Poland from the carcass of the Tsarist empire. Now they were riding motorcycles from South Africa to Poland. Witek had a computer business and Bartek was a translator.

We talked about places we knew in Warsaw and Addis Ababa, and the roads of Sidamo and the villagers north of Dessie who had thrown stones at their motorcycles. Their Swiss friend ('Drives a BMW K100 – real nice') had been held up at gunpoint on the China road.

'Refused to come any further north with us,' said Witek. 'They are savages, he said. Can you blame him?' Witek had lit a cigarette. He was smoking it with a girlish languour.

'We will meet him in Gondar!' Bartek's smoking was altogether more assertive.

'That's a real interesting place, I hear,' said Witek. 'You know Gondar?'

I told them about a night I'd spent there twenty years ago with some Soviet helicopter pilots. 'They said they were working for the famine.'

'Sure they were working for the famine!' said Bartek.

'Like they were helping the people of Afghanistan,' said Witek.

They lapsed into silence, dwelling on Soviet duplicity.

'Do you want some tinned fruit?'

'Thank you, no.' Witek politely put up his hand. They were happy with their cigarettes.

In the morning they left early. I listened to the fade of their machines, rising and falling as they climbed through the gears. They were taking the road to Aksum.

That morning we unpacked everything. We cleaned, we sorted, we mended. I drank another bottle and a half of Highland water. I shared another tin of fruit with Hiluf and fell into conversation with Abbai Tsehaye, the owner of the hotel.

Abbai was a round sleepy woman with an ink-blue cross tattooed on her forehead. She wore gold rings on her fingers and a man's watch on her wrist. She looked around the yard of her hotel.

'It used to be beautiful here. Everyone came. We had a hundred women working different shifts.'

'Under the emperor?'

'No – under the Dergie. Our life was much better under the Dergie.'

Which was surprising, because in the emperor's time Abbai's family were rich. They lived in a big house. They were related to the Wagshums. She said that when her father rode on his horse a group of 'ordinary men' ran alongside him. Her father was head of the justice department in Sekota, or at least until he killed a man and had to flee.

'For many years we did not see him. But when the Dergie came to power he returned home.'

The hotel cook shuffled across the yard and said she was going to market. Abbai dipped into her cleavage and handed her some money.

'Our family were rulers in this area. They had ruled since

the time of . . . well, forever. They are buried in a holy cave – such a beautiful cave!'

I told her I'd seen it yesterday.

'You saw it?' She fingered her gold rings. 'Well, you know then.'

She looked away. She seemed overcome by an immense weariness.

In the famine, she said, farmers went to the vaults and broke open the coffins of the Wagshums. They were looking for gold. They scattered the bones. 'My father went to the church and picked up every one of those bones from the ground. He knew exactly which bone was which. He put each of the Wagshums back into the right coffin.'

'And where is your father now?'

'He lives there, near the cave. He is just a farmer now.' She rose and crossed the yard. Her slippers flip-flopped on the concrete.

Hiluf and I went off into the town. We needed mules and we needed boots.

Sekota was a higgledy-piggledy place. There were few right-angles. Above rubble walls, eccentric pepperpot houses rose to conical roofs of thatch. Bisecting it all was a narrow, crowded thoroughfare where bare-legged farmers hardly broke step as they strode down from the hills, where the townsmen stood in twos and threes, only half-turning to piss into a dry culvert full of cattle bones and rags, where donkeys hoofed their way through mounds of wood ash, and stands of bamboo clicked and swayed in the breeze. Beside the path was a line of women squatting before stupas of garlic and green chillies and rust-red *berberi*. Down a side-alley, two guards were sliding bottletops around an old draughtsboard and a man with an adze over one shoulder lurched out, glared at me before waving his arms: 'Oh – let them rule us now! Let those foreigners rule over us! Let them increase with their children and take the last grain from us! Let them rule!'

As he paced off into the Muslim quarter, another man took me by the arm: 'Look, look, *farenj*! Here it fell, and here and here!' He pointed at the splash-marks of the bombs whose craters were now no more than gentle bowls in the dried-out mud.

All through the Derg years, Sekota bounced back and forth between government and rebel armies. Mengistu's forces replaced the imperial forces in 1974. Then in 1977 Gugsa Amdaw marched down from Amda Worq and ousted the Derg. The Derg ousted Gugsa. The EPDM ousted the Derg. The famine weakened the EPDM so the Derg ousted them but only for a year because the EPDM regained their strength and came back. After that, the Derg never recovered Sekota. Instead they bombed. Eleven times they sent in bombers. The town became a night town. The market happened after dark. Meetings happened at night. Saints' days were celebrated at night. By day the townspeople fled to the hills.

'The Derg promised us the modern world,' said one trader. 'But we ended up living in caves like animals.'

Sekota was flush with boots. We saw infantry boots hanging by their laces from bamboo stalls. We saw piled-up boots among stocks of forge-bright tools. We found shops in the new quarter crowded with *Made in China* suitcases and *Made in China* boots

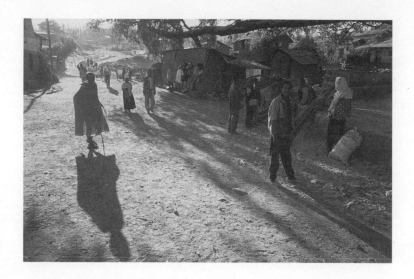

and shoes. Hiluf prodded every one with the sceptical thumb of a soft-cheese merchant. In the end we chose a pair of desert-brown boots with padded ankles and a sole with a good deep tread.

Mules were much more of a problem. 'Try Habtu Gabre,' they said. We tried Habtu. He was standing in the middle of his yard, scouring one of his nostrils with his index finger. He couldn't help us. He was due to take his mules to a wedding. 'Have you asked Getachew Yohannis?'

Getachew was a wild-looking man with thin hair that curled like flames from his scalp. 'What use are mules nowadays?' He had sold his last week to a man from Lalibela. Getachew suggested Wudaj Aderra.

Wudaj, it turned out, had never had mules. But he did have a Star of Victory medal from 1941, awarded for his loyal resistance to the Italians. From a goatskin trunk he pulled a certificate and read: '. . . *for those who fought for the love of their country. Our trusted servant Wudaj Aderra.*' The certificate was a roll of *faux* parchment stamped with the imperial seal of Haile Selassie. More recently he had been imprisoned by the Derg. When they killed his brother, Wudaj slapped his service pistol into the palm of his only son and packed him off to the rebels. The Derg put him and his wife in jail as a result.

'Terrible,' I said.

'Not at all. We were proud to have a son who fought.'

Behind a pair of fishbowl glasses, his eyes looked as big as tennis balls. He gazed out through the open door. A washing-line looped across his yard and his wife was hanging out a pair of plastic shoes.

'You can ask my son about mules.'

'Where is he?'

'He works in the finance department of the *woreda* office, revenue section.'

The *woreda* office was on the other side of town. Behind Molla Wudaj's desk were felt-pen bar charts and tables of figures. He was a shy and softly-spoken man. 'My father, he is the true patriot – I am just a revolutionary.' He gave a sweet smile.

He was eighteen when he carried out his first rebel operation, capturing a Derg lorry and twenty Derg soldiers. Then there was a disagreement in the EPRP and they began to fight with each other. Molla laid down his arms and went south. He became a teacher in Addis.

'I don't know why it is,' said Molla, genuinely puzzled, 'but our people have always liked to fight.'

Molla took us outside and pointed to a house across a patch of waste ground. There we found Alemu. 'Yes,' he said, 'I have two good mules. I will bring them to you at dawn tomorrow.' He had a charming, open face. Best of all, he was an Agaw. He spoke Agawigna and knew the road north.

111

He could take us as far as we wanted to go – Nirak! Yerchila! Abi Addi!

Abi Addi was in Tigray and for the first time I thought: We are making progress.

That evening in the bar of the Tadessa Hotel, a dense crescent of men gazed up at the TV screen. The Arab satellite station was showing *Octopussy*. Roger Moore schmoozed from one scene to the next, from caricature London to caricature Jaipur, dressed mainly in a white dinner jacket. The raised faces of the men flickered in the screen's glow.

At the far end was a party of farmers, and a taller man with them. The bottles of beer were thick on the table; a sizeable tape recorder stood among them.

The taller man was from Tel Aviv. He had been only four when his parents fled the famine to Sudan. From there they'd been airlifted to Israel with Operation Solomon. Now he'd come back to bring money – and a tape recorder – to his cousins. His T-shirt read: *Tiberias – New York style Pizza's and sub's Tel Aviv 925–879*. He had a twitchy, nervous energy.

'So you are a Falasha,' I said, 'an Ethiopian Jew?'

He gave a sly half-smile. 'I am now.'

When they stood to leave, he rose a good foot above the others. One of the farmers was clutching the tape recorder in both arms.

It was still dark when Alemu arrived next morning with the mules. We pulled open the gates of the Tadessa Hotel and set off north into a cold dawn. The moon was low over Sekota's rooftops. A blush of pink clouds glowed to the east. The wind rose and fell among the acacias with a lonely, seashore sound.

Alemu swivelled his stick and *thwack!* beat the mules' rumps. They rose to an easy trot. They looked keen and healthy, Alemu looked keen and healthy, and it was good to be on the move again.

The Story of Tekla Haymanot's Leg

Tekla Haymanot was a monastic holy man who lived in Ethiopia in the thirteenth century. He was of the sacred line of Zadok the priest who anointed Solomon king of Israel. Even in the womb, Tekla Haymanot worked miracles. A few months before his birth his mother was captured by a pagan king who reached out his rough pagan arms to embrace her. At once the sky filled with lightning, thunder rolled around the hills and the Archangel Mikhael struck that pagan king down with a terrible madness.

At the age of fifteen months Tekla Haymanot could turn water into wine. By seven he knew the psalter and all the books of the Bible by heart. In his lifetime it is said he managed to perform every miracle in both the New and Old Testaments. His worldly skills were no less prodigious, and for his part in restoring the Solomonic dynasty he received for the Ethiopian Church one third of all the kingdom's territory.

Tekla Haymanot's example shines down through the centuries. In damp caves and windy elevations, in the distant forests and on the ledges of great chasms, thousands of holy lives have bloomed in his name. His powers of intercession are perennial, and every hour of the day in Ethiopia someone is bowing before his image or whispering his holy name.

Near the city of Gondar is the church of Debra Berhan Selassie. On the walls of the church can be seen a painting of Tekla Haymanot. It was commissioned by a local king, Egwala Seyon. The king is lying down below the saint and his crown is removed. The king's humility before the saint is emphasised by his own boastful inscription: 'How the King of the Universe, Egwala Seyon, sought his help.' The king is also shown devotedly clutching the leg of Tekla Haymanot. The leg is not attached to his body.

Tekla Haymanot once prayed without interval for twenty

years. During that time he did not sit down and his right leg rotted and fell off. His praying though was unaffected, and he carried on for another seven years on his left leg. Tekla Haymanot's leg is now kept with the *tabot* at the monastery of Debra Libanos, and once a year, on his feast day, it is taken out and pilgrims are permitted to drink the water used to wash it.

9

In Sekota an elderly monk told me about his monastery of Bahir Kidane Mehret. It was on our route, he said, forty-odd miles to the north, and it was very near the main road.

'The road?'

Remoteness was the normal condition for monasteries.

'We need the road to sell our fruit.'

Fruit! At Bahir Kidane Mehret, he explained, they grew papaya. They grew limes. They grew the lemon-like fruit known as *bokra*, or 'first-born', for its great size. They grew guava and peanuts. But most of all they grew bananas.

So as we left Sekota that morning, heading north, and crossed the old Italian bridge, and saw the road ahead drop another thousand feet to a wide and endless plain – lower, hotter, drier than anywhere we'd yet been – I was savouring the image of sparkling streams and fruit groves, of ascetics hoeing and digging and weeding, living out the Pachomian ideal of contemplation mixed with a vigorous regime of gardening.

The survival of Ethiopian Christianity – and therefore, to a large extent, of Ethiopia itself – owes more to its monasteries than to anything else. The royal court spent much of the time roving in tents, quelling rebellions and dispensing justice. The monks meanwhile, with the nation's lifeblood preserved on goat- and calfskin manuscripts, stayed put on their mountain-tops. Warriors and kings made the climb to pay homage, to consult them, or to ask them to bring a certain *tabot* into battle. But the monks' world was intact, like a mysterious upper room, free from the frippery of the daily round.

It was in the mid-fifth century that a group of ascetics arrived in Ethiopia from the Egyptian desert. They brought with them the coenibitic Rule of St Pachomius. His work was one of the first texts to be translated into Ge'ez, and tales from his life have provided a model for the good Christian ever since.

Although he is the father of all the Christian world's communal monasteries, Pachomius's struggles were, like most celibates', largely private. He was plagued by demons. The greater his following became, the more the little fellows appeared. They operated with the permission of God, to test him and to provide an example to others. Sometimes as he knelt to pray, they would open up a great chasm below his knees. As he humbly went about his duties they would file before him like the footsoldiers of some great commander: 'Make way, make way for the Man of God!' They would come and rattle his cell to frighten him. They would try to make him laugh by appearing as a group of burly men struggling to haul a tiny leaf. They would come to him in the form of naked women and recline beside him as he ate. Pachomius dealt with them all in the same way. He made them vanish. To him the soul was made up of a series of chambers, and it was possible, with purity of thought, to sweep each one clean.

The physical harshness, the isolation and height of Ethiopia gave the monastic life there something of a head start. Pachomian groups spread swiftly south from Tigray. In their quest for abiding peace, many raging spirits have pursued the more severe, eremitic life. *Bahtawis* wander the highlands alone, taking the discipline of fasting, isolation and self-torture to dangerous extremes. The painted walls of churches are covered with exemplary privations. Gabre-Manfus lived for 363 years and never even thought about water or food. Abba Tadewos would bow forty thousand times during the day and forty thousand at night. One Ethiopian monk, having moved to the United States, carried on with his nightly vigils in the snow; he was quietly removed to an asylum. Sometimes in the forests of Ethiopia, wrote the scholar Getachew Haile, a shepherd will come across a pile of bones and amongst the bones will be the glint of a silver hand-cross. In such cases 'it is impossible to tell whether predators found them dead or alive'. Ethiopian monastic life is not for the faint-hearted.

The plains were spread out below us. Mile-long shadows stretched across the land from columns of rock. Far to the north the misty folds gave way to a pale horizon. Beyond Bahir Kidane Mehret was a string of monasteries running up into Tembien, then up into the Gheralta and, weeks and weeks ahead, to Debra Damo, the first Ethiopian monastery of all, the one founded by Abuna Aragawi who is remembered on the fourteenth day of the month of Teqemt:

And on this day is commemorated our holy Father Aragawi. This holy man became a guide to the servants of God on the road. And he went up to the holy Debra Damo holding the tail of a serpent and there he fought countless noble fights ... He established among his children the rules of the Monastic Life which he had learned in the house of his Father Pachomius. Salutation to Za-Mikhael who was surnamed Aragawi!

Hiluf was wearing his new boots. He was in good spirits. He was walking his strong, unshakeable walk. With a happy grin he raised his finger and pointed to the east, where a distant peak was silhouetted against the sun.

'It is Amba Alagi!'

On the night of 6 December 1895, some three months before the decisive battle of Adwa, one group of Italians had marched far ahead. Major Toselli stood on the slopes of Amba Alagi and looked south. In the immense darkness below were the flickering fires of the Ethiopians. He broke into song: *Ave Maria! Gratia plena, Maria Gratia Plena!* Toselli had only two thousand men under his command but he was confident of reinforcements if the Ethiopians attacked. They would push further into this strange land, and his name would be remembered long after his death. *Et in hora mortis nostrae, et in hora mortis nostrae* ... In the morning the Ethiopians did attack, Toselli's reinforcements failed to arrive and his force was destroyed. The Ethiopians chased the survivors off the mountain. Toselli announced to his fleeing officers: 'Let them do what they like!' He turned to face the enemy rifles, and was instantly killed.

It was not just the patriot's pleasure in victory which drew Hiluf's gaze to distant Amba Alagi. Somewhere too on the far slopes of the mountain was the place where he had been born, where even now his shepherd brothers would be rising to shake the dew from their hair.

Alemu in his own way was also animated. Suddenly he squealed. He ran down a bank to hug a young goatherd.

He pressed a banknote into the boy's hand before running back up the slope. 'My eldest grandson!'

We walked all morning. The road was empty. Its bone-white grade rose and fell over low hills. Hornbill squawked among the rocks; twice I watched an augur buzzard soar down from the cliffs and land heavily in the roadside scrub.

We saw only one vehicle. Four Chinese engineers were driving out to inspect a bridge. 'Car broke? You wun'ride?' I said I was OK. We watched their dust trail rise in the windless air. An hour later they came back, waving as they passed.

At midday we reached the settlement of Tsamara. Children crowded and giggled around us. The younger ones piggy-backed on the older. From behind, the group opened up like curtains, and a man with a fighter's jaw stepped through. He glared. He flexed his forearms. He thrust his fist at me and dropped a small mound of dried peas into my hand. He laughed at my efforts to chew them.

'You foreigners – you grind everything in fine mills. In our country we use our teeth!'

We rejoined the road. An oven-heat rose from its surface. The fringe of grass was burnt blond. The land all around was a waterless brown. After an hour we stopped in a gully and lay beneath some eucalyptus. A couple of weed-green pools of water remained among the dry pebbles.

'There was drought here last year,' scoffed Alemu. 'Now there is drought every year.'

He was a tall, vigorous man. He wore a mint-green suit, patched at the knees and with a ladder of torn thread down one side of the jacket – but a suit nonetheless, tailored and stitched and pad-shouldered.

'In the famine did you stay on the land, Alemu?'

'I had livestock so I could stay. I watched everyone else leave.

Then my cattle started to die. They grew thin and died. When the last one was dead, then I left.'

Above the gully, the sharp line of the rock gave way to a deep blue sky. We heard the tap-tap of a stick and an old man appeared. He gazed at us from a distance, raised his stick in greeting and carried on to the east.

That evening we crested a ridge and another vast stretch of country opened up at our feet. The low sun drenched everything in its honey-coloured light. To the west the cliffs fell to a narrow gorge and a riverbed. The riverbed was a pale and parched grey. Alemu let out a cry which filled the emptiness before us: 'Look at our cursed country! Rivers, rivers, rivers – and no water!'

Darkness was falling. We were still a few hours short of Bahir Kidane Mehret. Just above the road was a group of huts and in the first of them lived a newly-married couple called Inay and Mesret.

Inay had just killed a calf. He was bare-chested. His hands and torso were scabby with blood. On the ground he had pegged out the skin, a taut two-dimensional abstraction of the young beast. He was squatting over it, slicing it into a long spiral strip with a hook-bladed *bilowa*.

He waved the knife in the direction of the henhouse. 'Put your tent there.' He spoke softly.

Mesret sat in the doorway crushing chillies. Her skirt was hitched up to the thigh. With slow thrusts she was pressing the heel of her hands down into the bowl in her lap. She had a fierce beauty. Her plaited hair fanned out behind her neck and she threw inquisitive glances at me as I cooked onions over our stove.

A year ago, after the ploughing season, Mesret had come up from her village in the valley below. She brought with her a mirror, an umbrella and an embroidered *kuta* dress for saints' days. She moved into the hut that Inay had just completed. Together they fenced it round with thorn and at night they brought in his goats and the three cattle to join the hens. The calf they'd killed that day was the only survivor of that year's calves. Below their hut was the main road, built by the Chinese. Inay and Mesret felt it was a very good thing to be living near the road.

After dark we sat in the hut. Mesret lit a lamp. Her face shone in its yellowy light. She slopped water into the wooden bowls and rubbed her hands around the rims to clean them. She stoked the fire. She stirred the *wot* and spooned it onto a small rug of *injera* bread. She tore off a corner of the bread, dipped it in the sauce and Inay leaned forward and took it between his lips. The sauce ran down her wrist; she scooped it off. Everything she did was with a lithe and expectant energy.

'Tell me,' I asked, 'is the road busy?'

'Very busy now,' Inay said as he stood to go outside.

'There is a car every day.' Mesret's eyes glittered with excitement. 'Two days ago we heard *putt-putt-putt*! Like a bicycle. Two of them.'

That would be the Poles.

Inay brought in his new calfskin strap. He ran it through his hands, then sat beside a bed-frame cut from *goza*, the soapberry tree. He tied one end of the strap to a corner of it and started to weave it in diagonals over the frame. It was a small bed, no more than four feet long.

'By the end of the rains,' said Mesret, 'our baby will come.'

Inay yanked the strap tight.

A pool of moonlight lay in the open doorway. Outside I could see the mountains' distant silvery backs, the mountains of the coming weeks. Inay and Mesret's cattle stood motionless in the yard.

May the Chinese road bring you good fortune, Inay and Mesret. May your springs never run dry.

We left early. A dawn wind blew up the cliff. Ravens launched themselves from the rocks and we looked down on their black shiny forms. Far below, the valley was dotted with tall huts.

When we reached the bottom the wind had ceased, the sun had risen and the huts turned out not to be huts but baobab trees. For an hour we walked along the valley floor. There was no settlement. The trees' huge, bulbous purple trunks were topped by spindly little branches. They looked like cartoon hearts, ripped from the bodies of some tribe of giants.

We entered a narrow gorge. Egg-shaped pebbles rolled at our feet. The mules stumbled on slabs of rock. Rounding a corner, we reached a place where several large sycamore trees spread over a spring. Beyond I could see more trees, more vegetation, and the green of banana fronds.

A novice was at the spring. He was listening to the sound of water rising in his jerry-can. With good spring manners, he stood aside.

I splashed water on my neck and down my front. 'Is the *memhir* here?'

'He's away.'

'When will he come back?'

'Maybe today, maybe tomorrow.'

'You have fruit?'

'We have fruit. But you can't have any.'

'What?'

'Not without the *memhir*.'

I looked at him. His face stared back at me. There is no 'no' less open to question than the 'no' of an Ethiopian cleric.

So we waited. We wandered up through the trees. We sat on a council-ring of logs listening to the whistling of weaver birds and bishop birds in the jungle-like foliage around us. Hiluf took off his boots and tutted.

'What's the matter with them?'

'They hurt.' He put them in his pack and took out the old pair with their flapping soles. He began to stitch them. I felt the disappointment of having given an unwanted present.

* * *

Down at the river I sat on a rock to wash. A monk was sitting on a neighbouring rock. He was washing his feet, pressing down between each of his toes as if pushing peas from a pod. He then washed his sandals and put them on another rock to dry. He then joined me in the important business of staring into the water. The threads of new-hatched fish flicked in the stream.

'In the rains,' I said, 'you must get big fish.'

'Big fish, yes.'

'Are they good to eat?'

'Eat? You can't eat fish.'

'Why not?'

'In the Bible it says you must not eat beasts without blood.'

'Fish have blood.'

'No, no – they don't have blood,' he explained, smiling at me with a teacher's patience. 'That is why you cannot eat them.'

He put on his sandals, and sauntered up through the trees to his cell.

Bahir Kidane Mehret is not an old monastery. Only in the late nineteenth century did the first monks gather here. They looked up at their brothers on water-scarce *ambas*, at those hidden away on islands in the lakes, at the *bahtawis* in their never-seen-by-mortals caves, and decided that that was not the way for modern monks.

Based on Pachomius, they devised a set of rules. Nuns could be attached to the monastery, but should live on the other side of the river (at his monastery at Faou Pachomius established a convent across the Nile). Nuns could share the monks' food – strictly one meal a day – but they could not prepare it. Being

women, they would make the food too tasty, so that should be
left to the monks. The *kebbero* drum would not be permitted
at the monastery because of the shiver of excitement it causes.
Such shivers are not good for contemplation.

The monks planted fruit. They channelled the spring water
towards the plantations, and even then found that throughout the year there was water to spare. Those springs were
blessed and they dedicated the *tabot* in the church to Mary
and her Kidane Mehret, or 'covenant of mercy'. Because they
were on the Wag–Tembien route, they had many visitors. The
visitors bought their fruit.

But closeness to the world has proved a mixed blessing.

One night in 1981 a rebel, expelled from the EPDM, came to the monastery. He stood in the compound and clapped his hands. An old monk, Abba Hadara, stumbled out of his hut and rubbed his eyes. He saw the rebel's gun and at once fell to the ground. The abbot at the time was Abba Gabre-Hiwot, a Tigrayan. He had been abbot for nearly forty years, and he tried a different tack with the rebel. He sat him down. He served him butter and honey. He gave him bananas. But the rebel still looted the monastery and made off with six hundred *birr*. Abba Gabre-Hiwot called the monks together and they all agreed why it had happened: they had failed to observe the memorial day a week earlier of the late Abba Gabre-Mikhael.

At the same time a land dispute had broken out between the monastery and a poor farmer. It reached a head when the farmer hanged himself in the monastery grounds. Being good progressive rebels, the EPDM had less sympathy for the hoary old clerics than for a poor farmer, particularly a dead one. They arrested Abba Gabre-Hiwot and Abba Hadara. Nothing more was heard of them. Five years later their bodily remains were returned to the monastery by a rebel officer.

And now there was another problem. At two that afternoon we heard the wasp-whine of a two-stroke motorcycle. The whine stopped, and two policemen came through the trees. One of them had an automatic rifle, the other wore sunglasses. The one with sunglasses was the more senior.

The policemen had heard there was some trouble at the monastery. The trouble had something to do with the Chinese roadmen. But they weren't sure exactly what the trouble was. They had arranged for the Chinese roadmen to be here. They asked the monks if they had arrived. No, they hadn't. They asked the monks what the trouble was. The monks couldn't tell them because the abbot was away. So the policemen asked for some fruit. They were told they could not have any fruit. They sat down. They came over to check my papers but could find nothing wrong. From then on we eyed each other from a distance.

We all waited for the abbot.

Emuhoy Ameta Maryam was a nun. I found her sitting in the shade beside the spring, and for an hour or more wallowed in her strange and placid presence. She wore a sun-paled *kobe* and was completely blind. For thirty years she had lived in a hut across the river.

Long ago, Ameta had been married. Her husband had been a *leiba shai*, a thief-seeker. He was part of a small group whose task it was to flush the *shifta* out of the area. One day he engaged a group in the mountains. He killed three of them – but then he was killed.

In rural Ethiopia the term *leiba shai* embraces several types of traditional crime-tacklers. At one level they were vigilantes whose violence sometimes fell on the guilty, and sometimes on the innocent. An account in C.H. Walker's *The Abyssinian at Home* (1933) shows an altogether more effective method. If something was stolen, witnesses gathered and an adolescent boy, a *leiba shai*, was called. He was given a substance like 'coarse tobacco':

> Having smoked a little, the boy collapses like a drunken man and lies extended. Then the Chiqa Shum [district officer] three times passes round the boy's head a short yellow wand and strikes him thrice, intoning the word: '*Diras!*' or 'Arrive!' So the boy, rising with fixed eyes, reels

here and there like a drunken man, at another time flying like a winged bird, while all follow behind. The Chiqa Shum keeps hold of a sash tied round the boy's waist and, when they come to water he (or the witnesses or servant) will carry the boy across, lest he touch and suffer contamination. If they see animals on the road, the boy may run towards them, but the Chiqa Shum will seize him in his arms till they pass. If they meet a man the man will at once squat in the road, for the boy will slap and cuff him. So the boy follows the thief, and if he comes to the hut where the thief lived, will enter and make as if he were carrying out the stolen goods.

Emuhoy Ameta spoke of her husband in the present tense. It was after midday when she rose to her feet. 'I will join him soon in the next world. I think next year, after the rains.'

A novice took her arm and led her down to the river. Warm sunlight seeped into her sightless eyes. She left the boy at the water and crossed on stepping-stones. She knew every one of those stones.

From the river came the crunch of shingle. In a black soutane, Memhir Endriyas climbed up the bank. He saw those waiting for him: several strangers, a foreigner, two policemen. He managed to smile at each of us. He then went to his hut with two monks. At once they came out with bowls of bananas and papaya and guava. Soon we were sitting amicably with the policemen, eating the fruit and comparing each other's knives.

Washed and glowing, the *memhir* reappeared. He explained to the policemen what the trouble was. The Chinese roadmen had been killing goats at the spring and feasting. The spring was a sacred spring and no one was allowed to kill goats there, especially not foreigners. The policemen nodded. The Chinese still hadn't arrived but the case was clear to the policemen. The foreigners were to blame.

The *memhir* came over and sat with us. He had been *memhir* five years and before that performed his pastoral duties among the large Ethiopian community still in Khartoum.

'The emperor used to send money here. There were 250 monks and nuns then. Now we are very few and we are old. It is hard to grow enough bananas.'

Memhir Endriyas mentioned another monastery, the monastery of Meskal Krestos some three or four days' walk to the north.

'It is on an *amba*, with cliffs all around. It has fields on top.'

'How can we find it?'

'You must ask. I haven't been for many years. The only way up is by ladder,' he warned. 'Whenever they choose, the monks can just take the ladder up.'

And in that I thought I heard a hint of envy.

10

A boy at the monastery joined us on the road to Meskal Krestos. He had been sitting beneath the trees, eyeing us, and when we left, he left too. When we stopped to eat, he ate with us. When we spent the night in a *tella bet*, he stayed too. He was fourteen – thin and big-eyed and very shy.

In the morning, approaching the town of Nirak, the road went over a high bridge. We slid down the bank to wash in the river below. It was the old crossing point. Just downstream the river sluiced into a gorge and made a continuous roaring sound. It had been days since we'd seen so much water.

The boy was squatting on a rock. He gazed into the river where it tumbled into a deep pool. At his feet, a layer of slow scum revolved in the backwater.

'Where is your home?' I took off my boots and started kneading my toes.

He said nothing.

'Do you live in Nirak?'

'I am looking for my father.'

He put his head in his hands and peered into the pool. His story came out in a slow whisper.

He had left home. As a goat trader his father was always on the move. But now he had come of age, the boy wanted to be with his father. He needed to be with his father. His voice barely rose above the sound of the water, but when he turned his head to me he had a look that could move mountains.

'If I do not find him in Nirak, I will go to another place. I will go to every place in the country. I will go to every place in the world until I find my father.'

We climbed out of the valley. The settlement of Nirak lay in the distance, a strip of shiny roofs above the plain.

'Look!' cried Alemu. 'Like Addis Ababa!'

The town was a dismal collection of mud-walled buildings. The new road sliced it in two. Outside another *tella bet* we tethered the mules. An *azmari* was playing inside, leaning against the olive-wood column in the middle of the room.

'Our men are proud when they drive in cars!
But foreigners – they are proud when they are pilots!'

He was young and plump. He wore a *Titanic* T-shirt. He looked around the room. No one was listening to him.

'In the Derg time, we were going to prostitutes.
Now there is HIV, we must get married, look after our
   lives!'

Still they paid him no attention. He finished his *tella*, took up his *masenqo* and left.

Hiluf asked the drinkers there about the boy's father. Yes,

they said, we know him. He was here a week ago, said one man. Another said he'd gone south – to Tsamara.

The boy took in each comment with deer-like attention. When he heard the word 'Tsamara', he gave the first hint of a smile.

Alemu put down his beaker and spat a husk of barley at the floor. 'I am going back to Sekota. This walking is too hard.'

'But you said you'd come with us to Tigray!' I spluttered.

'It is too hard on the mules.'

'Maybe you need more money, Alemu?'

He shook his head. He'd made up his mind.

I left Hiluf and walked with them to the edge of town. The mules trotted off light-stepped into the brightness of noon. Alemu was distinct in his mint-green suit, with the skinny figure of the boy beside him, each of them dissolving into the shimmer of the plain.

Now we were stuck. I turned and walked back between the spaced-apart buildings. Nirak did not look like a place with many mules.

A little questioning turned up a man named Asgedum who did have pack animals. He was tall, with an incongruous high-pitched voice. But he couldn't help us. He had only one mule and his donkeys had just returned one short from a salt-trip to the Danakil desert. Asgedum was fully engaged with trying to recover the missing donkey.

I offered him a good price and he thought for about a second before changing his mind. He said his cousin had another mule. We would leave at dawn.

'Do you know Meskal Krestos?' I asked him.

'Meskal Krestos? Of course. It is high, high up! Cut into the rock by God!'

So I spent a happy afternoon sitting on the flat roof of Asgedum's store. The upper floor of the *hidmo* covered me in its shadow. It was the laziest few hours I'd had in weeks. I gave the land ahead a slow binocular scan. The kiln-hot plain rolled northwards in a series of bulges and folds. Do not be deceived by that flatness, I told myself; in each fold is a knee-breaker of a valley. On the far-off horizon I took in the ridge-line with its sudden drops, its interlockings, the slabs of its sandstone cliffs. I conducted imaginary hikes up its gullies. Twice, on plinths of rock I caught the flash of a church roof and thought: Is it that one? Is that the monastery of Meskal Krestos – cut into the rock by God?

From the compound below came the low chatter of voices. The women were plaiting the hair of a young girl. Asgedum's donkeys stood exhausted after the desert, their heads down. His one mule was shaded beneath a frame heaped with drying sorghum stalks. All was quiet.

I looked out again at the mountains. I read.

There was a sudden commotion below. The mule of Asgedum's cousin had arrived. The sight of so many dozing donkeys proved too much. It trotted towards them, its log of a penis dangling below its stomach. The donkeys woke and bared their teeth. They brayed loudly. The mule offered its weak, laryngitic whinny and backed off. It retreated to the other mule and dropped its head. The silence resumed.

I picked up my binoculars. Against the red cliffs to the west drifted a number of vultures. A dust devil followed its drunken course across the plain. In the compound below, the plaiting was finished. The girl stood. She ran her fingers over the ridges on her scalp before skipping across the yard. She threw a cake of dried dung at her little brother and it hit him on the shoulder. There was a brief pause before he began to wail. His wailing woke the mule, whose penis swelled again. The mule lunged at the donkeys who brayed at the mule who again backed off, and at that moment a sudden wind funnelled between the buildings and choked the entire homestead with dust. The women and the children ran for shelter. Both mules and donkeys turned their rumps to the wind and forgot about everything else.

I was hungry. I came down from Asgedum's roof and asked him where in Nirak it was possible to find a meal.

*   *   *

Mesfin was Amhara, from Addis Ababa, and he ran a small restaurant on the main road. There was no one in it. Across the road were the district's two cathedral-sized tents of emergency food aid.

Mesfin had come here years earlier to work on the road-bridge below the town. 'I was young. It was a year after the Derg fell and it was New Year, September, and everything was green.'

Six months later the land reverted to semi-desert and the isolation began to get to him. But he discovered that here in the lowlands his lifelong asthma was gone. So when the bridge was finished, he had a choice. He could return to Addis and wheeze, or he could stay isolated in Nirak, and breathe easily. He chose Nirak. He married a local woman. He opened a restaurant and now he stood amongst its empty tables, tense with anger.

'Look, they don't work, these people. You see those tents? Full of free food. They get married – one month later, twelve and a half kilos of grain, litre of oil. *Thank you very much.* They have a baby – twelve and a half kilos. *Thank you very much.* So they have another baby. Why work?'

'I see. Can I order, Mesfin?'

'What do they talk about? They talk about one thing. Sex. They eat and they talk about sex. They drink and talk about sex. They drink again and they do sex. What do you want?'

'Pasta? Tomatoes?'

'Tomatoes? Tomatoes? There are no tomatoes here. This is a remote place. You want tomatoes, you go to Makelle.'

Mesfin turned and stood in the open doorway. He looked up the street, he looked down the street. One way went to Addis, the other to Makelle. There were no vehicles. None of the sauntering figures on the road came near his restaurant. This was his prison yard. He clenched and unclenched his fists. He went through to the back.

Dusk threw its sack-coloured light over the town. The wind crackled at the polythene window. The ceiling was made from stitched-together grain-bags stamped: *Gift of the USA Not to be sold or exchanged Use no hooks*. Mesfin had decorated the walls with hyper-coloured posters of Alpine scenes with English captions:

LOVE IS THE MASTER KEY THAT OPENS
THE GATES OF HAPPINESS

and:

GOD BLESS YOU WITH HIS LOVE
THAT MAKES EVERY DAY A JOY TO LIVE

Mesfin came back. He placed on my table a candle in a saucer. He tried to light it but it kept going out.

'Sorry, it's the wind.'

'It's OK,' I said. I took out a Maglite and placed it end-up on the table.

When he came back again, he was carrying a plate of chopped onion and tomato. 'I have put chilli here, so you can add it as you want. And I will bring the spaghetti.'

I was so overwhelmed, I could hardly eat.

At first light we assembled in Asgedum's yard. His cousin Asrey was coming with us. Asrey was a member of the militia.

'Shall I bring my gun?' he asked me.

'Are there *shifta*?'

He shook his head.

138

'I think we can leave it behind.'

'*Usshi, usshi.*' I could see he was disappointed.

The noises of Nirak faded behind us – the cock-crows, the lowings and barkings. We entered open country. Pinpricks of light marked the fires of distant *hidmos*. The sky was yellowing to our right.

Where Asgedum was tall and long-necked and handsome, Asrey the militiaman was much shorter. He had a shambling, fussy manner. Every so often as we walked, he had to do a little jog to keep up with his long-limbed cousin.

'*Uuf-uuf*,' he went.

We had walked no more than a mile when Asrey's mule bolted. The load bounced and rattled on its back. The more it rattled, the more the beast panicked and the faster it ran. The load slipped round beneath its stomach, then unravelled. Piece by piece it scattered its parts through the thorn-scrub – all my pots and pans, the unnecessary utensils. Then there was no more rattling. But still the mule ran.

'*Ya-yee!*' Asgedum sprinted after it.

Asrey puffed along far behind. '*Uha-uha . . .*'

Asgedum caught the mule and led it back. Asrey gathered the baggage from the scrub. 'This is very noisy.' He held up a knife and fork. He waved them at me. 'Why do you need it? Very bad, very bad for the mule.'

We crossed into Tigray. Tigray! The border was not a river or a watershed but an arbitrary line across the valley. A young girl was coming towards us with a donkey. She was hopping and dancing down the road. She was picking out a course of her own choosing. Her hair was tied in plaits which fell from squares on her scalp. She was about eight years old.

'Do you go to school?'

'No. The teacher punished me.'

'Why? What did you do?'

'I didn't bring water for the plants.'

'But you can go back.'

'The teacher always punishes me!'

And she went on, skipping into the morning, following her donkey with its oil-drum panniers.

The heat rose. The path turned to sand, a fine black sand which flashed with mica. In the town of Finarwa, Asgedum peeled away. He was trying to trace his missing donkey. He returned breathless and despondent. No one had seen it.

Beside the Biza river a line of men was preparing a field. They had scarves wrapped around their heads to keep off the sun. The soil was so fine it looked like water as it spilled from their spades. Beyond them the river was dry but they had dug a fist-sized hole in the shingle and water had seeped into it to form a pool. I knelt down before it. I broke my own reflection to brush the dust from its surface. Using a plastic top I transferred the water scoop by scoop into a bottle. I dropped in a chlorine tablet and shook it. I waited five minutes and drank.

It became hotter still. The sky was a flawless blue, the rocks beside the road bulbous and brown. We climbed a low ridge and entered a broad open area covered in *euclea* scrub. For some time we walked up the riverbed of the Afareh until, well beyond midday, I flopped beneath a tree. '*Bakka*! Enough.'

We were above a small sandy beach. Some way upstream was a spring. Its water flowed to a point just in front of us, then sank into the sand. A group of purplish starlings flitted up the river.

Asgedum unloaded the mules and they rolled, their flailing legs spreading sand-splashes high above them. Asrey crawled onto a shelf of rock. He pulled a *gabbi* over his face.

'Oh, my head, my head! The sun is so hot –'

'Get up, bellied one!' Asgedum gave him a good prod with his *dula*.

Asrey groaned. 'I am too old to do this.'

Asgedum laughed and took the mules to drink.

Downstream the pebbles pumped their shimmer into the air above. Asgedum came back with a handful of persimmon. They looked like unripe tomatoes but had a little date-like flesh around the stone. He sat down and reclined against a saddle.

Asrey passed him a water bottle. He drank from it, poured the last drops into his hand and flicked them over Asrey. Then he spotted a group of goats on the far bank.

'What do you think? We take one and eat him?'

Asrey glared at him. 'You're a bandit, Asgedum!'

'Let debts be paid. I lost my donkey.'

'Always a bandit.'

Asgedum reclined a little deeper against the saddle. Propping one leg on the knee of the other, he flexed and unflexed his ankle, watching his foot rise and drop against the sky.

Asrey said to me: 'You know the problem with this region?'

'What's that?'

'We have no experts. They are sent here but they do not like it. It's too far away – so they leave.'

'What do you think about that, Asgedum?' I was hoping for an opposing view.

Asgedum was still watching his foot. 'He is quite right. We need experts.'

Asgedum had twenty children. He had nine from three marriages and eleven from 'other women'. Out of the twenty, he said, 'about eight' had died.

'What did you do during the Derg time?'

'What do you mean?'

'Did you fight? Were you in the EPDM?'

'He didn't fight,' said Asrey.

'Nor did you!' snapped Asgedum.

'I was recruited. I spread propaganda for the EPDM.'

'Why?' I asked.

'I didn't like the Derg. They said "Land to the Tiller" – but nothing happened. They did many bad acts. They killed educated people and –'

'This way,' Asgedum interrupted. 'They came this way, the donkeys, from the Danakil. Maybe it was hyenas.'

We crested another ridge and were looking down into a broad valley. To the west were the distant roofs of Yerchila. To the east spread an island of rock. Its sides were sheer sandstone and they glowed orange in the late sun.

'Meskal Krestos monastery!' Asrey took a deep breath and puffed out his chest, as if it was his mountain.

In front of it was a satellite *amba*, a rood-tower of matching rock. And in front of this *amba* was the village of Amda Meskal.

Asgedum and Asrey had another cousin in Amda Meskal. Aregash was a wiry, load-bent woman. She spread a calfskin onto the shelf of rock below her hut. She brought a can of washing water, lashed the growling dog with a rope, picked up a brick of dung, threw it at the goat, then went to roast coffee. It wasn't every day she had visitors.

Later we all sat in her store. Clay vats of *teff* and sorghum stood against one wall. Their low apertures were plugged with maize cobs. Candlelight flickered on the leathery mask of Aregash's face.

'I'm looking for my donkey,' explained Asgedum.

'You lost a donkey?' Aregash shook her head in disgust. 'So the *farenj* wants to visit Amda Meskal?'

'Yes,' I said.

'They won't let you.'

'Why not?'

'Because that devil robbed the *tabot*.'

A few years ago, someone had broken into the sanctuary and stolen the *tabot*. Because the *tabot* could not even be looked at by anyone but a high priest, the theft of it cast a pall of doubt over the entire area, over all those who lived in the sway of that sacred tabletop mountain. A lot of praying took place. In the end the *tabot* found its way back to the mountain and into its *maqdas*. But the priests had been fined out of their own money.

'They won't let you go. You're a *farenj*.'

Aregash then told another story to convince me further of the extreme holiness of the mountain of Amda Meskal. It revolved around the colourful figure of Ras Gugsa Araya.

In the days before the revolution, the land around Amda Meskal was governed by Ras Gugsa Araya. (He and his family were some of the more notorious members of the Ethiopian nobility. After a famously dissolute life, Ras Gugsa heard of a doctor in Switzerland who would restore his failing health. He mounted his war-mule and set out to see him. But in the nearby town of Adigrat, when the people came out to greet him, they found him already dead in the saddle. Somehow Ras Gugsa had managed to marry off his son, Dejazmach Haile

Selassie, to the favourite daughter of Emperor Haile Selassie. She was fourteen at the time. She died two years later in childbirth while the priests refused her a doctor. Dejazmach Haile Selassie sided with the Italians when they invaded in 1935, and when the emperor recovered his throne some years later he imprisoned his treacherous son-in-law in chains of silver. By the time the *dejazmach* died, it was said, his skin had grown over the chains.)

Ras Gugsa lived in the palace at Makelle but he also had land in the Simiens. Once a year, explained Aregash, the people of that land came to pay tribute to him. They would bring grain and livestock. They followed the road below the monastery of Amda Meskal.

One year as they passed, an ox fell down. It wouldn't get up. They beat it and beat it but it remained on its side. They were forced to leave it. When they reached Ras Gugsa, he said: 'You are short of one ox.'

'Yes, master, it fell down. It wouldn't get up.'

'Was it near a church?'

'That's right, master! Beneath God's mountain at Amda Meskal. It's still lying there, on its side.'

Ras Gugsa detected a faint knocking on the door of his conscience. He knew why the ox had fallen. It was because he had failed to give his own tribute to that monastery. In future, he told the peasants, you will take your grain and your oxen and give it all to that monastery.

Aregash finished her story and in the half-darkness I could feel her stare: *Do not take this mountain lightly, do not think that outsiders can go up it.*

11

In the morning we went to see a priest and the priest leaned on his staff-cross and scowled. 'The monastery is not accessible to outsiders. You cannot go up.'

'It's all right,' I told him. 'I have a letter from Abuna Pawlos in Addis Ababa, from His Holiness.'

The priest mouthed his way through the letter. It had all the right stamps. It had the signature of the Patriarch of the Ethiopian Orthodox Church.

He handed it back. 'Who is the patriarch to us here?'

But the priest agreed to talk to an ex-monk who lived in another village. He went to find the ex-monk. The ex-monk wasn't there. He left a message. He went to find another priest. That priest was ill. We waited five hours. Then the ex-monk appeared and said: 'You cannot go up. The mountain is not accessible to outsiders.'

So we took it to the authorities in the village. The administrator was out. We sat on the ground and waited for him, outside his small mud-walled office – Hiluf and me and the original priest, waiting.

It was mid-afternoon. The sky dropped from blue at its height to a horizon of hay-yellow. I shielded my eyes and looked up at the cliffs. I followed the hairline shadows running down the rockface. I looked at the tiny ledges and the sharp edge of the summit with its hanging roots and thought: How in God's name do you get up there anyway?

'*Yeee!*'

A pair of legs shot out through the window beside us. Then a woman. She ran clear of the building. '*Bewist!* In there, in there!'

She was shaking.

Inside, coiled up on the mud floor, was a fat green snake. When he saw it the priest, St Patrick-like, took his cross and jabbed at it. The snake slid under a shelf. The priest jabbed under the shelf and the snake dashed out through the open door.

Perhaps it was the snake that decided it. After it had gone, the priest ushered us up towards the cliffs. He set a brisk pace across the sand. We followed a rocky path up the mountain's skirt of rubble. At the eastern end we passed into shadow. A deep vertical scar was slashed back into the rock; a gully ran up it, to the point of a slender V of sky. The cliffs were overhanging.

Pebbles bounced down from above, and a troupe of vervet monkeys scampered away, knuckles-down, along a narrow ledge. They were followed by a line of slower, pillow-shaped marmots.

The path entered the gully. It became steeper. The wind increased. The sweat was cold against my cheek. This was a desolate place. We climbed up foot-worn ladders of tree jammed against the cliff. We came up under an overhang until only rock was above our heads – rock and a trapdoor. The priest tapped at it with his staff, and sat on the top step to wait.

'How many monks are up here?' I called, but the wind took my words. I repeated them.

The priest looked down. He raised one finger.

There was a rattle of chains. The trap rose and above it was the grinning face of Abba Wolde-Mikhael. He had been watching us come round the mountain. He'd probably been watching us all day.

A path led up to the flat summit of the mountain. We came out into the sun again, and in its thick syrupy light it was warm. The wind soughed in the dry grass. I had the sense we had entered some parallel kingdom, inhabited only by this lone monk. We arranged ourselves on rocks outside his hut. Beyond it a line of euphorbia ran down to the cliff and between the trunks the land fell away, then reappeared in bird's-eye view. I could see tiny circles of thatch and the dots of cattle moving towards them. Down there on earth, evening was spreading across the plain.

Abba Wolde-Mikhael was rubbing his feet. He had long toes and long twiggy fingers. I asked him what had made him a monk. He did not answer at once, but continued the task of foot care.

'Being alive was not enough.'

'What do you do up here?'

'Do? I prepare for the life hereafter. I read holy books.'

'Which books?' I asked.

'Holy books.'

'Do you know the *Book of Enoch*?'

He nodded. 'But I do not have that one.'

*   *   *

For a thousand years the *Book of Enoch* was one of the great mysteries of the Judaeo-Christian world. Originally written in Palestine, in either Hebrew or Aramaic, it was thought to have influenced both the content and the phrasing of many passages in the New Testament (the Sermon on the Mount, for instance). It is referred to in the epistle of Jude. Its ideas crop up in the great kabbalistic work the *Zohar*. It is perhaps the most important of all apocryphal texts – but around AD 800 it vanished. Fragments of *Enoch* in Greek and Latin and Aramaic served only to tantalise, and to prove the significance of the full text. In an age when biblical truth was the only truth, finding such a book was like finding a whole continent.

In the seventeenth century, rumours emerged of a complete version of *Enoch* in Ethiopic, or Ge'ez. At that time reaching Ethiopia was impossible. The Portuguese Jesuits had converted Emperor Susenyos to the Roman faith and caused such outrage that the entire country was plunged into civil war. The Jesuits were driven out and foreigners of all shades banned from the country. (In the 1640s a couple of Lutherans were discovered in Gondar disguised as Copts; they were strung up by their own girdles.)

The French were at the forefront of the quest for the lost *Book of Enoch*. Louis XIV's minister Colbert tried to find a copy for the king, but his envoys were denied entry to Ethiopia – or killed. It was one of France's greatest polymaths, Nicholas Fabri de Peiresc, who made the breakthrough.

Peiresc's passion was for the world's diversity. He was a botanist, an astronomer, a lawyer, numismatist, archaeologist and bibliophile. All that was rare and unexplained excited Peiresc – and in the early seventeenth century, there was plenty of each. Two hundred years before Champollion, he made a fair stab at translating Egyptian hieroglyphs. In Aix-en-Provence he had his own observatory, and one of the world's earliest micro-scopes. He kept chameleons to examine their mysterious traits, and made progress in solving the intricacies of mammalian eye-sight. He owned the first Angora cat in Europe and used the promise of an exotic kitten to persuade fellow book-collectors to part with unusual texts; other deals were closed with flasks of scent made from his own imported jasmines. When his scouts in the Middle East announced that they had found a complete copy of *Enoch*, he leapt at the chance to acquire it. Neither cats nor scent was a part of the deal; Peiresc paid a lot of money for the Ethiopic *Book of Enoch*.

By the time it reached him several years later, his health was failing. On the evening of 23 June 1637, from his deathbed, he dictated a letter to his brother: 'A final thought for scholarship – please press ahead with translating the *Book of Enoch* which I have obtained with so much trouble and expense, which has been unknown for so long and for which a frustrated public has been waiting . . .' The next day Peiresc died.

But the manuscript was not translated then, and it was some years before Europe's greatest expert on things Ethiopian, Job Ludolf, managed to inspect it. Peiresc had given the book a beautiful tooled Moroccan red binding. On turning the thick vellum title page, Ludolf read in Ge'ez: *Metshafa Henok*, the 'book of Enoch'. But it was soon clear to him that Peiresc had been sold a pup. He found that all the other folios were from an indigenous Ethiopian work entitled *The Book of the Mysteries of Heaven and Hell*.

Such was Ludolf's disappointment that he could hardly bring himself to read it. These were, he wrote, *'futiles et absurdissimas narrationes, crassae ac putidae fabulae etc'* – 'point-less stories of the greatest absurdity, crass and worthless fables'. Ludolf became convinced that the *Book of Enoch* did not exist in Ethiopia. And if it didn't exist in Ethiopia, it probably didn't exist at all. His view was widely shared. Ethiopia remained forbidden territory and the search for *Enoch* cooled.

Then in the late eighteenth century the Scottish explorer James Bruce managed to reach Gondar. Bruce had learned a little Ge'ez, was a fine horseman, and 'hated Jesuits like rats' – all of which endeared him to the xenophobic Ethiopians. On 14 February 1770 he spent his first evening in Gondar buried in a copy of the *Book of Enoch*. Two years later when he left he brought out no fewer than three copies: 'I think it is the most curious and most rare thing I brought from my travels.'

So curious and rare was his own account of Ethiopia that Bruce's contemporaries were convinced he was making it up. He was dismissed as 'Liar Bruce', Pindar satirised him, Dr Johnson doubted he had even been to Ethiopia, and a new edition of Baron Munchausen was dedicated to him. Only when others finally managed to reach the country, and witnessed its true strangeness, was the value of his account recognised – by which time he was long dead.

In 1821 the first English translation of the *Book of Enoch* was made from one of Bruce's copies. It too proved a little potent for credibility. A reviewer in the *Christian Observer* was appalled at 'the absurdity of its legends, and the grossness, and even obscenity, of some of its descriptions'. He doubted its authenticity. If it was the divine word, how would God have allowed it to remain lost for so long?

It took less faith-bound souls to appreciate the *Book of Enoch*. Byron drew on it for his poem 'Heaven and Earth', but it was William Blake – his imagination already a crowded bar of spirits and prophets – who responded most graphically to *Enoch*. In his erotic drawing, *Two Watchers descending to a Daughter of Men*, inscribed 'from the Book of Enoch', Blake shows a naked and submissive woman with a pair of celestial men. The woman is reaching for one of the men and gazing at the other, at the rays of light that shine from his vast, goose-necked phallus.

Who was Enoch? He is described in *Genesis* as the great-grandfather of Noah and only six generations from Adam; he is reported as living for 365 years and walking with God and then being taken by Him. After that there is a lot of begetting and some even longer lives – but no more Enoch.

The *Book of Enoch* is an account of what happened on his walk with God, and when he was taken. It survives as one of the richest examples of 'mission' or 'travel' literature. It is also the earliest, not just of this form but any form. In the Judaic tradition, Enoch was the first man to see the wonders of the world, its horrors and its workings, and the first to record them. It is an astonishing piece of writing. Although dating from not long before Christ, its stories are clearly of huge antiquity. Its fantastic imagery is not even allegorical. Every line rings with the conviction: this is the shape of the wide world, these are its ways. The story begins with God selecting Enoch to convey to a group of fallen angels the full details of the torments that await them. In order to do so he has to travel to the furthest extremes of the earth. He goes to the far north, the far west, the far east and the far south. From a certain mountain he sees the place where thunder is kept, where lightning is stored as bows of fire, and arrows and swords of fire. He goes to regions where no living thing exists and nothing is completed. He encounters trees of judgement, trees of fabulous scent, almond trees and cinnamon trees and trees with no known name. He is shown the tree of knowledge. He sees the burning place in the west into which the sun drops, and a river where fire flows like water. He goes to the dark mountains of winter and the great abyss from which gushes all the waters of the world. He stands and watches as, one by one, the stars leave the gates of heaven to follow their given course and he writes down the times and the seasons of each one. In the storehouses of the winds, he understands how the Lord fashioned from them the entirety of Creation, and he sees the cornerstone of the earth. At last he reaches the ends of the earth, where the heavens stretch high above it, and there he turns to the south. He comes to six mountains. They are made of wonderful layers of precious stones – of pearl and jasper and a fiery reddish stone – and in the middle of these six mountains is a seventh, and this is made from alabaster and its summit of sparkling sapphire reaches up to heaven.

Then he is shown the prison of those stars which have failed to follow their true course. He sees a great chasm and columns of fire rising to heaven and in the fire rolls the errant stars. He exclaims: 'How terrible is this place and how difficult to explore!' He has reached the region to which the fallen angels are condemned.

The fallen angels of *Enoch* are known as the Watchers. They are a group of about two hundred. One day they looked down from heaven and noticed the great beauty of women. They made themselves flesh and took their pick of those women and bred a race of giants. The giants devoured men, attacked the birds and the beasts. Meanwhile the Watchers taught men the secrets of metallurgy and they made swords to attack each other. The world was altered and corrupted.

Enoch approaches the Watchers and tells them of the fiery torture that awaits them and they are afraid. They beseech Enoch to appeal to God on their behalf – thus making him Enoch the Scribe. He writes a prayer. He leaves the Watchers and takes the prayer with him over the waters of Danbadan. Falling asleep, he has a vision in which he is taken up to heaven. He reaches a wall built of crystal, and a palace of crystal with floors of crystal. Its roof looks like the running stars and inside the palace it is as hot as fire and as cold as ice. But he passes on to another palace still more splendid and here the floor is on fire and the roof also a blazing fire. Here is a throne as large and bright as the sun but which looks like frost, and from behind a flame and tens of thousands of angels the Lord addresses him. 'Tell the Watchers,' He says, 'they have forsaken the eternal state of heaven to become flesh and lie with women.' He made men on the earth to perish and die and therefore allowed them wives so that they might conceive. But the Watchers are spirit and do not die and have no need for wives, and because of that God gives Enoch a message for the Watchers: 'Never therefore shall you obtain peace.'

The truths revealed to Enoch are unusual in the Judaic tradition in not being for the Jews alone, but universal laws.

Thus was he shown the mechanics of the cosmos and the forces which govern the passing of winter, the turning of the stars, the movement of water in the oceans, and the phenomenon of thunder and lightning. He has the wonder and the arrogance of the explorer; he had seen the extent of the old world, the world before the flood: 'And I, Enoch, I alone saw the sights and the end of all things and no one has seen what I have seen.'

Darkness was falling. I rose and walked to the cliff-edge. In the valley below, grey scarves of woodsmoke were wrapped around the homesteads. Overhead the first stars were marching out through the gates of heaven to follow their appointed course. It was an intensely still and beautiful evening. The bowl of the sky slotted neatly over the shadowy disc of the earth, and the mountain of Meskal Krestos stood precisely at its centre.

The morning sun was ablaze behind us. Its rays fanned over the back of Meskal Krestos. Abba Wolde-Mikhael, its lone inhabitant, was walking with us across the plain. He was barefoot. Before him was an elongated shadow – the *kobe* on his head was a column, the cruciform of his staff-cross rippled on furrows of bare brown soil.

The priest had worried poor Abba Wolde-Mikhael. He had warned him that if the authorities hear of a foreigner on the mountain they will make trouble – unless you come down from the mountain and go to the *woreda* office in Yerchila.

The administrator sat at the head of a T-shaped desk. He had a chunky wristwatch and some impressive desktop stationery. Form dictates that all foreign visitors to *woreda*

offices should first have the boundaries of the *woreda* explained to them, that they should be told how many *kebelles* there are in the *woreda* and should know the name of each one of those *kebelles*. Form dictates that the visitor must listen.

Abba Wolde-Mikhael worked to a different set of rules. He was hunched at the far end of the table, scratching at its varnish with his fingernail. Insects were making merry in the thicket of his beard. His tongue was clenched between his teeth – *scratch, scratch, scratch*. He blew the flakes away to reveal a perfect square of bare deal. A tiny triumph. A beautiful smile spread across his face –

'Abba!'

Abba Wolde-Mikhael looked up.

'What – can – we – do for you?' The administrator spoke to him as to a child.

He blinked.

It was Hiluf who explained. The administrator said he would vouch for us on the abba's behalf.

We said goodbye to him outside, waving him back to his solitary life on the *amba*.

'Be well!' he called after us. 'Blessings of the Mother of God be on you!'

The heat in Yerchila was stifling. We found a small *migib bet* and ate. Then I went out to sit under a bamboo awning, to watch nothing happen on the wide and empty main road.

Across the road was a man leaning on the counter of a stall talking to the young woman inside. The young woman was laughing. A little girl was standing near them, balancing on one leg; she was watching her shadow in the dust. Outside the pharmacy a woman was washing clothes in a plastic bowl. A man was looking at the ground. Two other men were standing. In the heat the minutes of the afternoon melted one into the next.

Down the middle of the road trotted a dog. His fur was the colour of ripe sorghum. He was a high-tailed, high-stepping dog. The heat did not bother him. He glanced right and left as he walked and he sniffed the air.

Around the dog's neck was a short rope. The other end of the rope was around the fist of a man. Beside the man was another man and this man held a gun. They walked to where the buildings ended. There was a single building there with a wire fence around it. They went behind the building.

All the people – the man and the woman, the little girl, the women, the men and the *farenj*, then stopped what little they were doing and looked at the building. The heat pulsed from the road. It pulsed from the roofs and the walls of the buildings. They waited.

Bang! A single shot. The bare rock multiplied it, chased its

156

echoes out beyond the town to bounce over the hills. All those who were waiting then stopped waiting. Slowly they carried on doing what they had been doing before.

'That,' announced Asrey as we left town a little later, 'was a very dangerous dog.' As a fellow militiaman, he was in full agreement about the need to shoot such a dog.

Asgedum looked down at him. 'How do you know? You're just guessing.'

'It was dangerous. Anyway you lost an animal in –'

'You just like authority too much.'

'To lose an animal in the Danakil country is very bad.'

'A man with a gun is always right, eh?'

Asrey's head dropped. He fixed his gaze on the hooves of the mules and began a muttering monologue. 'Twenty times I went and not once did I lose one . . . Five days' walking, God willing, and then you're down in the Afar country and if you lose the mules if you lose just one of them you can be all day just looking . . . Twenty times I went and never lost one . . . not like you – you who lost a donkey and not even in the darkness of the forest nor in the desert but here in the open . . .'

Asgedum ignored him. We were heading north again. It was another day to the town of Abi Addi.

At dusk we came over the top of a hill and spotted a small settlement below. Its low, flat-roofed dwellings were half-camouflaged against the slopes. In the yard of a man named Berhane we unloaded the mules. With the stock in, and the breach in the wall closed for the night, we all sat on rocks. I fried potatoes on the kerosene stove, stirring them in the pan by the light of my headlamp.

'How was the harvest last year, Berhane?'

'We had no rain. We lost many animals.'

'When was the last good year?'

'Before five years.'

He turned to Asrey and said: 'What is his country?'

'Britain.'

'Do they have churches there?'

'Yes,' Asrey assured him. 'Every country in the world has churches.'

All night Berhane's beasts pushed at the tent. At dawn I crawled out and shook the goat droppings from my boots. On the flat roof above, I watched his family rise one by one – five small figures silhouetted against the paling sky. Then two more, and another and the last of them, a girl of about twelve with a baby in her arms.

Yohannis was a student of Natural Resources. He was sitting by the road waiting for a vehicle to take him back to his studies in Makelle. But there were no vehicles. He ran to catch us up.

'The answer to our development,' he was holding a clipboard to his chest, 'do you know what it is?'

'What?'

'Water harvesting. The farmers practise rain-fed agriculture, but where does the rain go? It just goes away – so we must stop it, keep it. Water-harvesting and soil conservation. They are the answers!'

We were walking between dry hills. In the distance the eccentric line of the Simiens was etched against a harsh blue sky. The rocky plain stretched ahead in all its waterless expanse. But beside us the vision of another country was taking shape – an irrigated land of ten thousand microdams, check-dams, boreholes, household ponds, gabions and reclaimed gullies. Yohannis's belief in the future, in the restorative powers of modernity, was prodigious.

'... food-for-work ... we have constructed one hundred and thirty thousand kilometres of terraces just in Tigray ... forty-five million new trees ...'

We entered the wide basin of the Giba valley and saw seven hills, seven volcanic mounds all in a row.

'Sho'ata Hegum,' said Yohannis. 'We call those the Sho'ata Hegum.'

Sho'ata is 'seven' in Tigrinya, and after some debate we established that *hegum* was a kind of medical cupping device similar in shape to the hills.

'It's actually quite funny – they had to change the name of the *kebelle* because people were superstitious!'

The Tigrayan authorities found it hard to post officials to a *kebelle* named Sho'ata Hegum.

'So what is it called now?'

'The government changed the name to Debre Berhan.'

Debre Berhan means 'mountain of light'.

'Do people still use *hegums*?' I asked.

'Oh yes, they are used for ill people. Look.' Yohannis rolled up his sleeve – Yohannis the faithful technocrat could vouch for the powers of *hegum*.

'You see, all the hot blood collects in this place. For me even to look at the sun either at dusk or at dawn is very danger-ous. It burns the heart. It brings out the hot blood. It is very bad.'

We reached Abi Addi after dark. The power was down and the streets were full of people. They parted as we walked through the centre of town, a gauntlet of staring faces. At the gate of the guest house we said goodbye to Asrey and Asgedum. They merged back into the crowd, another team of mulemen gone. Hiluf and I were alone again with our bags.

The Lesson of the Ant-Lion

In the Institute of Ethiopian Studies in Addis Ababa there hangs a wonderful and somewhat bizarre painting. It shows a monastic group solemnly sitting down to a refectory meal, a slab of meat at each place. A monk stands reading from a sacred text. Not an unusual scene in Ethiopia – except that each of the figures is an animal. The reading monk is a lion, and a mouse squats on the text before him. At table sit a mule, a hyena, a leopard, an owl, a boar, an oryx, an elephant and others. Cats are serving the food. The painting is an elaboration of Isaiah's vision of a new Jerusalem, in which predators sit peacefully with their prey. It goes by the touching title *Ya'awri Mehaber Tafakeru*, or 'Community of Animals Loving Each Other'.

Animals feature in sacred paintings throughout the highlands. At the cave-church of Yimrehanna Krestos, I had seen peacocks and ostriches, gazelles and lions, hares, a bird-like angel, and a half-raptor, half-human hybrid. 'The Ethiopian painter,' concludes Georg Gerster, 'apparently makes use of pictures of animals for filling empty spaces without even thinking about it.'

One of the earliest works translated into Ge'ez was the *Physiologus*. Its fables of the natural world proved as popular in Ethiopia as they did in medieval Europe, where only the Bible had more translations. Each fable is followed by a Christian moral which draws on the belief that the behaviour of animals is an innocent – and much more consistent – version of human behaviour, that the laws of God can be read in animals just as they can be in the passing of the seasons or the movement of the heavens.

While the exemplary feats of saints can be offputting and austere, lessons from the animal world work through comic charm. Who could forget the story of the sea-tortoise mistaken by sailors for an island? (Beware of anchoring to the devil.) Or the hedgehog who gathers grapes on its spines? (Thus gather the fruits of the Christian mysteries.) Or the unicorn who shoots medicinal hairs from its testicles as it flees the hunter? (Cast away from you all that is carnal and leave it for your hunter, the devil.)

My own favourite is the ant-lion. With the face of a lion and the body of an ant, its father eats meat, and its mother eats grain. The poor ant-lion goes hungry and dies. Thus 'The one who does not believe in his heart finds himself with two lives.' In fact, the ant-lion came about by accident, through a series of mistranslations. Its success as a fable, like that of a joke, depends on incongruity and juxtaposition.

In the *Physiologus*, real animals rub shoulders with the mythical, the lion with the phoenix, the otter with the unicorn, the ichneumon with the onocentaur. The early Christian authorities didn't like it at all and tried to ban it. They feared its fantasy creatures would undermine the seriousness of doctrine and provoke ridicule. But its survival long into the Middle Ages suggests something much more universal than theological orthodoxy.

In Ethiopia, the world is still understood largely through sign and symbol and allegory, and the playful spirit of the *Physiologus* is accepted without question.

12

In Abi Addi begins a region of squared-off mountains, eccentric cliffs and one of the greatest, and least known, concentrations of churches and monasteries on earth. As recently as 1963, Tigray could boast only nine rock-hewn churches; three years later, at a conference of Ethiopian studies in 1966, a list of more than a hundred was read out by Abba Tewolde-Medhin Josef. Even now, the list of them is probably not complete.

One of the first to study the churches was a British architect named Ruth Plant. In the late sixties and early seventies, her month-long mule and Land-Rover trips took her deep into central Tigray. She pace-measured the buildings' interiors, grappled their irregularities into ground plans, sketched their capitals, their friezes, triglyphs, metopes and frescoes. But the 1974 revolution put a stop to her work. She retired to restore a medieval house near Bristol and build up a herd of prize Herefords.

One June evening, shortly before going to Ethiopia for the first time, I went to visit her. A red sun glowed in the tracery windows of her hall; on an oak table she spread out a hand-drawn, dye-line map of Tigray. She was a small woman and already old. As she looked down at her own map, with its Rotring rivers and mule-tracks, she was overcome with nostalgia. 'Wretched Derg!' she hissed.

For two hours or more she spoke of the hollowed-out buildings of Tembien and Gheralta. Her technical language could not quite damp down her burning love for the region and its half-discovered treasures. 'The craftsmen who formed them were as inventive as those who built Europe's medieval cathedrals. The rock-hewn churches were cut from the roof down – they could not afford mistakes. Not one!'

Then, handing me a copy of that hand-drawn map, she gave two warnings. 'Once you've been to Ethiopia, it never really lets you go. And beware – the food! Those journeys ruined my stomach.'

I went to Ethiopia – I fell foul of both traps.

But in those years Tigray was always off-limits, and the map lay buried in a cupboard. Ruth published a book of her studies, *Architecture of the Tigre*, which lists more than 130 churches. It contains short entries for reaching the churches like this: '... walk along a narrow ledge with a sheer drop of several thousand feet to one side ...' That made me keener than ever. Ruth died in the late 1980s, without seeing the TPLF defeat the Derg, and without ever returning to her beloved Tigray.

Early that first morning in Abi Addi, I spread out her map in the yard of our hotel. It was still the only guide to the churches. Following its faded lines, I felt a surge of high spirits about the coming weeks.

'I suggest this,' I said to Hiluf. 'We go to these churches, here in Tembien – then follow this track east to the cluster here – in Gheralta.'

First was the monastery of Abba Yohannis. Hiluf dug a photo of it from his pack. Five hundred feet of cliff and a few holes in the rock halfway up.

'How do you get in, do you think?' I wondered.

'Perhaps we must learn to fly.'

We set off to find a new team of mules.

It was market day in Abi Addi. The streets were a crush of merchants, farmers, cattle, salt-laden camels and scuffling goats. *Berberi*, sweat and excrement pooled their smells in the rising heat. Work-gangs swarmed over the building sites. Through the crowds bobbed the white turban of a priest, halted every few paces by supplicants kissing his hand-cross. An

unstoppable grin filled his face. In the market square a man rolled up his sleeve and scooped honey from a sack into our container. Children slalomed among the squatting traders.

The wild hinterland of Abi Addi was just the sort of country to make the Derg twitchy. On 8 July 1977 there was a shortage of salt in the region and people came from far off to buy salt in Abi Addi's market. In the mid-morning, Derg troops entered the square. They rounded up these people. They said they were thieves. They held back the crowd with batons, divided the peasants into two groups and machine-gunned them against a wall.

'In that corner, and in that one they shot them.' We met Hirut in a tea-house on the edge of the town's market square. After the shooting she was one of dozens who joined the rebels. She was only fourteen and one of the first female recruits. 'My father was a priest. He had eight children and by the end all of us were in the field – every one! Also four of his grandchildren.'

We had the usual problems finding mules. 'They've all died,' a trader explained.

'The famine?'

'Bee stings.'

We found two donkeys and a young donkey-man to take us as far as Abba Yohannis next day; from there we'd trust to luck. Then someone mentioned the name of an old nobleman who lived in the lower part of town, a man who had also been a senior official during the Derg years.

Gabre-Hiwot was ninety years old. He had been ennobled *grazmach* – 'leader of the left' – when such things mattered. He and his wife now occupied a single-roomed house. A metal-framed bed stood against the wall; much of the mud floor was covered in a collection of jars, jerry-cans, urns and drums.

Gabre-Hiwot's wife was keeper of this collection, treading among it as if it were a bed of rare blooms.

Gabre-Hiwot himself was squatting on the bed. His elbow rested on one raised knee and a long-fingered hand curled around his forehead. He heard out my introduction without response. When I asked about the Derg time he peered at me down his nose.

I tried again.

He scowled.

I looked to Hiluf. We stood and crossed to the door. Outside the midday heat was intense.

'Wait ... wait – *farenj*!' Gabre-Hiwot's wife called us back in. He was still sitting on the bed, but with one hand gestured to us to sit down again. He began to cough.

'I fought –' he spluttered.

His wife selected an earthenware jug and poured him a beaker of water.

'I fought against the Italians ... under Ras Kebede. I was wounded – look, here in the thigh. We held them.'

'What about under the Derg?'

'We were only trying to defend our land. It is the land of our forefathers.'

He narrowed his eyes. Was it even worth trying to convince this *farenj*?

'In the Derg time, I was administrator of the town.' The confession released something in him and the words came spilling out. 'You cannot say that the Derg were good. They did many bad things. But the town was being attacked by the TPLF. Your land is attacked, you must defend it. If your forefathers died for it, how can you give it away? I acted with the will of God.'

When in 1988 the Derg were driven from Abi Addi for

good, Gabre-Hiwot left with them. He was afraid of retribution. He fled east with the Derg to Makelle, then south to Dessie. The army broke up and as it did so Gabre-Hiwot was left with a choice.

'I thought to myself, I would rather die in my own land than be killed in Wollo. So I came back to Abi Addi. The TPLF were in charge. Some of them wanted to kill me. I told them: Look at the papers. I showed them the papers in my old office. They looked at the papers. They saw I helped the poor. I did not arrest people. The TPLF have shown me mercy.'

As we stood to leave, he called after us. 'These things are not simple –' He started to cough again. He was bent over, trying to catch his breath. His wife was already among the jugs, fetching him another beaker of cool water.

Outside we blinked in the sunlight. Across the road, a group of men eyed us. I had the impression no visitor went near Gabre-Hiwot's house.

We left Abi Addi soon after sunrise. It was a beautiful morning. The sky was a cloudless blue, the mountains ahead glowed like honey and today was the glorious anniversary of the TPLF's founding.

Exactly twenty-nine years earlier, ten Tigrayans entered the town of Dedebit with a few old guns and lofty thoughts of correcting the deviant course of the revolution. Now the movement they established that day governed the entire Ethiopian federation. On the main road two columns of schoolchildren were marching into town behind the Ethiopian flag and the Tigrayan flag – a perfect Socialist Realist tableau, except that the children in the columns couldn't keep straight and kept bunching up like a blocked stream, and giggling. They were already late for the anniversary parade. 'No, no!' cried the teachers. 'For the sake of God – you look like dying snakes!'

We left the road for a path and the path cut down across a series of terraced fields to a dry river. There, on a rock, sat a man with a sack of grain and a stick.

Hailu had been to the mill and was on his way home. He was busy inspecting the sand at his feet. He lived near the monastery of Abba Yohannis. He ran his stick through the tied-together corners of the sack and hoisted it onto his shoulder. 'It is good to walk alone – but it is better to walk with others.'

He had a high, handsome head and a slurred and lisping voice. He was almost entirely deaf, so in conversation wasted little time trying to listen to others.

In the famine of 1984 Hailu fled to Sudan. There he found work with an aid group. Also with the group was a French girl called Stephanie. 'We used to do everything together – everything.' Hailu sighed. 'We drove in vehicles, 'Tephanie driving beside me. Even when we went to the fields, we drove in a vehicle.'

After some time Stephanie left for France and Hailu was very sad. In a camp he met a Tigrayan girl from his neighbouring village. 'She was even my relation. So we got married.' Hailu wanted to stay in Sudan, but when the Derg fell his wife insisted they came back. He had never ridden in a vehicle since.

At midday we were sitting on top of a low rise. An acacia tree spread its shade over our heads. The land below fell in a series of dusty terraces to a small village. A shepherd joined us while his sheep nosed at the dirt. The shepherd told us about two of his sheep which had been caught by a devil: the devil took them to a high cliff and made them fall over it.

Hailu wasn't listening. From his breast pocket, he pulled a

small package wrapped in white muslin. He handed it to me. Inside was a five-franc piece.

'She gave it to me in the Sudan.' With an illusionist's dexterity, Hailu took the coin and passed it between his fingers. He had clearly spent a lot time with that coin. 'Here she is sowing!' He pointed to *La Sommeuse* on the face of the coin, the barefoot woman with her floating hair, her floating robes, spreading seed across a wide plain. 'It looks like 'Tephanie!'

He held it up a few inches from his face and closed one eye: 'If you look at it in this way – it is bigger even than the sun.'

A woman was half-running up from the huts below with a large pitcher of water. Even before she reached us, the shepherd had rolled up his sleeves. She poured water into his palms. He threw the water over his neck and head. It formed pearly droplets in his hair. She gave him a towel and he dabbed his face.

'This is the woman I am going to marry.'

'What?' asked Hailu.

He leaned closer to Hailu and shouted. 'In one month we are going to be married!'

'You should marry a white woman. They're the best women.'

'You are wrong.' The shepherd handed the towel back to his fiancée. She waited while he drank a cup of the water, then hurried back to her hut. 'Our own are the best.'

But Hailu couldn't hear. He was holding up the coin again. He was passing it through his fingers, covering the hot sun with its silhouette.

13

At the monastery of Abba Yohannis a group of slow-faced monks were slumped in the overhang of the cliff. Rock-cut steps led up to one side, through an arch and a gate, towards the church.

I bent to catch my breath, leaning on my knees; a drop of sweat rolled down and dripped from my nose.

The monks stared at me with glazed expressions. I pointed up the steps, and they shook their heads.

'Church locked.'

'What?'

'Hudadie. Come tomorrow.'

Of course, Lent had begun – *hudadie*. Fifty-six days of semi-starvation now lay ahead for Ethiopia's Christians. Each day, shortly after noon, *kidassie* prayers would be said in the country's churches, which were then locked. The prayers sanctified the church interiors, and after that you stood a better chance of squeezing a camel through the eye of a needle than persuading the priests to open them up again.

After *kidassie* prayers the fast was broken, and the monks were about to eat. There had been a baptism and the baby's father was squatting under the cliff preparing bean *shurro* in a large bowl. Tying a shawl around his shoulder he began to serve. He placed the bowl in the middle of the men. They pulled back their sleeves and tore off corners of *injera*. The father brought a jug of *tella* and filled their beakers. Vitality returned to them like warmth to chilled fingers.

'This *shurro* is very sweet, Yefat.'

'It is like the *shurro* of Cheli district.'

'Cheli *shurro* is quite a bitter one –'

'Who is he – Italian?'

'*Farenj*!' Long fingers curled over my wrist. An elderly monk fixed me with his watery eyes. 'We are struggling.'

'Of course.'

'We struggle to inherit *Paradise*!'

Another shouted: 'Yefat! Yefat – come out.'

He washed his hands and came away from the food. He

stood before them as if before an examining board. As well as the monks there were a few priests eating, and they were younger and fuller in the face. Everyone was now very lively. One by one they stood and addressed Yefat.

First monk (thick grey beard, face of a prophet): 'Yefat! Forty days have passed since you were granted a son. We have blown on his face. We have anointed his skin in the thirty places. Now we are eating and it is all the will of God. We thank God and all the saints for the blessings! Also this *shurro* is very good.'

Second monk: 'You are the son of my relations! But I have never seen you before today. Your father was a high *debtara* and he fought against the Derg. I think also he died but I do not know . . . Well, he was certainly a hero. I say this: let your baby be a servant of God!'

Third monk (small, gentle voice): 'Actually, I'm not from here but because your baby maybe is a saint, I came to the baptism.' *(Begins a prayer in Ge'ez.)*

Priest (interrupting): 'I knew the boy's father. Yes, he was a *debtara*. He was a fighter. He joined the rebels and he was wearing truly the finest trousers. But the famine came and he could not provide for his family and he took them to the Sudan. He died in the Sudan in great difficulty. Then his wife was in great difficulty. She also died. This boy here, Yefat, became lost. After many years his uncle came to the Sudan and with God's help found him and brought him back and raised him. So he is a child precious in the eyes of God and that means his child is also blessed!'

Fourth monk (looking around): 'In fact I haven't got anything to say. Everything has been said.'

Fifth monk: 'May you live long!'

Second priest: 'For a week now there were few priests at this place – but all at once there are many priests. So perhaps your baby is a saint.'

Fifth monk: 'Also there is a *farenj* –'

Second priest: 'That is the work of God!'

Third monk: 'May your baby always be your servant!'

Sixth monk: 'You are very poor but today you brought much food and also very good *tella*. This is because of the prayers of your dead father.'

Third monk: 'May all our own prayers be successful like his – may they be written across the heavens!'

Glee and pride quickened Yefat's movements. He took the *tella* jug around again. He scooped out the last of the *shurro*. Everyone was talking at once. In the shadow of that cliff an ancient ideal was being enacted: communal living in the sight of God.

Then one of the priests said something and laughed. There was a sudden silence.

The monks glared. The eldest of them rose to his feet and pointed a finger at the priests. 'You have no Christianity, for you have been cut away by the sword –'

Another monk tugged at his sleeve.

Now the monks and the priests avoided each other's gaze. They finished the food without speaking. Yefat was very subdued as he cleared the baskets and bowls. We helped him carry them back down the cliff.

'Why must they do it?' he hissed. 'Why?'

'What happened?'

'The monastery is for monks.' Yefat's voice had dropped. 'But now they have built the road, visitors are coming. They give money and so the priests from the villages say: Why should we also not have some of the money? So they come to the monastery.'

Seventeen hundred years earlier, the coenibitic rules of Pachomius warned of the problem: 'Our father Pachomius did not want any clerics in his monasteries for fear of jealousy and vainglory. In the same way as a spark cast into the threshing floor, unless it is quickly quenched, will destroy a whole year's labour, so it is with a thought of vainglory.'

We walked down from the cliff in silence. Yefat showed us into a yard where the newly-built walls of a hut rose to a neat cone of thatch. The house was empty. 'You can spend the night here,' said Yefat. 'It is my cousin's.'

'Where is your cousin?'

'He has gone to the lowlands. He is a priest. In the dry season the priests like to go to the lowlands. They like to search in the rivers for gold.'

Yefat's voice faltered. He was close to tears. He took his pans and jugs and made his way home to his just-baptised son.

That evening we went to see the monastery's abbot, Memhir Za-Manfuskiddus Abraha. He was sitting like a stylite on a high rock. The *memhir* did not move as we scrambled up but continued gazing like a raptor at the land below. We sat at his feet. He wore a brown *kobe* and a green blanket around his shoulders. The sun picked out the map of his wrinkled face.

The *memhir* had lived in the monastery for over fifty years. He spoke faintly, as though his voice was no more than the overspill from some vast reservoir. He would not be drawn on the conflict with the priests. He saw much more relevance in the work of the monastery's founding father, Abba Yohannis.

'Let me tell you this. People make the journey to our monastery and I ask them, Why did you come? And they say, Because we saw the person of Abba Yohannis.'

He paused.

'He has many caves in the west of Tigray. Some are for guests and over some he stands guard with his sword. Did you see him, in your country?'

'No.'

Fifteen hundred years had passed since Yohannis's mortal ministry. I asked the *memhir* to tell me about him.

He looked at me with some disdain, but then began. 'There was a governor of Haghere Salem. It was the time of King Kaleb and the governor went to fight in the Yemen. Well, a year passed and the governor did not return. His brother went to the governor's wife. He told her: My brother, your husband, has been killed. Therefore I can marry you. She refused, so he forced himself on her. The following year by the Grace of God the governor returned from Yemen and asked: Where is my wife? She is giving birth, they said, in an upper room. The governor went to the upper room and took the baby and was about to kill it when a monk arrived and told him: That child has been chosen by God! The monk was called Abba Amoni and he lived in these cliffs here and the Archangel Gabriel had told him to go and save the child. So he brought the child to this place and baptised him Yohannis and the goats suckled him and he was raised on the path of God.

'When he was the right age, Abba Amoni took Yohannis to Aksum to be received as a deacon. But on the way they passed a river and the boy saw some women in the water. The women had their breasts exposed. Abba Amoni became afraid for the innocence of the boy and took him back to the cliffs. Then the Holy Ghost descended as a dove and Yohannis received the holy spirit. Thereafter he lived a holy life.'

The *memhir* pointed up to the head of the valley. The slopes were dotted with boulders. 'There are another forty-two up there.'

'Forty-two what?'

'Forty-two churches. But you cannot see them.'

'They are closed?'

'Only the saints can see them.'

'Where are the saints?'

'They are invisible. They live in the rocks, in caves. They live on berries.'

'And can you see the saints?'

He shook his head.

He paused. His body seemed to be slowing down, his energies withdrawing back into him. His voice grew even fainter. 'Sometimes in Aksum when we go there for holy days, the saints come up to me and touch my arm and say: Memhir, we see your works. We see you working in God's name. Blessings be upon you.'

He turned away. He resumed his staring at the earth below and his lids half-dropped over his eyes. As we left him, he had reverted to his rock-like stillness.

The next morning I rose early and stepped out of the *hidmo*. A momentary calm hung over the slopes, before the day's business began. Up here, it was easy to imagine living not in a linear world, where time and progress were one, but a cyclical world where dawn rolled round to dusk and dusk rolled round to dawn, where fast led to holy day and holy day to fast, and everyone knew that famine would give way to feast and feast would give way to famine and the lives of the saints were eternally present.

High up the cliff a dark shape rose against the rock. It was a hooded vulture. It had black-brown plumage and finger-like primaries. One easy wing-flick and it was gliding along the cliff, the sandstone a blur behind it. Then it was clear of the mountain and the sun was bright on its underwing and it was soaring into a milky sky. I watched it climb. I watched it spin and spin in slow circles. Then it stopped its spinning and returned to the cliff to dash along the rock face. It put out its feet, gave one braking wing-beat and landed on the cliff. In all its flight it had moved its wings only twice, once at the beginning and once at the end. Now I could see the heads of two young. They were standing on the ledge which was spattered with a white frieze of droppings. Several hundred feet below, but still high above the ground, were the windows of the church. How to reach it remained a mystery.

We climbed back up towards the cliff. The monks were rising in their cells, and in brush-roofed shelters in the rock. In bare feet we mounted the steps. A tunnel led blind through hidden folds of rock, burrowing in behind the cliff-face. It entered the church low down one wall. We were in a large, hollowed-out space. After a night of praying a group of monks stood unmoving in the semi-darkness. Columns of bedrock divided the interior into a series of bays, rising to arches and low cupolas. Chisel-marks covered the walls.

Daylight flooded through high windows; below them was a doorway. It opened onto a narrow ledge and I moved out onto it. Directly below was a scattering of treetops and boulders. A single step into space, just one step . . .

*   *   *

We found two donkeys and two donkey-men. Gabre-Mariam was a thin, athletic man; Solomon his cousin was a little younger. Over the coming days I grew to appreciate them more and more – their quiet good humour, their passionate faith and their breezy sense that difficulties are a natural part of everyday life.

In the rising heat, our small party left the monastery of Abba Yohannis and set off along a narrow aloe-lined path. As we passed Yefat's hut, a monk came running out.

'Wait – I am coming!'

14

Abba Tadewos had been at the baptism and now he was going home. He wore a black ankle-length soutane and had a black umbrella over his shoulder to keep off the sun. His face shone with goodness and his saintly presence lifted the labour of the morning's walk.

Abba Tadewos lived in a cave. He had lived there for thirty years on the eastern side of Debra Asa. He had gone in during the last months of imperial rule, had lived there through the revolution, the Red Terror, the great famine, war with the TPLF and the fall of the Derg. None of these things could touch Abba Tadewos in his cave. Except one day when he looked up at the sky and saw two planes coming to attack Debra Asa. 'Those *farenjis* dropped their bombs on the mountain – but there's not a bomb in the world that can enter my cave!'

It was after midday when he jogged up between two boulders and led us into a clearing shaded by a large *ficus*. Its serpentine roots coiled down over a swell of bedrock. The roots

divided over a small thatched vestibule and a wooden door.
Abba Tadewos folded away his umbrella and smiled a home-
coming smile.

The air inside was cool, and musty with fungus spores. In
one corner a clay platform served as a bed, in another was a clay
stove. Cobwebs thick with soot hung from the rock above.
From the back of his cave Abba Tadewos brought a jug of *tella*
and a jar of white honey. We sat on low stools, eating honey
and drinking *tella*.

Before coming here, Abba Tadewos had taught theology in
Makelle. He had been a priest and a teacher and he had had
a wife. When she and their daughter died from 'a shrinking
disease' in 1973, he sold all his things, gave the money away and
retired to his cave.

I took the opportunity to ask him the big question, the
question that distinguishes Christianity from all other faiths
and the one that so successfully sliced up the early Church into

little pieces: how did he define the nature of Christ? How do Ethiopians resolve the problem of a deity in a mortal body?

Over the years, I had put the same question to a number of Eastern clerics – to Armenians and Copts and Syriacs. I had never had a straight answer. Instead they gave analogies, proving that matters of essence are best conveyed by metaphor. Christ's nature, said one, combined the divine and the human in the same way as bread combines flour and water. Like the waters of a lake, said another, fed by two streams – one mortal and one divine. Or like coffee – the coffee is one part, the milk is another part, the combination is something new.

Abba Tadewos was no different. He took a deep breath and brushed some dust from his lap. With it thirty years of contemplation were swept aside; he was the teacher again. 'Think of it like this. If you look at his divine nature it was like fire, and his mortal was like iron. Together they allow the bent to be straight, the short to be long; and when the iron was held in the fire and beaten, the fire did not feel the beating but the iron did – in the same way that the mortal Christ suffered on the cross but the divine did not.' He smiled. 'But of course it is more complicated than that.'

'How?'

'If Christ was man, then there was a time he did not exist. But if he is God then he has no beginning and no end. That is only one example.'

Members of these Oriental Churches tended, like the Gnostics, to stress the divine side of Christ's nature. Much of their earthly struggle was with demons, and a more godly Messiah was deemed more effective against them. The appeal of a deity who had never been compromised by taking mortal form is one reason why Islam – with its purely divine God and its purely mortal Prophet – found so many converts among these Eastern Christians.

On 8 October, AD 451, five hundred bishops gathered together in the Byzantine town of Chalcedon. After the bishops had exchanged opening pleasantries – a barrage of explosive insults – they managed to agree the definition of Christ's nature. It is this definition that has, with various compromises and modifications, suited both Western and Orthodox Churches ever since: 'one Christ in two natures, without confusion, without change, without division, without separation . . .'

But it was seen as a fudge by the Oriental Orthodox Churches – Armenian, Syriac, Coptic and Ethiopian. The Ethiopian Church dismisses Chalcedon as the 'Council of Fools' or 'Council of Dogs'. Exactly why is harder to establish. The more you try to clutch the opposing definitions, the more they run like sand between your fingers. There is as much politics in the schism as theology. The great Christological disputes teach us less about the Incarnation than about man's perennial urge to factionalism.

One thing the Ethiopians deny passionately is that they are 'monophysite'. So do the Copts, the Armenians and the Syriacs. But look in any history of Christianity and you will see reference to these Monophysite Churches. The Ethiopians do not believe in a single nature of Christ. They distinguish a 'composite unity' from an 'elemental unity' and are more correctly 'miaphysite'. 'Monophysite' is clumsy and pejorative, seen as a term coined by others to dismiss the dissenting Eastern Churches.

In Ethiopia itself, isolated from other Christians for a thousand years, many of the finer points of Christology were forgotten. That changed in the sixteenth century when the Portuguese Jesuits arrived. The Ethiopian clergy knew they were not supposed to agree with these Catholics, but were not quite sure why. They began to argue among themselves, and they carried on arguing, and fighting, for the next two hundred years. The country broke up into a series of fiefdoms.

In 1878, Emperor Yohannis IV called a council in central Ethiopia. A native of this region of Tigray, Yohannis was trying to re-establish the unity of the state, and in this the role of the Church was vital. Hammering out an orthodoxy on the nature of Christ proved successful. Only two clerics refused. The emperor ordered their hands and feet to be amputated and their tongues to be sliced out. Since then the Ethiopian Church has been known as Yethiopia Tewehado Bete-Cristyen. *Tewehado* is from the verb 'to unite' – a reference not to the unity of the Church but to the position on the nature of Christ.

'When we say *tewehado*,' explained Abba Tadewos, 'we mean that God and man are united in Christ, and that God does not lose his identity nor does man lose his identity.'

Over his shoulder, a man appeared in the mouth of the cave. He stood there, haloed by sunlight, before hobbling in. A hand-towel hung over his head with the faded words *Tigrai Hotel*. He was so stooped that his eyes were level with his shoulders. He put an arm out to the rock and stood there, his rasping breath a drone to Abba Tadewos's soft voice. He nodded in agreement with all that the abba said.

'Now, the difficult place is with Mary. But we say when she was pregnant, Christ was still a spirit. He had been a spirit even before the beginning of the world. Even before the world He was there. He is descended from apes but He was also created from Mary without a father – then He became flesh.'

It was late afternoon when we stepped back outside. Abba Tadewos looked around him, at the sheltering tree and the flitting birds and the warmth radiating from the rock. His didactic expression was replaced by one of quiet joy. He sighed loudly. 'Words, words, words.'

The other man nodded and the towel on his head swung from side to side.

I asked Tadewos how to reach the monastery of Abba Salama.

'You are going to Abba Salama?'

'If we can find it.'

He pointed to a blue-grey line of mountains to the east. 'You see the one with two points, and behind that another? It is between them.' He gripped my arm. 'But be careful.'

'Why?'

'You must pull yourself up on chains. They are like the chains of heaven! If you look down, it is like looking down on *hell*!'

The other man opened his arms in imitation of some hell-dwelling demon, and chuckled.

We entered a broad valley. The plain beyond was a pale shade of tan. In the heat, dust-devils veered across it. At dusk we reached a scattering of *hidmos*. The men were all off celebrating St Mikhael's Day and the women were reluctant to let us in. We tried several houses before one said: 'Well, he will be back at any moment.'

We bought feed for the donkeys. We put up the tent in the corner of the yard, driving the pegs into layers of impacted dung. I was unpacking the stove when the man of the household returned. He wore the white head-dress of a priest.

'Good evening, Abba!' I greeted him.

'What?' He looked over my shoulder. 'What is this?'

'A tent —'

'Take it down!' He stretched an accusing finger towards it. 'Take it down at once!'

He then sat on a rock and put his head in his hands. '*Wai-wai-wai!*'

The women were silent. One of them was suckling a baby. The three children beside them were also silent.

'You come with your tent!' he wailed. 'It's a sign. Another child will be taken. Each time when the babies died they brought a tent like that.'

I was already ripping out the pegs.

'In the name of the Mother of God! Now which one? Which child will you take now, oh Lord?'

Had a hole appeared in the ground, I would have happily jumped into it.

'*Wai-wai-wai!*'

Another man entered the yard. He looked at the priest, he looked at us.

'What's all this?'

'The tent – the *farenj* put up the tent. It's a sign!'

The man looked at the tent-bag.

'Have we not suffered enough?' cried the priest.

'It's just a foreigner's tent.'

'Not even in Aksum do they allow tents –'

'Yes they do.'

'In the compound of St Mary of Zion in Aksum tents are never permitted.'

'What are you saying? On Palm Sunday, Aksum is full of tents!'

The priest put his head in his hands again. 'Oh-oh – I can see the little bodies, I can see the shroud. That *farenj* has brought death to this home again. Why do we suffer, in the name of Mary, help us . . .'

The man put his arm on the priest's shoulder. The priest allowed himself to be led away.

'How many places have you visited, Abba?' said the man, in a low voice.

'*Wai-wai* . . .' They stepped out through the gate and along the edge of a ploughed plot.

The man returned. 'I am sorry. That priest has been drinking.'

'So this is your house?' I asked.

'Yes, it is.'

'And you have lost children?'

'Well, that's certainly true. Two died last year.'

For a long time after dark, the women were still laughing about it. 'The foreigner's tent. The priest! It's a sign, he said. A sign! Oh, that nervous priest . . .'

I rolled out my bedding on the bare rock. Lying back, I looked up at the canopy of stars. That night I dreamed of high cliffs and an Enochian wind fanning the flames of hell; I woke to an ox breathing on my cheek.

Dawn was already bright behind the hills, and I lay watching it pick out every tiny serration, every leaf and rock along the skyline.

15

Shortly after seven, we left and headed east, following a stony path between rows of euphorbia and agave. The low sun flickered between their spiky limbs. I had grown to love these early mornings, waving goodbye, setting off into crisp highland air with shreds of mist and an unknown day before us. And I was fit now, with that physical confidence that comes with fitness. In the town of Amda Worq – another Amda Worq, another 'golden pillar' – we collected water from a pump and found two papaya. We pushed south towards the mountains.

Two hours later we entered a long, high valley. The first sight of the monastery of Abba Salama was innocent enough – a flash of corrugated iron roof at the far end of the valley. But as we drew closer, so the land between fell away, until we were standing on the edge of a dizzying chasm. The monastery was an island of rock connected to the main plateau by a broken isthmus. Even after weeks in the highlands, the scale of those cliffs was overwhelming.

In Ruth Plant's *Architecture of the Tigre*, the relevant entry says this:

> The monastery of Abba Salama must be one of the most inaccessible in the world ... it is necessary to follow an extremely narrow ledge, invisible from a distance and lacking handholds of any kind which cuts across a tremendous precipice ... the visitor must then ascend a chimney, then clutch a bundle of chains which enable him to surmount the final cliff-face ... on this last lap the unseen monks above assist the climber by hauling at a thong around his middle.

The entry for Abba Salama is not written by Ruth but by David Buxton, who comments drily: 'Women, happily for them, are debarred.'

The monk who could allow us up was judging a dispute in a neighbouring village. So we unloaded the donkeys and settled in the shade to wait. The monastery cliffs rose across the gap like the gates of another world.

I took out a knife and divided the papaya into slices. I handed one to Gabre-Mariam. He was the elder of the donkey-men. He was in his early forties and had a kind, devout face. His eyes flashed with a boyish enthusiasm as he spoke.

He was talking about his ploughing. Tigrinya has four words for ploughing. In one of his fields he had done the first ploughing (*tsigi*), the other he had ploughed twice and that was *aymi*. Third and fourth ploughing were *tselas* and *raba*.

I asked if he had been to Abba Salama before.

'Yes, I know this place.' He tossed the papaya rind over the cliff and wiped his mouth.

One day during the time of the Derg, he had developed a

sickness. A terrible sickness! His limbs grew heavy, his head beat like a church drum, his eyes went strange and he could not work. (As he said this he dropped his head and made his body sag.) He prayed to Abba Yohannis. Nothing. He prayed to Mikhael and Giorgis and Urael – but the sickness became worse. He went to the *debtara* and they gave him herbs but the herbs did no good. He was told that the right medicine for his sickness could be found only in Makelle.

He set out for Makelle. It was very difficult walking because of the sickness and because there was little food in the country at that time. After a week, though, he reached the hospital in Makelle.

'Where is your ID card?' they asked.

'I don't have an ID card; I'm a peasant.'

They told him that if he did not have an ID card the Derg would say he was a rebel. Then they would make trouble for the hospital and they would throw him in prison. Anyway, they did not have the right medicine. So Gabre-Mariam began the long walk back. The sickness now felt as if there was a big rock on his shoulder and big rocks on his feet. As well as that he was now worried the Derg would arrest him. Whenever he saw soldiers he pretended he was just working on the land. Then he met a group of men. They were three men and they had such a nice look in their faces that he asked them: Where are you going?

'We are pilgrims,' they said, 'and we are going to Abba Salama.'

'Where is that?'

'It is on the holy mountain of Debra Medhanit.'

Well, because of the name of the mountain (it means 'mountain of medicine') and because of the nice look in their faces, Gabre-Mariam joined the men. They came to this place. He looked up at the cliffs and thought: I cannot climb it. But they tied a rope around his waist and the strange thing was that by the time he reached the top he already felt a little better. He drank the holy water and the sickness rose from him and opened its wings and flew away. Now Abba Salama was always part of his prayers.

Across the gorge, a monk was walking around the flat rim of the cliff. Beneath him the rock was in shadow and fell hundreds of feet to the scree below. It took him a long time before

he was standing before us. The wind flicked at the frosty tufts of hair behind his ears. He had settled his dispute. He could take us up.

This is what it entailed, reaching the monastery of Abba Salama. (Looking at my notes now brings it all back: the writing is rushed and angular, the pages smudged with dust and sweat.)

The monk led us down a ladder, across the narrow saddle of rock to the main cliff. A ledge ran around one side. There were no handholds but the ledge was a couple of feet wide. What made it perilous, what made you place each foot so carefully and press your hand to the cliff on one side was an awareness of the vast space on the *other* side.

After thirty yards, there was a gap in the rock above and a short scramble up a ladder. You were now in a narrow chimney – a cliff behind and a cliff in front, and on either side a bird's-eye view of the gorge below. The wind funnelled between the rocks. A ladder rose in front of you and you craned your neck and looked up. It was two ladders welded together, made from rust-brown iron. It began at a slight angle to the vertical but flexed until it was flush and sheer with the rock face.

The monk was talking about the bottle of water he dropped the other day. It bounced on the rock and did not roll on over the precipice. It did not even break! Because it was holy water!

You did not want to hear that; you did not want to hear about things falling. You began to climb, one rung at a time. There was no sign of the waist-rope mentioned by Buxton and by Gabre-Mariam. You were now halfway up the ladder and it was straight up and down. It was secured at the top with a wire and had a couple of inches' play. It came away from the rock as you climbed – but that was OK because it had dug itself into the soft sandstone and you needed to pull it out from the cliff to get a toe- or hand-hold. You looked along the cliff-face. A couple of ravens hung in the wind. Their wings were flexed against the updraughts, their feathers back-blown. You envied them their wings. You did not want to look up; you did not want to look down. You examined the bloodless white of your fingers as they gripped the ladder. Reaching these places, you thought, these clifftop monasteries, is a rite in itself.

One rung at a time, one at a time . . .

Then the ladder stopped. The summit was still some way up, still out of sight. To one side was the chain. It was three or four arms' lengths away. Even by leaning you could not get close to it. You now had to leave the ladder. The wind was pressing at your ears. You had to traverse the cliff-face and make a grab for the chain. You stepped away from the firm hold of the ladder. You pressed your fingers into cracks in the rock. You reached the chain and gripped it. But then you had to remove your hands, one at a time, because they were so sweaty they were slipping down the links. You leaned back and pulled yourself up the last twenty feet of cliff. And that was the worst part. Because this last section was *overhanging*.

'That chain gives me so much pleasure!'

Abbaminata Gabre-Mariam Gabre-Mikhael was the monastery's abbot and he was waiting at the top. His face wore a look of ageless calm.

'Look at you – sweating so much! When I climb I just put my faith in God.'

We were back on the flat. We followed a path beside a shabby plot of biscuit-coloured stalks. 'That's where we tried to grow barley, but the monkeys ate it all.'

He pointed out the huts of the dozen other monks, the grass shelters of his seminarians, the papyrus-rimmed well. He bent to run his fingers over the back of the monastery cat. And I could think only of the strange sensation of coming on land after being at sea, with your legs weak beneath you and the impression of having landed in an alien element.

On the eastern edge of the cliff, the Abbaminata led us to that mountain's holiest site, the reason for coming here. We scrabbled down a gully and came to a ledge. Far below, the boulder-bed of the river wound between rocky slopes. Beside us was a small hut and in the hut were the remains of the man who in the year 330 first brought the faith to Ethiopia, who became the first bishop of Aksum, Abba Salama himself.

In the Ethiopian *Synaxarium*, each day has its saints. The entry for Hamle 26 (3 August) reads: 'On this day also died

Abba Salama the Revealer of the Light. And he arrived in the country of Ethiopia during the reign of Abreha and Atsbeha and he preached the peace of Christ in all the regions thereof and because of this he was called Father of Peace, Abba Salama. And after he had saluted the men of Ethiopia, he died in peace. Salutation, salutation, I say with joyful voice to Abba Salama!'

Abbaminata Gabre-Mariam looked out into space. 'When Abba Salama arrived here he was already one hundred years old. He had been among the people of Gojjam when God appeared to him and said, You must seek out a place to suffer alone. He chose this place. He lived here another fifty years.'

The abbot himself had been a monk here for only forty years. He wore the butter-yellow robe of a hermit.

'What has kept me here?' He gave a beatific smile. 'It is the chain.'

The chain, he said, was less a chain than a thread between one level of being and the next. By this thread he had been coming and going all these years. He was never afraid.

I asked him if anyone was ever hurt.

'No.' He was toying in the dirt with some barley-stalks. 'Well, last year one man died. But he worked for the electricity company.'

Once a long time ago, a boy fell from the chain. By God's will the boy was caught on a ledge and survived. In time he left the region. Years later a team of builders arrived at the monastery. They said they had been paid to restore the church and to build a rest-house on the cliff for pilgrims. Who paid you? asked the abbot. We don't know! A man in Canada sent the money! All they knew was that when he was a boy the man had lived near here and one day he had fallen on the cliff and been saved.

'That is how he works, that is how Abba Salama works.'

We lingered up there. I was reluctant to leave – or reluctant to deal again with the chain. It was late afternoon when we stepped out onto the overhang and began the descent. Below the cliff we took a steep path down into the gorge below. High above, Abbaminata Gabre-Mariam stood on the ledge and watched us go. The wind was inflating his yellow robe, and as dusk flattened the shadows he appeared to be hovering against the cliff like some brimstone angel.

That evening our small party became separated. We had sent Gabre-Mariam and Solomon on ahead with the donkeys. They had to take a slower route, a donkey-friendly track down the cliffs. We came later, taking the steeper way. We had arranged to meet at the bend in the river visible from above.

But the rule applies in the fastness of Ethiopia as it docs everywhere else: if meeting arrangements can go wrong, they do. Because we had lingered at the monastery, when we reached the spot they were not there. The light was failing. Were they also late, or had they gone on ahead?

'There are wild animals.' Hiluf was nervous. 'The monk said there's a leopard here. I think they would want to get the donkeys out before dark.'

So we set off down the gorge. It became darker. The slopes above us closed in. Sometimes we were on the bank among squat spreading salix. At other times the cliffs narrowed and we followed the dry river itself through pebble-fields, squeezing around house-sized boulders. There was no sign of habitation. We searched the sandy places for signs of donkey tracks. There were none. We walked for an hour, two hours. Our pace quickened to a half-run. Then the cliffs opened out and the star-thick sky dropped to the horizon. We stopped and caught our breath.

In the darkness was a distant dot of firelight. We stumbled across rocky ground to get there. They turned us away. Others did the same. In the end we found a family in a stone hut. We had no food, no coats and no bedding. All night we shivered on a calf-skin.

We rose early. We called in at several homesteads but no one had seen Gabre-Mariam and Solomon and the donkeys. We reached a small dam and waded its irrigation channels. Then, high up on a rock, was a figure waving. It was Gabre-Mariam.

It had taken them four hours to climb down. Several times they had had to unload the donkeys and pass down the loads.

'We were worried,' I said.

'We were behind you! We thought you ... something had happened. Oh-oh!' Gabre-Mariam took my hand and gripped it and a great tide of relief flooded between us.

'Thanks be to Abba Salama!'

The sun was just rising behind him.

The Ethiopian Book of the Dead

The Virgin Mary, according to Ethiopian tradition, was once taken on a tour of hell by Her Son. She was shown a great abyss, and if a soul fell down that abyss for fifty thousand cubits it would still not reach the bottom. And she saw a mighty man being stoned with red-hot stones and beaten with rods of lightning and another whose tongue the angels were slicing out with a red-hot razor and also they were slicing off his nose. And the Virgin Mary pleaded with Her Son to redeem the souls both of these men and all men and He was unable to refuse Her because it was She who had borne Him. He wrapped around Her seven pavilions of fire and joined Her inside and in the fire too was the Lord God Himself and they were all invisible even to the angels. Then Christ took a pen of gold and wrote for His mother His own secret names, his *asmat*, in which reside his power.

When a Christian dies in Ethiopia these *asmat* are written on a strip of linen between three and six inches wide. The cloth is cut exactly to the height of the deceased. It is wrapped around the body and the *asmat* ensure its safe passage through the many gates of the underworld, across the terrible river of fire to heaven.

The names appear in the Ge'ez text the *Lefafa Tsedek*, or Bandlet of Righteousness. In the British Library there is a copy of the *Lefafa Tsedek*. Raise its bareboard cover and on the first folio you will see an annotation attributed to the missionary and Ethiopic scholar Dr Isenburg. It was he who donated this Ge'ez manuscript, and it is clear that the *asmat* exerted their power over him too: 'One of the most striking pieces of abyssinian absurdity & superstition. The names of Christ real and invented, some of them shocking (eg Satanael etc) used as a spell against unclean spirits, against all evil, & death.' (Over the years his ink has faded to a watery sepia, while the older reednib script of the *asmat* remains pure black.)

The magical tradition of *asmat* explains much more about Ethiopian faith than many would care to admit. Secret names allow mortals to perform godly feats, and avoid devilish scheming. *Asmat* enabled Moses to part the Red Sea, and David to defeat Goliath. They suggest a belief system in which God and man are engaged in a kind of game. Man spends his life trying to dodge the work of demons, and in death the fires of hell. Acquiring *asmat* is one way to ensure this. God in turn tries to maintain His omnipotence by preventing man from acquiring the names. But he is vulnerable in certain areas – by taking mortal form in Jesus, for instance, He lays himself open to mortal weakness and filial obligation. (In Ancient Egypt the story of Ra and Isis is an exact parallel. Isis has Ra bitten by a certain scorpion, and in exchange for healing him Ra in his death agony reveals to her his secret name.)

Christian Ethiopians still wear amulets containing neatly-folded squares of parchment written with *asmat*. Many daily prayers revolve around the invocation of secret names. If you ask a highlander how many children he has, he will be vague as to the number, and if he does have to count them he will not tempt the demons by mentioning them by name. He will point at the heads of each of his children and say: 'One rat . . . two rats . . . three rats . . .'

16

For a whole day we headed north-east across the plain. A scattering of acacias rose from the dusty soil. They each grew to the same invisible ceiling, then spread out flat.

The plain on the right was bordered by a dark line of hills. Twenty miles ahead they broke into a natural architecture of sheared-off spires, splintered buttresses, colonnades and chimneys. That was Gheralta. No other part of Tigray is quite so pitted with rock-hewn churches and cells, all that remain of countless thousands of ascetic lives and mountain-minded loons.

We spotted rivers ahead, folds of land running back to their own gaps in the cliffs. When we reached the rivers they were dry. The sun rose higher. I could feel it pulsing at my back. A shadow slid over the soil and I squinted up to see a vulture gliding to earth on beam-still wings. It landed and hobbled across the ground towards a meeting of other vultures, all picking over the carcass of a camel.

A woman was sitting in the shade. She had a baby swaddled

in her lap, and hurried over with it. 'One *birr* – just one *birr*! Look!' She unwrapped the baby and I handed her the money. It was a large *bokra* lemon.

We entered an area of rounded hills. The land became a biscuity pale brown – pale brown terraces holding back pale brown plots. The brown was so pale in places that it was almost white. The thorn trees were burnt black and their branches were bare. Everywhere the shadows were retreating: the dead silence of noon crept over the land.

Gabre-Mariam and Solomon were fasting. Hiluf and I sat under a thorn tree to let them catch up. We could see them dragging their legs through the dust. The laden donkeys swayed like ships beside them. Then Gabre-Mariam raised his stick high above his head, leapt to one side and hammered at the ground. When he held up the stick again, the squiggle of a snake hung from it.

'*Farenj – farenj*!'

In a small settlement a man came running towards me, waving his arms. 'We tried to tell them. We said you cannot cross the river – after two hours they came back – they had bicycles – big motor-bicycles. I am so sorry!'

We reached the river. The waterless bed was littered with *keremt*-driven rocks. I was feeling light-headed from the heat. I pictured the poor Poles trying to wrestle their bikes across. They had wanted very much to reach the churches of Gheralta. The road had been a road during the Italian times. It was planned to be a road again but for now it was a mule track. The only other route was hundreds of miles round.

We ate the *bokra* lemon in the shade of an acacia; it was more pith than flesh. I wandered off and lay under another tree to read. I picked up a clod of ploughed soil and it crumbled to a fine dust. Was that *tsigi* or *aymi* or was it *raba*?

On a hillock some way off, a shepherd boy was leaning
against a tree, playing a *washint*. Its flutey notes rose and fell
with a sound like the wind. The terraces below him chopped
a harsh symmetry from the land. During the war with the
Derg, this had been *hana merit*, 'free land'. The government
never controlled it.

All around the horizon were mountains – a fish-grey ruff
of rocky undulations. Gheralta was close now. Its vellum
cliffs were an endless spectacle, projecting a different face with
every mile we made towards them. The clouds above them
had thickened.

I was woken by a sudden breeze. Gabre-Mariam and Solomon had now eaten. I could hear them talking with Hiluf in
throaty Tigrinya.

We walked another two hours, following the foot of the
Gheralta cliffs. A dry wind came dashing down from the
heights. It made a mask of the sweat on my face and dried

my lips. Then it started to rain. Soon we were running, heading for a few huts on a small rise. It was raining hard when we unloaded the donkeys and ducked through the doorway of a single-roomed dwelling.

Negisti was rattling a pan of coffee beans over the heat of a brazier. She was sitting on a stool. She glanced at us as we stumbled in – then resumed her rattling. The brazier was made from an old tin of cooking oil donated by the WFP. Four children sat on a clay ledge. A baby was a low mound on Negisti's back.

The rain continued. We drank coffee. As it grew dark Negisti stood to light the lamps. We drank more coffee.

The room contained her entire life – a bottle of shampoo on a shelf, a few clothes, schoolbooks, a bed each side of a crooked column of goba wood. On the wall was taped a government poster, divided into two sections: one was a cartoon picture of a line of sturdy-looking maize, the other a smiling family with two sturdy-looking children. The slogan beneath read: *Family planning and straight planting gives strong results!*

Negisti had no land. Her husband was in prison – 'He burnt something in his work.' She supported herself and her five children by serving coffee and *tella* to passers-by. The beauty of her face was somehow frozen, but when she smiled, it revealed a sudden undefeated joy.

Once, when Negisti was young, a man came to her village. He had a soft voice and spoke like a priest. He told them all that they were ruled by bad people. They'd always been ruled by bad people. What the bad people most wanted in this world was for everyone else to stay poor. The old rulers were bad people and had been driven out, but the Derg who replaced them were also bad. The most important thing to understand, he said, was this: *the bad ones can be bad ones because the good ones do not fight.*

Negisti became a fighter. She went west to the rebel stronghold in Sheraro. She began training. She met a man there but they couldn't be together because it was forbidden. Negisti told herself that when they had defeated the enemy, then they would marry. One day the Derg came in planes and bombed the camp. The man was killed. The attack made everyone want to fight even more. But Negisti did not want to fight. She now believed that fighting just made everyone unhappy. She stopped her military training. She helped the movement with food distribution but when the famine came she fled to the Sudan. She met another man and married him. She went to Asmara, divorced, married again and had five children. It was only three months now since her husband had been sent to prison.

We spent the night in a small shed in her yard. I woke to the sounds of the morning cock-crows, goat bleats and donkey brays, the muttering of Solomon at his *tselot zezewota* and the slow rattle of Negisti's coffee pan over the brazier.

The rain had cleared. One or two high clouds were ranging in the western sky. I struck out ahead on a straight, clear path. The path was bordered by aloes. If you looked closely you could see orbs of moisture cradled in their fronds. If you looked closer still, each of the orbs was ringed by drinking ants.

The ridge above performed its tricks. The rock-towers and cliffs rearranged themselves into different shapes with every step. There was a space rocket, there the teeth of some monstrous jaw, there a clutch of minarets. Somewhere amidst them too was the excavated church of Abuna Yemata.

On the path ahead appeared an elderly man with a sack of grain over his shoulder. He had busy bare legs. His deep-set eyes glittered with life.

'Health be on you,' I said.

'Thanks be to God! Health be on you.'

'Thanks be to God. Where is Abuna Yemata?'

He pointed at a line of rock-towers. They ran out from the main plateau like a set of broken organ-pipes.

'You cannot see it – not from here. Follow that path and you will reach the base.'

'Is there a pump near?'

'No. In Megab.'

'Megab?'

'An hour that way. But that pump's broken.'

'Oh.'

'You'll find a river just here.'

'With water?'

'No.'

We stood a moment longer. He inspected each of my features and clothes – but asked nothing.

'Beneath the church is the spring of Abuna Yemata.'

'With water?'

'Have you ever known the spring of Abuna Yemata to run dry?'

I watched him go, his legs making quick work through the sand.

At the spring, a trickle of silvery water oozed from the rock. I knelt and drank straight from it and let the water spill down my chest.

When the others arrived, we settled down to wait for the priest.

*

They were holy wanderers, men who would rather perish in the desolate places than compromise their faith. They scorned the worldly formulation of Chalcedon, skipped ahead of those who would persuade them of its truth with spear and knout. Their wandering took them from Syria to Egypt, to Arabia Felix and finally to the distant uplands of Ethiopia. There they became known as the Sadqan, the Nine Saints.

Over a century had passed since Abba Salama brought Christianity to Ethiopia in 330. It had had its converts in the Aksumite court and on the caravan routes. But beyond that, the land was still a place of sky-gods and sacred groves, *zars* and *budas*, demons and night-hags.

The Nine Saints each chose a mountaintop in the Tigrayan highlands. Abuna Aragawi hauled himself up the cliffs of Debra Damo on the serpent's tail. Of the others, it was Abuna Yemata who pushed furthest to the south. He crossed the Wari river and came to the rocky wilderness of Gheralta, to the assembly of pinnacles above us.

And that's really about it. That is almost the sum total of knowledge about Ethiopian Christianity in its first thousand years.

The priest of Abuna Yemata arrived from his fields. He had an under-chin beard and an Old Testament face. In silence we followed him up to the foot of the cliff and began to climb. We reached the top of a stump of rock. We took off our shoes and stepped out onto a narrow ledge. Tigray rolled out at our feet like a map.

208

At the far end of the ledge was the church. Abba Alem took the key from around his neck and unlocked the olive-wood door. Daylight flooded the scooped-out interior. Its walls and ceilings were covered in paintings. Nowhere else in Ethiopia had I seen such paintings. Their presence filled that cave of a church with a theatricality that made me smile. Here were prophets and patriarchs in yellow ochre and Venetian red. In the ceiling were a number of shallow domes. In one was painted the Sadqan with Ottoman-scale turbans. Looking up

at it gave me the feeling that the dome was a well, open to the sky, and the saints had gathered round the edge of the well to peer down into the church.

Abuna Yemata himself was not included in the ring. He was on a horse on the north wall, and the horse wore a cowrie-shell bridle and a cheeky devil-may-care expression: *Look at me*, it was saying, *I am bearing him – I am bearing Abuna Yemata!*

We sat on the floor. Barley stalks were scattered on the bare rock. The doorway framed an improbable arch of space, distant cliffs and the great plain beyond. Abba Alem sat with his legs up and his forearms on his knees.

I asked him how Abuna Yemata came to choose this particular place for his church.

Abba Alem nodded. He began to speak and spoke without pause until his story was told. His voice took on a liturgical detachment. Fifteen hundred years of oral use had reduced the story to an inventory of received Ethiopian ideas.

Here then is the fear of strangers and the licence to slaughter them; here is the gradual triumph of the Christian saint over the pagan sorcerers (using a fair bit of sorcery himself); here too is shape-shifting and resurrection, the terror of snakes and wild animals and the protective power of the Word. The glorious outcome is not the provision of pastoral care but the harsh and exclusive example of monastic life. The strangeness of the landscape plays it own part – proving that these sculpted mountains are not only a refuge for the faithful, but also a springboard for the imagination.

'Yemata came. He came walking in the night and at dawn he reached the river below the rock. He was thirsty so he touched the rock with his *tau* and the water burst from it and to this day it has never ceased.

'He looked up and climbed the rock. At that time two

devils lived in the area and they went to the village below and said: Look, there is a stranger up there and you do not know his country. What will you do? Eight people came to the rock. They tried to throw Yemata down the cliff. But Yemata had a very small prayer book and because of it they couldn't harm him. Then 150 people came with wooden clubs and rope. As they approached Abuna Yemata, he saw them and turned their clubs into leopards and lions and tigers, and their ropes into snakes. The 150 were all killed by those beasts and Abuna Yemata saw them and they were lying on the ground like dead flies.

'The people then became afraid of Abuna Yemata. They came to him and said: What can we do for you? He told them: Bring me the bones of four dead people. So they went away and came back with the bones and Abuna Yemata turned them back into living people. He then began to question those people and they told him: We were alive during the time of the kings Abreha and Atseba and we have been suffering in hell ever since.

'After that Abuna Yemata also brought back to life the 150 people. He baptised them with holy water and they kissed Abuna Yemata's foot but he said: You must not kiss my foot but only the foot of God. Ten of the people remained with Abuna Yemata on the rock and then six left and only four remained. Yemata told them they must cut their fingernails and shave their hair and they could never go back to their villages and they must never see the face of women nor hear their voices. They must grow cabbages. Suddenly the soil became soft and the leaves of all the trees were sweet like honey.

'But still they had no church to worship in. So Jesus Christ appeared. He announced that at that moment four great rocks were having a battle in the north. They were fighting to see which one would house the church for Abuna Yemata. The rocks were from Wujarat, from Hamassien, Tsada Amba and Abergelle. They fought and fought and the hills were filled with the sound of the fighting rocks. The struggle was won by the one from Wujarat and when it came to this place, when it arrived at Guh, the church was already complete inside it.'

For several days we wandered the region of Gheralta. We climbed its bouldery paths, its shadowy gullies. We slid down stone tunnels and clambered up scree-runs. We scuffed slabs of yellow limestone, steps of red sandstone, grey sandstone, pink sandstone, quartz-streaked sandstone, confectionery-striped sandstone, sandstone with a grain like pinewood. In the fierce heat of midday we stepped into hollowed-out churches, abandoned cells, high-sided ambulatories until it became clear that

there was no stone in Gheralta that had not at some stage been chipped at, or had not propped up the head of some star-yearning ascetic.

One evening we were sitting in silence on the edge of an overhanging cliff. 'Forty-five years I have sat in my hut,' said Gabre-Mariam. 'But now – what history! What places we have seen!'

'Tigray has many historical places,' said Hiluf – who, of course, worked for the tourism commission.

Far to the north, across the central plain, was a line of blue-grey mountains. Hiluf pointed out the towns they rose from. 'Adigrat ... Enticcio ... that sharp one there, that is above Adwa.'

'And Aksum?'

'Beyond that last one.'

Aksum! It was in our sights, although we were following a very roundabout route to get there.

Hiluf eased himself to his feet. From the cliff he picked a lozenge of *opuntia* cactus.

'I used to do this when I was a shepherd.' With his boots he scraped off the needles.

With the lightest of flicks he let it go. It spun into the void. It curved and levelled but did not fall. It remained on the horizontal long after it should have dropped. It was suspended, a black disc shrinking against the evening sky. Then, very slowly, it began to tilt. And it was falling – down through the sky, past the far-off mountains, faster across the plain until the land was blurred beyond it and with a scuff of dirt it struck the slope below and burst into shards of broken flesh.

'*Phweeee*!' Gabre-Mariam clapped his hands. 'It flew, it flew, it flew – like a bird!'

Hiluf shrugged. 'It was not a good one. Sometimes we used to do it and it was up so long you thought it would never fall.'

We stayed there for some time, each contemplating the panorama in his own way. Gabre-Mariam sat on his hands, swinging his legs against the rock and taking in every detail below him. 'What places, what places.'

It was dusk when we climbed down the mountain. At the foot of it Solomon was sleeping under an olive tree. We reloaded the donkeys and set off towards Degum and a church dedicated to Kidane Mehret.

The weeks were slipping past. Already it was the middle of Yekatit, the fifth month in the Ethiopian calendar, and the annual festival of Kidane Mehret was approaching.

Of all the tenets of Ethiopian belief, none is valued more highly than Kidane Mehret, the 'covenant of mercy'. With this the Virgin Mary was granted the capacity to spare souls from the torments of hell. No saint has as many holy days as the Virgin; Ethiopia is the 'land of Mary', one of those Christian countries where Mariology counts for as much as if not more than veneration of Christ. But it was not always so. Just as her cult had a sudden twelfth-century flowering in Europe, so in Ethiopia she emerged to sit alongside Her Son only in the middle of the fifteenth century. Her elevation was very largely the work of one man – King Zara Yaqob.

Holy warrior, scourge of Satan, Zara Yaqob united the corrupted elements in his kingdom with the sword of Christ. He re-established the status of the holy city of Aksum, exempting its people from tribute and talking of its most sacred site as 'Our Mother Zion, the cathedral of Aksum'. Such is his stature that it is hard now to imagine the existence of Ethiopia without him.

One afternoon in 1982, Teklu and I had gone to see him.

17

'Is it man?' The monk thrust a flickering taper in my face. 'Or woman?'

Teklu and I were in a dank shed at Lake Tana's monastery of Daga Istifanos. A couple of wedding-cake crowns were just visible in the half-darkness, sitting on slatted shelves. Various leatherbound manuscripts were stacked with them. The island was accessible neither to women nor hens nor nanny goats.

Teklu smirked. 'Man.'

The monk remained doubtful. But he led us into a window-less back room. He bent to hold the taper to an open-sided coffin. 'King Zara Yaqob,' he announced grandly.

Tallow dripped down the taper and onto the bare-earth floor. Inside the coffin was Ethiopia's greatest medieval ruler. The skull was detached from the spine; leathery scraps of skin still hung on the bone. It could have been anyone.

'Look, the foot.' The monk moved the light down over the legs. I could see the shin bone partly sheathed in dried skin. The phalanges of the right foot were clearly arched and twisted.

'Always on one leg, always praying. Like Tekla Haymanot. King Zara Yaqob was a very holy man.'

Indeed he was. He wrote a great number of tender and affecting prayers. He wrote homilies and hagiographies which are still in use. He commissioned many more, and the largest part of these were dedicated to the Virgin Mary. They leave little doubt about what he felt for her: 'Our Lady Mary is purer than the angels. Our Lady Mary is the mind of God. Every form in our Lady Mary is the form of God ...' He ordered a copy of the Book of Nativity to be sent to all churches so that his people could stop worshipping devils and trees and donkey-idols and dedicate themselves to earning the eternal compassion of the Virgin.

Zara Yaqob towers above Ethiopia's medieval centuries. He transformed both state and Church. It was his brand of myth-driven zeal that has enabled the nation to survive. He was also a vicious and paranoid tyrant. He viewed the world as fatally weakened by the malignant influence of fallen angels; he believed his own realm was besieged by their Muslim and heathen agents. His horror of magic and sorcery stemmed from the conviction that he himself was living under an insidious hex. All around him he saw the work of devils – turning good women into prostitutes, corrupting monks, stealing the lives of babies and cattle, constantly trying to infiltrate his court. Twenty-four hours a day a rota of clerics patrolled the palace, spreading holy water and reciting psalms and prayers.

He decreed that the entire Bible – New and Old Testaments – should be read during church services. In his campaign to purify the land he encouraged denunciations. Anyone accused, rightly or wrongly, of worshipping the devil was at once stoned to death. All Christians, he ordered, were to fix a cross to each of their possessions and to have branded on their foreheads the names of the Trinity. On their right arm they should write: 'I deny the devil!' and on the left 'I renounce the accursed Dask, I am the slave of Mary, mother of the Creator of the universe!' (Many Ethiopian Christians still tattoo their foreheads and wrists with crosses.)

He was mercurial, like all true despots. He ordered his own wife to be flogged. When she died as a result he had his son Ba'eda Maryam tortured and imprisoned for lighting a candle in her memory. Several great monks came to petition him. They told him that Ba'eda Maryam was protected by Tekla Haymanot, and Zara Yaqob immediately released him, showered him with favours and made him his heir.

Zara Yaqob's elevation of the cult of the Virgin Mary helps to give Ethiopian worship its peculiar flavour, by providing an object for the very deepest devotion. Stories from the Gospels or the Old Testament are part of the canon; they are text, immutable. But those of the saints contain the playful traits of oral tradition. In the case of Mary, the stories are further animated by a mutual and limitless love.

The *Ta'ammere Maryam* – 'Miracles of Mary', gathered together by Zara Yaqob himself, are better known than most Biblical stories. A story about Ras Makonnen, the conquering father of Emperor Haile Selassie, shows King Zara Yaqob's enduring legacy. Visiting Britain in 1905, the *ras* was presented with a copy of the Ethiopic *Miracles of Mary* by the collector Lady Meux. Ras Makonnen at once dropped to his knees to give thanks to the Virgin and placed the sacred volume on his head.

The miracles number in their hundreds. Some of them are duplicates, many have loose equivalents from medieval Europe. A glance at them gives an idea of how Mary's powers are seen, and the particular way she dispenses them:

How a bishop cut off his hand which had been kissed by a woman during Mass, and how the Virgin Mary re-attached it to his arm . . .

How, while the monks slept inside, the Virgin Mary removed a monastery from the desert to a place beside a running stream . . .

How the Virgin Mary saved a drunken monk from a lion and a savage dog . . .

How the Virgin Mary enabled a man to slay a hundred-foot snake and how the man took from the serpent's brain a pearl which he placed in a martyrium of Mary . . .

How the Virgin Mary saved a beautiful lady from committing adultery by causing her to read the Prayers of the Dead by moonlight in the garden where she was to meet her lover . . .

How the Virgin Mary forgave and protected a noble woman who committed incest with her son and conceived a child . . .

But favourite among Ethiopians is the story of Beilya Sub. A rich man and a Christian, Beilya Sub was also a cannibal. He ate his friends. He ate his neighbours and his servants; the rest of them ran away, leaving only his wife and two children. He ate them too. He was forced to go out to hunt for food, and while travelling came across a beggar. The beggar's leprous body was covered in sores and scabs and smelled so bad that Beilya Sub didn't eat him. The beggar pressed him for water but he refused. Then the beggar invoked the name of the Virgin Mary and Beilya Sub recalled her merciful ways and gave him a couple of drops. In time, Beilya Sub died and was taken to the depths of Sheol. There the Virgin saw him and called on Her Son to redeem him. The Lord sent for scales. In one side the angels placed the seventy-eight men Beilya Sub had eaten, and in the other the drops of water he gave the beggar. The scales tipped in the cannibal's favour.

In the early Christian centuries, the cult of the Virgin Mary slipped behind other cults because she left behind no body parts to worship. But in later years their absence helped establish her pre-eminence. Like Enoch and Elijah and Moses (according to the apocryphal *Ascension of Moses*), the Virgin was believed to have been taken straight to heaven. It was there, according to Ethiopian tradition, that she received her Kidane Mehret, the 'covenant of mercy', the divine promise which allows her to intercede on behalf not only of the afflicted and the damned, but all mortals.

In the *Miracles of Mary*, Zara Yaqob gives a colourful version of how she attained the Kidane Mehret. It involves a glimpse of the next world, owing a little to that first mythical journey, that of Enoch.

On the sixteenth day of Yekatit [23 February] the angels raised the Virgin Mary to the heavens. First they showed Her the good places. She saw the souls of the patriarchs and the prophets, of Abraham and Isaac and Jacob and they all bowed down before Her. She was then taken to a curtain of fire. As it was drawn so She saw, standing behind it, Her Son. He kissed Her on the mouth and said: 'Did you come, my bearer?' He seated Her on His right hand and revealed to Her the divine joy that transcends the senses and even the imagination. Then the angels showed Her the place of sinners, the region of outer darkness. There She witnessed the eternal torment of souls who had followed Satan: 'Woe to them and alas to them!'

The Virgin began to plead with Her Son for their redemption. 'He who builds a church in my name, clothes the naked in my name, visits the sick, feeds the hungry, gives water to the thirsty . . . reward him, O Lord with divine joy that transcends the senses and even the imagination. I petition you, O Lord, and supplicate to you for every one that believes in me: Make him free from hell.' The Lord Jesus Christ said: 'Let it be as you said. I shall fulfil all your wishes. Was I not incarnated for this?'

All three of the great monotheistic religions have in their store-houses of myths a similar story. The godhead takes a chosen mortal towards His realm and offers a covenant. In exchange for alms or righteousness or the promise not to 'go a-whoring' after false gods, the deity agrees to dispense His divine services.

Thus Moses disappeared up Mount Sinai to intercede for the Jews; Muhammad went on a dream tour of heaven and later received the word of God. The Christian covenant was reaffirmed in the death and the resurrection of Jesus.

In Ethiopia, where the nature of Christ is still held to be more divine than human, the saints, and Mary in particular, act as His divine agents. Each of the saints makes a pre-death covenant with the Lord and it is this covenant that is invoked in prayer.

Every visitor to Ethiopia learns early on that the Ark of the Covenant is housed in a mysterious and never-entered chapel in Aksum. They learn that at the heart of every Ethiopian church is a representation of the Ark, known as the *tabot*; and on holy days it is this, hidden in gold-threaded silks, which is paraded around outside the church, carried on the head of a priest.

The Ethiopian claim to have the actual Ark is unique. Jewish history loses track of it after the destruction of the First Temple. The question of whether it is actually in Aksum can be left to the myth-seekers, grail-chasers and Indiana Joneses. Much more revealing is to examine what it is *believed* to be.

One of the ideas brought to the fore by Zara Yaqob is that Mary's covenant of mercy, the Kidane Mehret, has precedence over all other covenants: 'The Covenant of Our Lady Mary . . . did not start after the Ascension of Our Lord Jesus Christ but when Adam was expelled from the Garden . . .'

Mary was deemed to have existed at the time the world was made. (*The Ascension of Moses* suggests a similar idea for Moses). So all the saintly covenants in Ethiopia are merely branches of her arch-covenant. Even when Moses descended the slopes of Mount Sinai, he was, in effect, holding a version of the Virgin Mary's covenant, the Kidane Mehret.

222

The association of Mary with the Ark of the Covenant is found on the fringes of other Christian traditions. Luke suggests it in his account of both the Annunciation and the Visitation. It is picked up in the apochryphal *Book of James*, a version of which survives in Ge'ez. But nowhere else do the two come together physically as they do at the very heart of Ethiopia, in Aksum. The compound of the Cathedral of St Mary of Zion contains the Chapel of the Tablets of Moses, the country's most sacred place.

No one knows what is actually in the Ark – tablets of stone, the letters of divine law, a mound of dust or some mysterious ether, or nothing at all. But in the early seventeenth century, a Portuguese Jesuit asked Emperor Susenyos what was inside. His enigmatic answer confirms perhaps how embedded the cult of the Virgin Mother had become: 'The figure of a woman with very large breasts.'

It was the eve of the festival of Kidane Mehret. We were walking beneath the Gheralta scarp. Streaks of late sun dropped behind a bank of cloud and against them rose the rocky façade of Debra Seyon, the 'mountain of Zion'. At the foot of the mountain was a low stone farmstead. A man was following his cattle in for the night. He glanced at us, threw one end of a *gabbi* over his shoulder and without a word led us into his yard.

The years had not been kind to Hailu Makonnen. He had lost two children in the great famine and another one just ten months earlier. In the corner of his yard lay a dying calf. His surviving five-year-old son was trying to interest the calf in a bowl of milk. Its flank heaved with the effort of breathing;

it did not even have the energy to drink. When we started to put up the tent, the boy abandoned the calf to watch.

'Look!' He ran around the tent as it rose. 'Look – it is coming out! Father, look – it is growing!'

Suddenly the tent took shape. The boy stood still. 'Father, father – loo-ook! What they've made! It's a car, Father!'

Hailu was not listening. His face was half-hidden by the hood of his *gabbi*. He was leaning against the wall of his house. He was looking out over the backs of his stock, over the top of the wattle tree, to the cliffs of the Mountain of Zion.

Dawn was cold. Hailu heaved a stuffed goatskin on to his shoulder and we crossed the valley. Around the base of the mountain ran a necklace of white-shawled worshippers.

The church of Kidane Mehret itself was tucked in under the cliffs. We eased our way through the crowds. They looked submissive and expectant. Along one side was a line of supplicants. A man was sitting on a cloth; where his right leg should have been, the cloth was scattered with coins. Next to him was a woman rocking back and forth. Beside her was a man with no face – nostrils flush with his cheeks, upper lip ripped away to leave a row of peg-teeth. A blind woman beside him fumbled each offering as she heard it fall, burying it deep inside a leather pouch. 'In the name of Mary . . .'

Near the door a priest was guarding the church's pool of Kidane Mehret gifts – cloth-wraps of bread, curled-up bank-notes, fingerbone tapers. Hailu untied his goatskin and a stream of precious white wheat gushed onto a grain-mound already two feet high. I watched him closely as he did so. His face gave nothing away. It was as if he was paying some long-agreed tithe.

I squatted against the limewash wall and let the trance-like mood of the service flood over me. Incense and the drone of Ge'ez began to stretch out the minutes. In the half-darkness I could see the bowed, turbaned heads of priests and *debtaras*, the mounds of squatting women, the dozing drummers.

An elderly priest was leaning into a prayer book while a boy held a taper over it. 'May he build the threshing floor of your harvest with blessing, amen let it be.' The murmuring chant was hypnotic. 'May he remove from your cities the invasion of arrows and spears amen and amen let it be –'

Just beside me was a man in a lemon-yellow towelling hat. He had bare legs and a staff-cross against his shoulder. A smoky hermit smell came from him. His face was pressed down hard on a shelf, and his cheeks had rucked up in creases against the rock.

'– by the mouth of Our Lady Mary, the throne of fire, forever and ever, amen and amen upon me and upon you, let it be, let it be –'

Above our heads a flycatcher flew back and forth. No one paid it any notice. Between two standing figures, I spotted the raised head of a woman. Her cheeks ran with tears.

'– for the sake of Mary, Mother of Light, amen and amen let it be, let it be; for the sake of His body and blood, the sacrifice of the faithful, amen and amen upon me and upon you let it be let it be let it be.'

An hour or more passed. Readings began, overlapped, rose and fell or faded to a mumble. Dawn spread the top of the doorway with its buttery light. The man beside me did not move an inch; I wondered if he was even breathing.

Then a long, low note filled the church. It was like the voice of the earth itself. It came from one of the *debtara*. All other noises ceased. One by one the other *debtara* added their voices. They shuffled into line. The note dropped. Soon there were a dozen singing. They roamed the scales; they were tentative and distant, as if looking for something. The metallic tinkle of their sistra trotted behind them.

Then – *Bom*!

With the drum, everything changed. Not at once, but imperceptibly, irreversibly. The worshippers' trance was lifted: each beat sealed the covenant. The promise of compassion and redemption spread throughout that dawn crowd. The *debtara* raised their tempo. They coalesced around the drummers. An excitement seeped into the church. Handclapping rose from the perimeter. The women began to ululate. The *debtara* raised their prayer sticks. They rocked back on their feet. The drummers stood. Their double-beat drove the *debtara*. One line advanced. The other retreated. Their bare feet slid back over the rugs. Day was now streaming through the open door.

The *bahtawi* beside me raised his head. His face had a far-off expression. Then he took his staff and disappeared into the crowd; I saw him emerge a few minutes later, above the bobbing heads, leaping up over some lumpy boulders and into a narrow gorge.

Back at his house, Hailu pulled off the hood of his *gabbi* and smiled for the first time. We ate bread and honey. He told us about his father. 'He was born on the mountain – he lived among the rocks. He loved those rocks!'

'My father lived on the mountain of Debra Asa. He died up there.' Gabre-Mariam picked a thread of plastic from a grain sack and begun to stitch one of his shoes. 'My mother died and he went up to the mountain.'

'Perhaps he is still there,' said Hailu.

Gabre-Mariam grinned, without looking up from his stitching.

From the open doorway ran a cat. Behind it came Hailu's son, waving his stick. The cat hopped onto a lying-down ladder, onto the top of the wall and under a lean-to roof; it padded to safety behind the only cow still in the yard, for whom the Kidane Mehret had also done its work. Beneath her, shunting its nose against her teat, was the sick calf.

In the evening we reached the town of Megab. One or two lights glowed in open doorways. The sun had long since set but its light still glowed creamy white on the clouds.

Music was throbbing from a *tella bet*. Several priests were sitting in front of beakers of custard-yellow *tej*, spinning out the last hours of the feast-day. The floor was spread with fresh grass and reeds. On the bar was a tape-recorder playing Eritrean dance music while three boys stood and shuffled their feet in a half-hearted way. A bored-looking girl sat beside the bar.

We put up the tent in the yard. In the morning, the girl was sweeping the grass from the floor, steering her broom around the slumped bodies of the dancers and the priests.

*   *   *

There was one more of Gheralta's monasteries I wanted to see, and it stood on a thousand-foot-high cliff above Megab. I stepped out onto the road and looked up. Dawn had smeared the rock-face in honey-coloured light; the tiny shapes of eagles spun around its heights.

The monastery of Mariam Korkor played a formative part in Ethiopia's greatest religious schism. In the fourteenth century a young monk named Ewostatewos studied here, becoming ever more convinced that the Church was in error, abusing divine law by failing to observe the Saturday Sabbath. As his following increased, so did the persecutions against him. He was forced to flee the country. In Egypt he was appalled to find the Copts committing the same mistake. In the monastery of Scete he was thrown in chains. He fled to Jerusalem. From there he went to Cyprus and Armenia (probably the Cilician kingdom), where he died.

This lonely life and death had a profound effect back in Ethiopia. Ewostatewos came to represent a divide deeper than the Sabbath dispute. It became a fundamental clash – between Old and New Testaments, between Judaic and Christian traditions. And beneath it all was the perennial Ethiopian urge for independence – in this case from the Coptic mother-Church, itself cowed by Mameluke rule. A hundred years later, a majority of Ethiopian monasteries were Ewostathian. It is probable that when Zara Yaqob came to the throne he too was a supporter – but, paradoxically, he was the one who settled the dispute by ruling against the Ewostathians.

We followed a path round beside the cliff and entered a narrow gully. Because of the skew of the rock, the sky was not always overhead. Leg-like roots dangled in the overhang. The gully opened out and Gabre-Mariam bent to kiss the cliff where it had been chiselled into a cell. We carried on up the bare rock.

We heard the chimes first. Alloy pendants hung from the eaves of the Dej-es-Selam, the 'gate of peace', and we entered the monastery. A bowl of open ground led to a space between two high rocks, and the abrupt edge of the cliff.

A family from Addis had just climbed up to the monastery. The women wore delicate gold jewellery and the men white jogging suits. They were teachers and lawyers and had come to visit the grave of their father. He had once owned a large tract of land below Korkor but when the revolution came the land was nationalised. He died soon afterwards and his widow had arranged for him to buried here. She then took her young children to Addis.

This was the first time they had been back. They filled bottles with holy water. They asked a monk to pour it over their heads and the sudden coolness made them laugh. 'No! Wait – do that again . . . hold it!' They took photographs of each other.

On a rock above squatted the abbot, a lone, crag-faced ascetic, his *gabbi* pulled tight around his face. Far below was the town of Megab and the mosaic of ploughed and unploughed plots around it.

I asked him about Ewostatewos and he fingered the curls of his beard. He peered at me as if from a great height. He did not reply.

'Famous monk,' I said. 'Caused a great split in the Church. Ended by Zara Yaqob.'

His fingers dug deeper into his beard. His cloud-high gaze grew cloudier. His reticence grew more reticent.

'Ewostatewos?' I prodded.

229

He withdrew his fingers and folded his palms together. His voice was a melodic purr. 'Ewostatewos and his men crossed the Red Sea to Armenia. They made boats from the skins of cows. His men's faith was weak and their skins sank. But Ewostatewos had a very strong faith and because of that his skin did not sink.'

He turned away. The details of the past were no more relevant to him than the world below.

On the way out of the monastery we passed the family from Addis. Something had gone wrong. They had found the grave, but another body had been placed over that of their father.

'You will remove it,' one of them was ordering the monk.

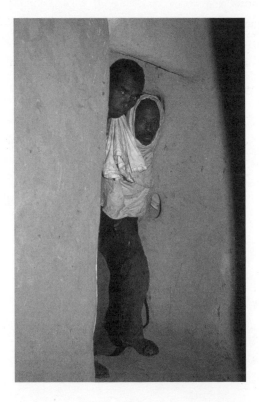

'Look, we do not mind which place you put it in,' said another. 'Just not there. This is the grave of our father. He was a landowner.'

It was almost dark when we reached the town of Hawzien. There we parted from Gabre-Mariam and Solomon.

'Thanks to Abba Yohannis for the hour that we met!' said Gabre-Mariam.

Solomon went from Hiluf to me, to Hiluf again and back to me, shaking our hands. 'We have seen all those places, so many places!'

We walked with them to the edge of the town. We watched them grow smaller in the thickening darkness. Goodbye Gabre-Mariam, goodbye Solomon – favourite of all our mulemen!

Emperor Menelik Learns to Drive

One night in 1843, Hayle Melekot, heir apparent to the kingdom of Shoa, was 'inspired by the Holy Spirit' to sleep with his mother's companion. The boy that was born was named Menelik, like the son of Solomon and Sheba, and it was predicted by the wise men of the court that he would 'restore the glory of the kingdom'.

Menelik did more than that. He became modern Ethiopia's greatest ruler. He saw off the Italians at the battle of Adwa in 1896, united the squabbling fiefdoms around him and then established an empire that pushed the borders of the country far to the south and east. It is those borders that more or less mark out today's Ethiopia.

Menelik had a great love for innovation. On wooded slopes he established his new capital of Addis Ababa, and built his own palace on a commanding hillock. There, with the help of a Swiss engineer, he performed a great miracle. He installed water pumps:

We have seen wonders in Addis Ababa.
Waters worship Emperor Menelik
O, Menelik, what more wisdom will you bring?
You already make water soar into the air.

On the last day of 1907, the first motor car arrived in Addis Ababa. It was an eighteen horsepower, four-cylinder, open-topped Siddeley and it had taken an Englishman named Mr Bentley and Wells, his engineer, five months to reach Addis from the coast. Menelik at once summoned them and their machine to his palace. He examined its instruments, its chrome-rimmed hubcaps. His ministers warned him it would explode if he rode in it – so Menelik ordered them to instead. He had the streets cleared and Wells raced off with them to

the market. Over the coming weeks Menelik spent more and more time in the motor car. He himself learnt to drive and had a couple of chauffeurs trained. He had long conversations with Mr Bentley and Wells about all the latest gadgetry. (They left Ethiopia without the car.) Menelik's wife Empress Taytu was more suspicious of machines and wouldn't go near the car, which Mr Bentley said was a great relief because 'she was so fat'.

18

Hawzien is not a large town, but it has witnessed several significant moments on Ethiopia's troubled passage towards modernity.

Menelik came here in 1890, and like us he was on his way to the sacred city of Aksum. In Aksum he was going to be crowned King of Kings of Ethiopia, heir of Solomon. But when the Tigrayan chiefs heard of his plan, they let it be known that they would kill him if he took another step north. He withdrew.

Six years later, he returned to Hawzien. He was at the head of a very large army. But now there was a common enemy – the Italians had invaded. In Hawzien Menelik remained for several days before the final march to Adwa.

Almost a century later, Hawzien played its part in the Derg's downfall. 22 June 1988 was market day. The alleys and squares were crowded with villagers. Towards midday several aircraft appeared in the cloudless southern sky – four MiG-21s and two attack helicopters. The rebels had pushed forward and, so it was believed, were using Hawzien as a base. But there were no rebels there that day. For six hours the aircraft bombed the town. They launched air-to-air missiles on the market squares. They strafed the fleeing crowds. An estimated eighteen hundred were killed. It was the single worst act of Derg brutality, and did much to swell the numbers of the rebels.

'Bombs fell there – and there ... and in that house many took shelter and they bombed it and in that one too. Here was the donkey market – it was thick with dead donkeys and dead people.'

Tadelle had not been in Hawzien that day; he was with the rebels. As they approached the town that night, they could smell the carnage from far across the plain. They tried to burn the bodies with kerosene. For three weeks the stench grew worse; only when the rains came did the air become clean again.

'Fatima!' Tadelle called into an open doorway. 'Fatima – are you there?'

A young woman came to the door. She was pulling a green chiffon scarf in front of her nose.

'Show him, Fatima.'

Fatima held up her right arm. It was amputated at the elbow.

'You see? She was standing here. A bomb destroyed the rest of the house. Her parents carried her for two days to the clinic.'

He jumped down from the step and we continued down the lane. 'What man will marry a woman with only one arm?'

Tadelle was a deputy in the Ethiopian federal parliament and Hawzien was his constituency. He had a boyish enthusiasm for his civic duties, and one of those duties was public relations

– relaying details of Derg terror, and publishing a magazine which sang of Hawzien's virtues, its impressive agricultural yields, and the perpetual joy of its people. The magazine was called simply *Hawzien*, and Tadelle had Issue no. 1 tucked under his arm.

'Look – I chose this photograph for the cover. You see this girl? She is almost a woman now, but she was born at the very moment the Derg bombing was happening. She is like – like a replacement. Look how strong she is! She carries that heavy water jug.'

Tadelle looked at the picture with pride. 'Yesterday I went to find her. I knew she would be proud to be on the magazine. I said to her, In the photo you are carrying a big water pitcher. Isn't it heavy? Do you know how she answered? She told me: I do not mind as long as we have peace.'

Tadelle recalled his years with the rebels. He chuckled at the memory of what they did to Hourri Asgedum. 'He was an important man in the Derg. He came to Hawzien to deal with the rebels, so we kidnapped his son. No, no – we didn't harm him. We just gave him propaganda. We said the Derg is very bad and so on. When we released him, his mother killed a sheep and gathered all the women. And they were all saying, These rebels are good! Hourri was so angry.'

We had reached the edge of town. Hawzien's rubble walls had thinned to an area of dusty brown wasteland. Lines of farmers were following the road back to the plains. Tadelle was suddenly reflective.

'The movement then – we never thought it would get this far.'

The farmers waved at him. He raised his hand and slowly waved back.

'I have served these people for two terms now.'

'You must be doing a good job,' I said.

'What? Yes, I am,' he was the politician again. 'Last time I got 99 per cent of the vote!'

On our quest for mules we met a man who had also served his people. Kidanu Rada had been the town's governor during the Derg years. He lived in a room that opened straight onto the main street. His doorway framed a constantly shifting cast of market-day stock and people. He was an elderly man, weary with his years, and he wore a white *gabbi* over a dark tailored suit.

Under the Derg, Hawzien was constantly taken and retaken by government and rebel forces.

'It must have been difficult governing,' I said.

'No, why?'

'Didn't the rebels take revenge when they attacked?'

'I supported the rebels. I never liked the Derg.'

'Well, didn't the Derg take revenge?'

He shrugged. 'I had letters from the Derg and letters from the rebels. When the rebels came, I showed the rebels' letters, and when the Derg came, I showed the Derg letters. Wasn't so difficult.'

'How did you get the job?'

'After the revolution we sent seven men to the Derg with letters, and seven men to the rebels with letters.'

'What did the letters say?'

'That they wanted me to be in charge.'

'Why you?'

'Because I was a *kenazmach*.' *Kenazmach* was an imperial title meaning 'leader of the right'. 'Of course, I'm not a real *kenaz-*

mach. The Derg thought I was, but I am not. I won it in a game.'

One evening, in the years of the emperor, he and some others were in a *tella bet*. At the time he was just 'an ordinary police-man'. He was drinking with his chief and a number of men from the administration. Everyone scribbled titles on a bit of paper – thief, traitor, Ras, Abba. The game was mock-serious; what gave it tension was the profound significance attached to names in Ethiopian belief. Thus those who picked 'thief' or 'traitor' suffered a degree of real shame. As a junior officer, Kidanu's relief at picking *kenazmach* was enormous. So much so that after that everyone called him *kenazmach*.

'Many in the current administration still think he is a real *kenazmach*,' said Kidanu's son proudly.

'They can think what they like,' said Kidanu. A tired smile spread across his lips. 'I get my pension.'

Hiluf went off with Kidanu's son to continue the mule-hunt; I walked down to buy supplies in the market.

Onions . . . garlic . . . potatoes – *potatoes!* . . . chillies (chilli a day keeps the parasites at bay) . . .

'*Farenj! Farenj!*' A trail of boys was following me through the rows of women. 'Give me pen!'

Tomatoes . . . no oranges . . . no papaya . . .

'*Farenj!* Money – money!'

Salt . . .

'*Farenj* –'

'HEY!' It was a voice from behind me. '*Hid!* Scram!'

A man was bending to pick up a rock. He made to throw it and the boys scattered.

'Jeez!' He chop-wiped the dust from his palms. 'They're like bladdy mozzies!' Fikre was Tigrayan but he spoke English with an Australian accent. 'Apologies!'

We crossed the square to a two-table café. A girl was sleeping on her hands at the counter and for a couple of hours Fikre and I talked – or rather he talked and I listened. Behind his odyssey crouched the horrors of recent Ethiopian history, but he delivered it like a vaudeville entertainment – one part tragic to two parts comic. He kept reminding me of Teklu. Both had come of age during the revolution; both were Tigrayan – Fikre was visiting his parents in his home town of Hawzien; Teklu had been born near Adwa. Fikre fled Mengistu's Ethiopia by walking to Somalia, Teklu by walking to Kenya. Fikre ended up driving a taxi in Sydney, Teklu running a liquor store in Denver. Fikre had returned with his savings to open a small hotel in Addis, and a few years earlier Teklu had, according to a cousin of his I'd met in Addis, done something similar. But it hadn't worked out. He had returned to Colorado. Fikre's hotel venture was also having problems. Two weeks ago, someone had lobbed a hand grenade into the bar. Ten people ended up in hospital.

'When I left Ethiopia, that sort of violence was only permitted by the government. Now anyone can do it. That's democracy!' Fikre gave a shoulder-shaking giggle. He had the rubbery movements of a born comedian. He did not so much tell his story as act it.

He was born and brought up in the 1960s. At that time Tigray was governed by Ras Mengesha and his court. 'These guys, they were like gods *[Fikre swells his chest]*. They were somewhere up there, in the clouds! And then suddenly *[whispers]*, suddenly we are hearing a song, a song about how these gods suck the blood of the people. We couldn't believe it – a song AGAINST THE GODS!'

One of the Derg's first acts when they came to power in 1974 was the *zemecha*. Fifty thousand students from high school and university were sent out to spread the good news of the revolution and set up peasants' associations. Fikre went to a camp in western Tigray.

'We was just getting used to this Derg when we started hearing about something else. Soon in the countryside every-thing – the wind, the trees, even the dogs – everything was whispering it – the TPLF! Suddenly we all had such a warm feeling for the TPLF, we were such big sympathisers! But secretly all of us were thinking *[drops voice]* – What the hell this new one? What the hell this bladdy *teepee-elef?*'

While Fikre was in the *zemecha* camp, his father died. He was given leave to return to Hawzien for a few days. When he went back to the camp he found it empty. 'Every one of those bladdy students had gone to fight for the rebels!' So he returned home – there he found his mother and all her neigh-bours celebrating.

'I see them all jumping about and singing and I am thinking *[cocks head]*, is father alive again or what? And my mother has an envelope from Addis Ababa! I have a place at bladdy uni! But when I saw the envelope, I cry and cry. They say, Why sad, boy? I tell them, Now who will look after mother? So then they fall quiet and all look at each other and start crying too *[loud wailing]*. All bladdy crying like a loada frightened sheep!'

'Did you go to university?'

'My mother say – Go, Fikre, I look after myself. When you have a top job – top job! *[straightens imaginary tie]* – then you send money to look after yer poor old mum. So I go to Addis, three days on a bus and I walk up and register at the biology faculty. In the faculty toilets, they have graffiti and I look closely at it and suddenly I am feeling at home! It reads: *TPLF are the only Real Marxists!* Didn't know what the hell it meant but I liked the way it sounded. So I found the other Tigrayans and we wrote it in every damn place we could.

'At night the soldiers began to visit the dormitories. They take us Tigrayans, one by one. I am lying in bed *[drops voice]* hearing the soldiers and thinking it is me now. Is it me now, and if it isn't me now will it be me tomorrow? So I enrol at the Pedagogical College in Bahir Dar and escape up there.'

Fikre leaned forward to drink his coffee.

'So what happens in Bahir Dar? *[feigns bewilderment]* What happens? The bladdy terror comes to Bahir Dar, 's all!

'Yes, yes. They used to have this damn thing. *Magalata,* they call it – revolutionary council confession. They call us all together and everyone has to confess and it is a very good thing they say because after confession everyone feels so damn clean and nice. So they point the guns at us and say – What have you done! They go down the line and I know to say nothing but some of the others said, Well, I did see a pamphlet or I did once listen to this man talking ... Those ones were taken ... You know what? One of those guys from Bahir Dar I saw last year. He was on the street in Addis. He was nothing, just a crazy beggar. They beat him so badly he went crazy. Is he alive now or dead, I dunno ...'

Fikre looked away and for the first time I saw a sadness cross his face.

'I graduate from that institute and apply for a job. When I saw the list, I had been sent to Sidamo. Sidamo! Sidamo is no bladdy good! Sidamo is too far from the border. Beside me is a man from Sidamo and the list says he must go to Alemayu College in Harar but of course he would rather be in Sidamo. So, we just swap round! *[crosses hands]* At the college, I am quiet, I am a good student. No one knows I am from Tigray and I am just waiting, waiting for the chance to escape!

'That is all damn fine but who should come to the college? *[throws up hands in despair]* Only a bladdy singing group from Tigray! And of course because I'm Tigrayan I had to put my arms around them and hug them. They were good Tigrayans now and went round all the places singing songs about workers and what-have-you. When they go up on stage they say there are still people around who are afflicted with "narrow thinking". Even in this room there is someone with narrow thinking. Someone here wants to do *magalata* – he wants to confess ... I just kept mum but after that I knew I had to be quick.

'I went to see the right people and those people knew the right people who could help me reach the Somali border. And one Monday I slip from the college and go down to Jijiga – and I wait, and I wait ... and the damn bladdy man doesn't turn up! What can I do? If I return to the college, the cadre will smell me *[sniffs]* – the cadre knows how to sniff well and he knows how escape smells. But I am a stranger in Jijiga and they have their own cadres there spotting strangers. Well I go back to the college and luckily that cadre is away in Addis. Next time I go to Jijiga I make sure it is on the weekend so I can return to college if it doesn't work.

'But there is the man! And he gives me Somali robe and Somali turban and we leave the town. There is a camel behind me and a camel in front and we are walking across the desert, we are walking for days ... walking ... walking *[bobs head in slow, camel-like fashion]*. And I am thinking each step, each damn step is taking me further from bladdy Mengistu!'

I left Hawzien early. Hiluf and the new mule-men would follow. I struck out into open country, watching my pinheaded shadow bob far along the road in front. A couple of hoopoes flew beside me. They flew with single wing-beats and a long dipping flight, like trackside cables seen from a train window. A camel stretched up its long neck to an acacia, closed its mouth over the distichous leaves and – *tu-ug!* The branch flicked back, and the camel's jaws began to grind.

We were heading for the monastery of Debra Damo, oldest of all the country's monasteries. It was two or three days' walk to the north.

I pulled the water-bottle from my bag and raised it to my lips. Along its plastic barrel the sky glowed its deep mountain blue. This was the best moment of the day – not yet too hot, the sweat already dry at the temples. The cool of the water spread down my throat and into my stomach. In a few hours the water in the bottle would be as hot as tea.

All morning the road pushed north and west and north

again. I dropped into tight valleys and flood-torn gullies. I passed road-gangs and farmers walking to market and elderly couples walking to weddings. I fell into step with a nun and her sister; they were travelling to their cousin's funeral. 'He died on Kidane Mehret,' said the nun. They left the road and I could see on a hilltop below a vast gathering of mourners.

Later the others caught up and we all stopped beside a river. Tsegaye was the lead mule-man. He wore a coat with an air-brushed image on the back: a Formula One car caught at speed and beneath it, in forward-leaning letters, the words *Fa-ast Tra-acking!*

'Where did you get it, Tsegaye?'

'In Gondar, when I was in the army.'

He was in his early twenties. A few years earlier he had fought in the pointless and brutal conflict with Eritrea. He had survived the charge across minefields towards the Eritrean guns but now he was angry. 'What did my brothers die for? For nothing.'

We sliced up tomatoes, sprinkled their red flesh with Danakil salt and ate them with the morning's bread. Tsegaye and his younger brother lay with their heads on his folded-up *Fa-ast Tra-acking!* coat.

Upstream, women were washing clothes. The white squares of their *gabbis* were stretched taut over hot boulders.

I stood and stepped out of the shade. A trickle of river was still flowing but it would be several months until the big rains. I peered into a pool. The water was already a cloudy green-brown. Revolving around it were a dozen or more perch. Their silver bellies flashed in the sun, but they were sluggish, and the pool was crowded. On the rock above, the waterline was a rim of brackish white flakes. The level was falling fast.

19

We were spilling out of Nebolet. It was evening. We were six wide and dozens deep on a stony road that pushed east up the hill. The market-day crowds were returning home, their trotting donkeys fat with grain; women carried egg-baskets and honey-gourds and folds of calico import, men were flush with *tella* and the fever of exchange, and Abba Gabre-Selassie ('servant of the Trinity') held a shoulder-borne pole from which wriggled, by its feet, one angry cockerel.

Abba Gabre-Selassie had a broad white-muslin turban and a broad white-tooth smile. He agreed to put us up for the night. 'Just here – I live very close!' He pointed to a hill. It was at least three or four miles away. 'And there – that is your road to Debra Damo!'

We crossed the valley. The crowd came with us. They were all from the same community around the ancient rock-hewn church of Wuqro Maryam.

'Look at the *farenj*!'

'*Wai*, is he soldier or priest?'

'Where is his car?'

It was dusk when we stepped over the threshold into the yard of Abba Gabre-Selassie. His daughters ran out to greet him; his wife stood in the doorway. He swung the pole down from his shoulders and squatted to untie the cockerel's legs.

'*Pii-pii!*' He prodded him with the pole. The bird stood, swayed a little – then toppled.

'Up – get up!'

From the far corner came the mumble of hens, and the cockerel found his feet. He shook his autumn-red plumage and pranced across the yard. Abba Gabre-Selassie stood satisfied, picked up his youngest daughter and headed towards his house.

The next morning was Sunday. We climbed the hill to the church. A sturdy gatehouse stood below the cliff and Tsegaye, with his swagger and his *Fa-ast Tra-acking!* Formula One coat solemnly bent to kiss the wall.

One side of the compound was cliff – rough on the outside and topped by vervet monkeys. Inside the cliff was a miraculous series of chambers, columns and cupolas all chiselled from the rock. They rose high above our heads. Bosses were carved into inkwells and Turks' heads; imitations of Aksumite detail ran as friezes in the coffered ceiling.

'Look, look – and here too!' Abba Gabre-Selassie's eyes flashed in the half-darkness. Not for the first time, I was overcome with awe at the thought of these places and what it took to create them – not so much the labour or the expertise or even the thorny problems of working with reverse space – but the *why*?

Outside the church gates, two hundred men had gathered for their monthly council. They sat in the dust, on bare banks and knuckle-like boulders. They were clustered beneath the cooling foliage of eucalyptus. I stood in the shade with Hiluf and we watched.

One among them rose to his feet.

'I bought fertiliser. The *kebelle* gave me the money and said, You can pay us after harvest. But the size of the harvest was too small. Now they want much more money.'

A *debtara* answered. 'You must be careful to pay back as early as you can. Even if your maize is not growing, the amount to pay still grows.'

Another stood. 'They told us we must dig a hole for a pond. They said they will give us a sheet. Well I have dug my hole and now they say there is no sheet.'

'I have dug a hole too. My cattle fell in and couldn't get out.'

'Put brush around it. At *keremt* God will provide water.'

'Last *keremt* the water did not fill the pond even half – now it is all gone . . .'

For some time the complexities of rural life were aired, a life in which development schemes arrived like the weather,

God-given: sometimes they brought salvation and sometimes they brought disaster.

Several men moved through the seated crowd with copper jugs of *tella*. Others followed with baskets of mud-coloured *injera*.

An old man near me stood and adjusted his broken glasses. His voice was faint. 'Bless those who brought this food. May the coming months be full of light for you. May God give you long life, may the blessings of Mary always be with you, may God –'

'Stop these blessings!' called a younger man. 'Blessings do not help the hungry. In a month's time, we will come here and bless you all with food and *tella*. Who can tell but in the meantime, if God and St Mikhael bring us EVERYTHING, then we will bring everything with us!'

Back at Abba Gabre-Selassie's house, we sat beneath the lean-to. Stripes of noonday sun sliced through the thatch and patterned our shoulders. One of his daughters was in the soapberry tree tearing off branches of fruit. 'Quick, quick! Pick it up!' The others had to rush to collect the fruit before the calf got it.

Abba Gabre-Selassie was not watching them. He was in a post-liturgical torpor. He looked at the ground and mumbled. Then from behind the wall appeared his new cockerel. In a blur of feathers the bird leapt down, clamped the neck of a hen with his beak and pinned her to the dust. He sat astride her – wings flapping, coxcomb wobbling – and Abba Gabre-Selassie's face filled with glee.

We packed the mules. Above Amba Seneiti was a muddy ceiling of cloud, and we carried on towards Debra Damo.

* * *

Late the following afternoon we arrived at the foot of a sheer cliff. The head of a monk appeared high above. A rope hung for a moment against the sky, then uncoiled and slapped down against the rockface. It was made from plaited oxhides. It was the only way up.

After Abba Salama, such an ascent presented few difficulties. We scrambled up the worn footholds and hauled ourselves over the lip of a ledge. There was the yellow-robed figure of a young monk. An elderly monk lay on the ground beside him, inspecting a tiny hole in the rock with his fly-whisk.

Debra Damo can, with its direct Pachomian lineage, claim a place at the top table of Christian monasteries. It is the most monkish of locations, the most monkish of approaches; and in a land of strange places it ranks among the strangest. The first thousand years of its history are unrecorded. So it will never be known why, for instance, there should have been found here a hoard of early Umayyad and Abbasid coins, or Kushan coins from even earlier and even further afield – yet only a single coin from nearby Aksum.

The flat summit of Debra Damo turned out to be a small town – refectories, churches, grazing cattle, rock-cut cisterns, dry-stone lodgings. Eucalyptus spread its shadows over *hidmos* in which monks cooked and read and sat, mainly sat. But walk a few hundred yards in any direction and your toes push out over thousands of feet of space.

For weeks now, the clergy of Gheralta and elsewhere had been deflecting my questions. 'Ask at Debra Damo . . . at Debra Damo they know all things . . . *wheeee* – such learning!'

So I had simply deferred the hope of this – of sitting in the dust while a wise and ancient anchorite explained the Ge'ez version of the Apocalypse of Baruch, or ranked the dictates of the Didascalia, or countered with devotional logic the rationalist philosophies of Zara Yaqob. Already we had asked several monks here, and all fingers pointed to the head of the monastery, to Memhir Wolde-Igziyabher.

He lived in a two-storey building. Prayer rooms and living quarters were above; below was a large high-ceilinged hall. Everything was old and dark and still. An empty iron-frame bed stood against one wall. We sat near the open door and dust motes drifted between us; a blade of late sun cut across the floor and buckled over the *memhir*'s feet.

'Does the monastery have land?' I asked.

'The Derg took our land.'

'How many monks are here?'

'Once we had six thousand monks. Now we are not even three hundred.'

I asked him about those early fathers of Ethiopian Christianity, the Nine Saints.

The *memhir* leaned his head back. His speech was slow and reluctant. 'They were in Aksum. They had been there twelve years when their leader Abuna Aragawi said – Look, we are living in the secular world. We must go to the mountains. We must go there and teach. So each of them found a mountain. Aragawi found this one. He climbed here on the tail of a snake.'

A cat, soft-pawed and high-tailed, padded out of the darkness and leapt noiselessly onto the *memhir*'s lap.

I asked: 'Do you use Pachomius's teachings – the *metshafa menaqosat*?'

'I know that book . . .' He was watching his hand run along the cat's back.

'But is it used still?'

'It says a monk must weaken his body with hard praying. He must prostrate himself five hundred times each day . . . except on holy days.'

Behind him, the empty bed creaked. There was a body in it, and it was slowly turning over.

I quizzed the *memhir* about various texts – the *Book of Enoch* and *Jubilees*, the accounts of Kidane Mehret. But he just shrugged. These things could not be discussed literally, not with the laity and certainly not with a foreigner. To do so is to dissolve the mystery in which reside the eternal secrets of this world and the next. Either that, or he just didn't know.

This was the head of Ethiopia's greatest monastery. Abuna Aragawi had told his fellow monks: Go forth and teach! But the *memhir* was of the obscurantist school, the one that put about the story of the Ethiopian peasant who burst into flames when he tried to fathom the Trinity.

He continued stroking the cat. Behind him in the half-darkness the figure of an elderly monk sat up on the bed.

'If you stay here a week,' said the *memhir*, 'I could talk to you. If you stayed a month I could begin to teach.'

My frustration dissolved into shame.

He looked up at me. It was neither a friendly nor an unfriendly look. Shoving the cat from his lap, he rose. The interview was over.

'One more thing,' I asked. 'Do you know the *Hatatas* of Zara Yaqob – the philosopher?'

He thought for a moment. 'I had that book once. I don't know where it is now.'

Behind him – *pitter . . . pit . . . pitter . . . pit . . . pit . . .* The elderly monk was sitting on the bed, trying to piss into a bucket.

The *Hatatas* or 'treatises' of Zara Yaqob are a wonderful piece of meditative literature and occupy an unusual place in

Ethiopian letters. They were composed in Ge'ez for a start, rather than translated, and they are infused with a very un-Ethiopian passion for plain truth.

This Zara Yaqob was poles apart from his namesake, zealous King Zara Yaqob. He was born 130 years after the king's death, in 1599, in Aksum. He was rational, open-minded and undogmatic. He trained in Church schools. He grew close to the court but became more and more disillusioned by the religious divisions of the time.

The country was in chaos. Emperor Susenyos's conversion to Catholicism had condemned it to a frenzy of suspicion and fratricide. Zara Yaqob found himself persecuted by both sides. He fled Aksum to a cave in the Takazze gorge and for two years lived a life of glorious simplicity.

'Alone in my cave, I felt I was living in heaven ... I built a fence of stone and thorny bush so that wild animals would not endanger my life ...'

When Susenyos died he left his cave, worked as a scribe for a wealthy man, married and late in his life wrote the *Hatatas*.

His two years of isolation afforded him a clarity which shines down through the centuries. The *Hatatas* are a series of sharply reasoned discussions. How could God create such divisions in those who follow him? (Because of the flawed interpretations of man.) Why are such things perpetuated? (Because the seeking of wisdom is a weary task; most shy away from examination and accept what they have heard from their fathers.)

All three faiths of the Book come in for criticism. Why was Moses given God's truth to teach only to one people? Why was slavery part of Muhammad's teaching when all men were created equal? Christian monasticism was wrong because it went against the demographic logic of creation. As for fasting, each of them was at fault. 'God does not order absurdities, nor does he say: "Eat this, do not eat; today eat, tomorrow do not eat."' Desires are God-given and to deny them is to deny the will of the creator. Monks, said Zara Yaqob, will be tempted by fornication, ascetics by wealth, hermits by company. His god was non-denominational, the god responsible for the natural laws and the natural beauty he witnessed from his cave.

The impact of Zara Yaqob's teaching derives in part from its coming from such a priestbound culture, one dependent on the disciplines of fasting and the example of monasticism. When the work appeared in Europe in the mid-nineteenth century, it struck a note of universality. It was translated into several languages. It represented 'a real contribution to the history of human thought' wrote Enno Littmann, its excited German editor. 'A man like Zara Yaqob gave utterance at the time of the Thirty Years' War to thoughts which became current in Europe at the time of Rationalism in literature.' That it was the work of a man from a far-off and ancient outpost of Christianity gave it added power.

Unfortunately it wasn't. The *Hatatas* of Zara Yaqob are, in all likelihood, the work of an Italian Jesuit, Giusto D'Urbino. He had learnt Ge'ez during a long mission to Ethiopia earlier in the nineteenth century. The length of the mission had also bred the profound scepticism about men of God. Enno Littmann revised his belief in its authenticity.

Yet the debate has continued. Doubters are accused of anti-Ethiopian prejudice. D'Urbino's Ge'ez, they are told, was not good enough to produce such polished prose. But then, research has uncovered a series of strange parallels between the lives of Zara Yaqob and D'Urbino (same birthday, D'Urbino's pre-ordination name was Jacobus, and many others). I have to say I favour the sceptics, although my first reading of the *Hatatas* was as a genuine text.

Perhaps it doesn't matter that much. It is a beautiful little story, full of refreshing wisdom and arresting truths. And in a way it *is* part of Ethiopia's legacy. Like Samuel Johnson's *Rasselas*, like the Letter of Prester John, like Coleridge's Abyssinian maid, like the cult of the Rastafarians, it reveals Ethiopia's perennial capacity to stimulate the mythical imagination.

The secret of its authenticity may be hidden in the text itself. Tagged onto the end of the *Hatatas* is the work of a pupil of Zara Yaqob's. In it he says: 'Believe nothing that is written in books, until thou searchest in them and findest them true.'

I walked out with Hiluf to Debra Damo's western cliffs. It was dusk. The sun raked across the flat ground. Yard-long shadows stretched from every stone. At the cliff-edge vervet monkeys scattered onto ledges. The bare rounded hills below rolled north like an ocean of frozen waves. Somewhere in there, two hostile lines were facing each other across the Eritrean border.

We hadn't noticed him at first. He was sitting on a boulder shielding his eyes from the sun. Hearing our approach, he turned to wave. He was dressed in white – white *gabbi* hooded over a white cap, white breeches. His hands, wrists and ankles were long and elegant. Though he was seated, I could see he was unusually tall (I remembered a very old Ethiopian monk I had once known in Jerusalem, equally tall, a man who did not know his age other than that when news came of the victory of Adwa in 1896, he had just learned to walk).

Tesfaye-Maryam had been here at Debra Damo for fifty-two years.

256

'Do you ever leave?' I asked.

He shook his head.

When I asked where he was from, he stretched a quill-like finger towards a cluster of huts in the valley below. His father was from there, and his grandfather.

'I am very bad.' He gave a self-deprecating smile. 'I have never been anywhere.'

'If you live up here,' I mused, 'perhaps there's no need.'

'No,' he said. 'If I was allowed another life I would go to all the places of God's earth. What better way to worship God than to look on all His works?' The late sun filled his face with a warm red glow.

Some way on, right at the edge of the cliff, we came across another monk. Gabre-Amlak was lying back against the half-globe of a boulder. One laceless shoe was propped on his knee. In the dim twilight he appeared to be perched on his own cloud.

For years he had served as chaplain to the armed forces. In the Ogaden, he had once witnessed a miracle. A man went to collect firewood and a Somali came and shot him dead. But the man's dog managed to take the gun in his mouth and fire at the Somali. The Somali ran off, the dog came back to camp and with the dog's help the Somali was captured. 'I saw that dog! I saw him carrying the gun in his teeth!'

But of all the things he'd witnessed in his life, the thing that had most impressed Gabre-Amlak was the Congo river. 'Such a river. So wide, so flat and so deep. Not like our rivers. You can stand by that river and watch it all your days.'

I carried on alone around the rim of the *amba*. When his work was done, when he had established the coenibitic law on Ethiopian soil, Abuna Aragawi stepped to the clifftop and vanished. A chapel marks the place. It was painted lime-green. I sat with my back against it and looked out over the cliff. Teklu had told me about Debra Damo that first afternoon in Addis Ababa. 'You have to climb up to it on a rope – it is like an island in the sky!' That image had grown with the passing years into something impossible and otherworldly. Now I was here, I found the image's work was done, and it too had vanished.

The light was failing. Colour was draining from the landscape but the sky to the west remained bright. Just below me a harrier was gliding back and forth along the cliff. Its wings were braced; the ends of the finger feathers flicked in the wind. It climbed high on the updraught and I could see the pale plumage beneath as it banked. Then it tucked in its wings and it was diving. I glimpsed its face as it passed, a fierce cluster of eyes and beak and then it was gone.

In the distance beyond, one or two lights flickered from the town of Bizet.

20

The dry season was drawing to a close. Aksum was less than a week away. We were resting at the foot of a pass when a farmer mentioned a village of Muslims some way to the south. It would mean a slight detour but in this sea of passionate Christianity, the idea of Muslim villages was pretty appealing.

Ethiopia was the first place to receive Muslims – seventeen of them. They were not proselytisers but refugees. It was the original *hejira*. Wearied by the persecutions of the ruling Quraysh, they were fleeing Mecca. It was Muhammad himself who suggested they seek refuge in Aksum. 'If you go to Habeshastan you will find a king under whom none are persecuted. It is a land of righteousness where God will give you relief from what you are suffering.'

The Quraysh were not pleased. They sent to Aksum an envoy of two men, one of whom was Amr ibn Al-ass (who was later converted to Islam and conquered Egypt in the name of the Prophet). They brought with them precious gifts of leather and told the Aksumites that the refugees were dangerous heretics. The Aksumite king refused to surrender them until he had heard their case. There then followed a scene, recorded in the *hadith*, which represents one of the most dramatic moments in early Islam: the first public defence of the faith.

The refugees went before the king. Lined up beside him were his clergy with their Christian holy books. He asked about their beliefs. It was Muhammad's cousin Ja'far who spoke: 'We used to worship images, eat the dead, commit lewdness, disregard the ties of our kin and the duties of neighbourhood and hospitality, until Muhammad arose as a prophet.'

The king then asked them for an example of Muhammad's teaching.

Ja'far recited from the nineteenth surah of the Koran. He chose well – it was the Surah of Mary, which tells how the Virgin received word that she was to give birth, and how she said it could not be so because she had 'neither been touched by any man nor ever been unchaste'.

When he heard this familiar story, it is said that the king wept with such abandon that his beard became damp with tears, and all the holy men beside him wept so that the tears fell into their open books, and the king addressed Amr ibn Al-ass of the Quraysh: 'If you were to offer me a mountain of gold, I would not give up these people.'

It is probable in fact that the king thought he was dealing with yet another group of persecuted Christians. Maybe they were like Montanists, or the *Sadqan*, the Nine Saints who had fled post-Chalcedonian persecutions. One biographer of the Prophet speculates that had he not found refuge in 622 in Medina, Muhammad himself would have fled to Aksum and Islam would have joined the roll-call of failed quasi-Christian sects. Or perhaps he would have won converts and Ethiopia have become the first Muslim state. Islamic traditions have it that the Aksumite king did secretly convert to Islam and is buried in the Tigrayan town of Negash – and his grave remains the holiest Muslim site in highland Ethiopia.

So the refugees were allowed to stay in Aksum. They returned to the Prophet in better times. As he lay dying, years later in the compound of the mosque at Medina, Muhammad was tended by some of those who had been in Aksum. When he fell into a fever one of the women administered a purgative. As soon as he tasted it, he cried out: 'Get out! This is a remedy for pleurisy, which she hath learned in Habeshastan!' He ordered all those in the room to take it too.

Then two of the women began talking of Aksum. They spoke of the great beauty of the cathedral, St Mary of Zion, and its walls covered in paintings.

'These are people,' fumed the dying Prophet, 'who, when a saint among them dies, build over his tomb a place of worship, and then adorn it with their pictures – in the eyes of the Lord, the worst part of all creation.'

He died the following day. Soon afterwards the Aksumites lost control of the Red Sea to his followers. The Christians were pushed up into the highlands where for a thousand years they pursued their beliefs in isolation.

'You will go over that mountain. After that you will walk some hours and you will see the houses of the Muslim people in the village of Mai Agam.'

On the slopes of the mountain we came across a madman. He was half-crouched in the dust, naked but for the rags of a shirt. His eyes burned through the dust-mask of his face. When he saw us, he ran off into the scrub and sat twitching beneath a euphorbia, toying with his genitals.

At the pass, a group of villagers was resting after the climb. 'Yes, that man lives on the mountain.'

'How does he survive?'

'They leave food for him, the people of that village.'

'One day wild animals will take him,' said another.

'*Wai-wai* . . .'

The villagers had been in Enticcio, collecting grain on a food-for-work scheme.

'But your mules are unladen,' I said.

'There was no grain!'

One of the women leaned towards me. 'A man told us we must come to Enticcio in two days. We all went to Enticcio and the man said, What are you doing? I told you to come tomorrow.'

'So now we are going back home.'

'We must go to Enticcio tomorrow!'

We carried on up to another ridge. Crossing it we were again looking down on central Tigray. Clouds were swelling from Gheralta, dragging streaks of rain across the low ground. In the late afternoon we saw the village of Mai Agam spread out below, a tongue of land sticking out above two gorges.

Mai Agam was little different from any other Tigrayan village. The Tigrinya they spoke was the same; the houses were arranged in the same way; the same combination of beasts and crops filled their days. But one or two things marked out the Muslims of Mai Agam. The men wore calf-length *jellabiyehs*, the minaret of a mosque rose on the skyline and everyone was very friendly.

Crossing the fields down into the village, several women

came out to greet us. 'Where are you from? Oh – come and talk with us!'

'Stay in our house!'

'No – stay in ours! Stay with us.'

'No – our house!'

There was quite an argument. We reached a Solomonic solution. Tsegaye and his brother and the mules spent the night in one house, Hiluf and I in another.

At dusk three elderly men stepped in over the threshold. Each of them laid his stick on the floor, greeted us and sat on the bed. A woman was shaking a coffee pan over the fire. A hen and four yellow chicks hopped in and began to peck at the mud floor.

'What are the origins of the village?' I asked.

'What?'

'We don't know.'

'It's no good asking us.'

'We're not educated.'

'Why do you want to know?' the owner of the house asked. 'Why does it matter?'

'I'm interested.'

'Look – we live, we pray. It's enough.' He looked at me calmly. 'That history talk is for town people.'

He stood and crossed the room. He knelt down, pushed his head into a tin chest and pulled out a prayer-rug. He lined it up and bent over it. On the rug was a fuzzy image of Mecca.

The hen and her chicks gathered around the edge of the rug and as he prayed they pecked fleas from the arches of the Great Mosque and from behind the Ka'aba.

'Now I know.' The old man beside me had a thin grey beard. 'Today I suddenly thought of him, after all that time!'

'Who?'

'The Italian, the one that came sixty-eight years ago. He had a pistol. I was thinking, Why did it come back, this Italian, why today? Now I know. It was because you were coming.'

In the morning, we walked up to the mosque. Its rocket of a minaret thrust up into the morning sky. A vast building was spread out at its base. Beside the mosque was a small, freshly daubed hut. It had a brand-new corrugated iron roof and new paint, but it was still just a hut. A fort-like wall ran around it.

'Who lives in that hut?' We were taking off our boots on the steps of the mosque.

'No one lives there.'

'It's empty.'

'Sometimes we put tools in it.'

'They just came and did it!'

We entered the mosque. Two rows of slender columns ran down towards the *mihrab*. As if shy of so much space, the few men there had tucked themselves away in a corner. The early sun came through the windows and the shape of their arches stretched out across the carpets.

'Look at that glass. What use is glass? This is a rural area. We need iron bars to keep out thieves.'

The mosque had come about like this. A few years ago a team of men turned up in Mai Agam. The men were experts and arrived with machines. They said: We have come to build a mosque. They stayed a long time and when they left, there was a very big mosque.

'They also restored that hut. Then they went back to him.'

'Who?'

'Al-Ahmoudi. They had to build another place. A school.'

'No – it was a big shop.'

Al-Ahmoudi is Ethiopia's richest man. He is the man behind the Sheraton hotel in Addis Ababa, a small town of Arab glitz. It has ballrooms, pastry-halls, chalets with private pools and a singing fountain – all discreetly walled off from the shanty around it. Al-Ahmoudi's father is from Qatar, but his mother is Ethiopian – from here in fact, from Mai Agam. In her name, Al-Ahmoudi had despatched a team to build the mosque and to enshrine the hut where she was born.

'How many can pray here?' I asked.

The men were eating, squatting one knee up around a bowl of bread.

'About two hundred,' said one.

'Two hundred?' scoffed another. 'More like two thousand.'

Two thousand looked closer to the mark.

Silently a cat pushed forward. As we looked around, it started to nibble at the bread.

'Away!' The man gave the cat a good swipe and it bounded off down the colonnade.

'And how many people live here?'

'In Mai Agam? We are thirty-seven families.'

21

Outside the mosque of Al-Ahmoudi's mother, we laced up our boots and pushed along below the ridge. Acacia scrub bristled against a gentian sky. We were now only a few days short of Adwa, and the road seemed ours: the labour of the journey was done.

We were moving back into rebel country. This tangle of valleys and mountains between Nebolet and Adwa has always been restive. In the fourteenth century, in order to avoid yet another revolt, King Amda Seyon eradicated the local chiefs and appointed in their place a number of gelada baboons. In 1896, as Menelik's vast and hungry army marched towards the decisive clash at Adwa, an Italian hostage recorded constant shooting from the heights. The people, he was told, were unwilling for 'the soldiers of the Negus to requisition supplies'.

The path ahead was pale and dry; its shingle scuffed beneath our feet. Stars of aloe burst beside us. In the hot mid-morning we fell into step with a woman on a donkey, slumped in the saddle. Her son, no more than eleven or twelve, was taking her to the clinic.

'Chest,' he said. He held one steadying hand on her back. On his own chest was a T-shirt with a grinning face and the legend HAYALOM – 20th CENTURY HERO.

They dropped behind us, and we could hear the woman's dry coughs.

'Who is this Hayalom, Hiluf?'

'Hayalom? You don't know Hayalom? One of the great TPLF fighters!'

'Did he fight here?'

'Here – and everywhere!'

Son of a noble Tigrayan family, Hayalom Araya became the TPLF's Scarlet Pimpernel. He joined the movement early, having chucked in his schooling when he had the chance. As a truculent and disruptive pupil, he was perfectly qualified as a rebel. He soon became famous for his swift and brazen raids. Such was his reputation that the strategists of the Derg despaired. Hayalom, they said, he is like a cloud – he appears in a clear sky, he throws us thunder and lightning, then he vanishes. It was Hayalom perhaps more than anyone who gave the TPLF the mystique vital for any outgunned guerrilla movement, the capacity to be both invisible and omnipresent.

Hayalom commanded one of the greatest sorties of the war. He led an attack on the northern edge of Makelle, the Tigrayan capital. It was a Derg stronghold and had a huge concentration of forces. But the attack was a feint. With the Derg engaged on one side, a small group of Hayalom's men sauntered into Makelle on the other side, broke into the main jail and freed twelve hundred prisoners. Many of them were rebel fighters. The re-addition of them to the front was significant. But the real success of the raid was in the mythology it earned the TPLF. In markets and churches throughout the province, and through the conscript ranks of the Derg, news of it spread: The TPLF can appear out of nowhere!

Once, said Hiluf, Hayalom was eating in a restaurant in Makelle. Sitting at a table in one corner were some Derg officers. Hayalom called the waiter: 'Who are those men?'

'Mengistu's top generals!' he whispered. 'They have come north to plan a new offensive!'

'In which case,' Hayalom handed over some banknotes, 'please let me pay for their dinner.' Signing his name, Hayalom then left.

*   *   *

We were in a deep valley. The bottom of the valley was flat but on each side the slopes rose to a line of high cliffs. It was evening and we were walking in shadow. A dry wind blew down the slope. The dust in the wind was blinding. We wrapped scarves around our mouths and noses and kept our heads down. But the wind made the mules nervous. Twice they bolted and we all had to lunge off into the scrub to catch them.

There was a place where the valley met another. Each of the valleys had its own wind and where they joined was a single thatched hut and a corrugated iron fence. The fence was rattling. Over the top of it peered a man's face and the barrel of an automatic rifle. 'Come in!' he smiled.

Beside the hut was a low building that had once been a schoolroom. The wind came slicing through its wattle walls. We fed the mules and rolled out our bedding in the schoolroom. We joined the man outside his hut.

Tekiste-Berhan had fluffy, white-edged hair. His pink striped shirt, buttoned to the neck, bore the sharp creases of the iron. He lived here on his own. He had a family, he said, and waved his hand up towards the plateau. But he preferred to spend his time down here, tending his bees. Each of his movements was calm and unhurried. He was as monkish as any of the monks I had met en route – except he had a gun.

'I know about the English.' He peered at me in the half-darkness. 'Their faces look like meat.'

Under the emperor, Tekiste-Berhan worked in the municipality. When the revolution came he joined the militia and defended this land against the Derg. But there was little need. During their seventeen years in power, Mengistu's forces never reached this valley.

Tekiste-Berhan had two sons. They had both joined the rebels. With pride he listed the places they had fought – Enticcio, Abi Addi, Makelle . . . They had both been killed.

'Why do you think the rebels won?' I asked.

He straightened his back. 'They were disciplined.' The sound of the wind rose and fell in the darkness. 'Also they were fighting for their own land.'

'Did you know Hayalom?'

'Hayalom? Hayalom came here once but I did not know him. You must talk to Berhan Gide.'

In the morning the wind had dropped. Tekiste-Berhan stood in front of his fence. His AK47 was over his shoulder; a different pressed shirt was buttoned up to his neck. He stretched an arm up the valley. The sun had just caught the top of the cliff.

'Your road goes up there. Just where that shadow is – that is where you must climb.'

We found Berhan Gide at the mill. He stepped out of a low, whirring shed. His eyebrows were dusty with flour and his hands powder white. He looked like an ex-boxer. He had a hero's head and a powerful body, but with the slight sag of muscle turning to fat. He washed and put on a green field-jacket and we sat in a *chai-bet*. The walls were painted red to waist height and sky-blue above; the blue was dotted with mosquito spatters.

Berhan was a soft-spoken man, with a quiet charm, and his story came easily. 'At the beginning I was just a farmer. I had a wife. I had four children. I ploughed my land.'

One day, shortly after the fall of Haile Selassie, the Derg

271

came to his village. They gathered the men and told them a Muslim army had invaded and that they must come and fight for their land. It was the Raza operation. Berhan went. But when he realised the Derg had tricked him, and he was fighting against his own people, he deserted and joined the rebels. As the movement grew, so did his dedication. 'I divorced my wife. I had to free her. Being the wife of a fighter was dangerous.'

His first operation was in the town of Nebolet. They defeated the Derg garrison and captured three hundred soldiers. That attack was led by Hayalom.

'He was like a brother to me – an older brother. He loved me. He gave me my clothes, my cartridge belt. He gave me this jacket. We were always together.'

He too listed the places they had fought – Bizet, Enticcio, Diudibor, Makelle. 'We were always victorious. When Hayalom was in an attack, everyone knew it would succeed.'

'What did he look like?' I asked.

'You know, he actually looked quite funny.' Berhan wrapped his large hands around the tea glass. 'He was quite small and had a big nose and a long moustache like a cat. He was always smiling. He wore tight shorts and button-up gaiters and just plastic sandals.'

For Berhan, his association with Hayalom helped elevate him in the movement. But in the mid-1980s he laid down his gun and joined the administration in Hawzien. When the war was over, he made a decision. 'I could have gone on in politics. I could have gone to Addis and had a good position. But I stayed.'

'Why?'

He shrugged. 'I was tired, and Addis sounded like a bad place. So I trained as a carpenter.'

Two years ago he had lost interest in carpentry and returned to the land. In thirty years his life had gone full circle.

'I am just a farmer again. I have a new wife, I have more children. I plough my fields.'

Berhan called over a boy and whispered to him. Two minutes later the boy returned with a woman. Mentewab was thin and anxious-looking. She too had been a fighter; she too had been close to Hayalom. 'He was my best friend. He believed in me and so I was brave. I believed in God and I believed in Hayalom.'

Mentewab scratched the back of her hand and looked out through the open door. 'I have problems now with hypertension. It is since he died.'

Hayalom survived the war, but not the peace. He moved to Addis when the Derg fell. One evening he was drinking with

friends in a bar. An argument broke out with a car salesman. The man left the bar and Hayalom carried on talking with his friends, but the man reappeared with a gun and shot Hayalom dead.

It was mid-morning. Tsegaye and his brother were sleeping in the shade of the mill; the mules were grazing the bank above. We carried on, following the rim of a vast, terrace-striped basin. We were heading for Adwa, where Ethiopia's long tradition of obscurity reached its climax.

22

The run-up to the battle of Adwa was a tantalising business. Like others before and since, the Italians were driven mad by the Ethiopian genius for ambiguity.

'Never, probably, in the history of the world,' writes G.F.H. Berkeley in *The Campaign of Adowa*, 'has there been so curious an instance of a commander successfully concealing the numbers of his army, and masking his advance behind a complete network of insinuation, false information and circumstantial deceptions.'

Rumour swilled back and forth through the Italian camp. Emperor Menelik's forces were thirty thousand strong, fifty thousand, eighty thousand ... A ship was unloading a million cartridges for them at Massawa ... The Italians' own local allies were all duplicitous spies ... Armenians were brokering secret deals ... Russians were training gunners ... Menelik's camp was in revolt. He had been struck by lightning. He had lost the power of speech. He was dead.

By the end of January 1896 Menelik and his army were

moving steadily through these valleys. The Italian scouts now had a clear view of their strength: more than one hundred thousand – six times the Italian force.

But being a good colonialist, General Oreste Baratieri was convinced of the superiority of his European-trained troops. He knew too that the size of the Ethiopian army presented Menelik with its own problems. One witness gave a picture of the Ethiopians' locust-like progress:

> Every trace of vegetation vanished under those hundreds of thousands of feet . . . A few thousands of individuals whom I saw were cutting furiously with their swords at the branches of trees; others with small hoes were toiling patiently at the stems of large plants in order to make their levelling more easy; others were cutting grass; others carrying stones; others clearing away little plants. It was a continuous noise caused by branches being torn off and thrown away; a continuous deafening sound of beating. All were working – it was for the Negus.

Baratieri was right. Menelik's immediate concern was simply feeding his army. Any local food surpluses would soon be exhausted. Once in position, he could not afford to wait long for battle. Yet in such terrain, whoever attacked first would be at a great disadvantage. Neither commander could afford to retreat. The prelude began to take on the form of a rather coy courtship: each side was desperate to engage, but neither would make the first move.

February 1896 was a month of waiting. Menelik took up position at the foot of the Adwa mountains. A herd of cattle driven from distant Harar eased the hunger for a while. But in every church that he could, Menelik bowed his vast imperial head into his imperial chest. He beseeched God and St George, Mary and the Kidane Mehret to make the *farenjis* attack.

The saints began their work. On 25 February, a telegram arrived in the Italian camp. It was from Signor Crispi, the prime minister in Rome. He accused Baratieri of inaction. 'This is a military phthisis not a war . . . we are ready for any sacrifice in order to save the honour of the army and the prestige of the monarchy.'

Eighteen miles now separated the two armies.

We were climbing. The path followed a dry stream, a torrent of boulders checked in their downward tumble. Everything was angles, chaotic planes of rock and dust. Tsegaye and his brother zig-zagged the mules up the narrow ravine. I hauled myself over the bank. Sweat on my cheeks and neck drew a cloud of flies; my legs were ripped by thorn. The path disappeared.

A gap in the trees exposed a tiny plot cut from the forest. It was bordered with a brake of scrub, and along one side by a lone house-sized boulder. Neat ranks of peppers and beans grew there. The soil was hoed into corrugations and was so fine and so free of stones it looked almost artificial. I stopped, and marvelled. High above was the rainbow flash of a priest's umbrella: among the rocks a group of men had gathered for a burial.

The slope flattened. Now water ran between grassy banks and high acacias. The mules brushed its surface with their muzzles and drank.

'WOMEN?' A voice came through the trees.

'No women!'

Upstream a man stood naked in a pool, washing.

We left the valley and climbed a slope of bare limestone. The mules' hooves scraped on the rock. Then we were on top again and far below was the valley of Feres Mai. Above it, in the mid-morning light, as if seen through clear water, rose a line of thrusting peaks.

'The mountains of Adwa,' said Hiluf.

For several hours as we walked, clouds thickened over the peaks and by late afternoon they were sweeping the slopes with broomlike showers.

Each afternoon, following the delivery of Crispi's telegram, General Baratieri watched clouds gather around the mountains. Each evening he listened to distant thunder, and each evening he was rewarded. At nine o'clock came the first tap-tap of rain, rising to a constant hiss on the canvas of his tent.

Another day when he could ignore Crispi's orders and hold the attack! Another day when Menelik's men needed feeding!

But his own supplies were also running low. On 28 February he called his marshals together and put the proposal before them: they should pull back.

Photographs of the Italian generals show a set of proud and determined faces. These were men perched on the very summit of earthly life, the height to which all evolution rose. Their uniforms were clipped, their gaze level, and each was blessed with a splendid moustache. Baratieri himself had one a good inch and a half deep. Major-General Dabormida's had a sharp sloping upper edge; it was gondola-shaped, with a tiny curl at each end. Arimondi's was a broad cocked hat while Albertone's, curled at the end, covered his mouth like the eaves of an Alpine hut.

Dabormida responded first. 'Retire? Never!'

Albertone also advocated an attack, saying the Ethiopians were vulnerable. Arimondi agreed.

'The council is full of spirit,' observed Baratieri, 'the enemy is brave and despises death; how is the morale of our soldiers?'

'Excellent,' replied his generals.

Baratieri was still looking for a way out. He dismissed the men, saying: 'I am expecting further information from spies, who ought to arrive from the enemy camp.'

What happened in the next twenty-four hours to change Baratieri's mind is not clear. But Ethiopians point to the role of Awalom (a name oddly similar to Hayalom).

Awalom was a sutler. The Italian advance had brought him a ready market for his eggs, chickens and grain. And now there was another source of income. Baratieri himself had offered Awalom a fee of two hundred thalers if he would go to Menelik's camp and report back on its strength and readiness.

Awalom crossed the ridges between the armies. Once in the Ethiopian camp, he reported at once to Ras Mengesha. 'I have been asked to spy by the *farenjis*.'

Mengesha took him to Menelik. Their plan was the obvious one: they would send Awalom back saying that the Ethiopian force was hopelessly scattered, foraging. Menelik in turn offered Awalom a fee for his work. Ethiopian sources record the instinctive loyalty of this man, who refused any fee and pledged his fee from Baratieri to Menelik's war chest.

So on the afternoon of 29 February, with Awalom's devastating intelligence, the consensus of his generals, and the chiding of his prime minister, Baratieri announced the decision to advance. Even then perhaps he hoped for a reprieve. He set the departure time for 9 p.m. – the hour that on previous nights the rain had begun to fall. Clouds had already massed around the heights. But that evening, they dispersed.

At 9 p.m. the first Italian troops left Enticcio. Smoking was prohibited and they marched through the darkness in silence.

At dusk we approached a tobacco-coloured homestead. An old man was asleep outside on a bare bed-frame. One of his arms flopped down towards the dust, and a boy was tickling his feet with a reed.

'Ff ... ff-FUH ...' the old man stirred and made a noise like a sneeze, but did not wake.

The boy tickled some more.

'Ay ... Ay-ayy! ... RASCAL!'

The boy ran off. The old man rubbed his eyes and spat on the ground. Then he spotted us.

'Who's this?'

We told him.

He grunted and pulled a brown blanket around his shoulders and led us beneath the arch and into his yard. The mules' hooves chinked on the stone threshold. With the bags taken off, they rolled in the dust. Bahata sat on a rock and watched them. Above his head a bottle of holy water hung against the wall. He was grunting and muttering. I set up the cooker and chopped up the last of our onions.

Later Bahata's mood improved, and he began to talk. He had been a judge in the emperor's time. 'I was a judge – a PEOPLE'S judge!' He had the habit of repeating his statements with booming emphasis. 'But the Dergie came and put me in prison – in PRISON! They took me to Adwa and I was there for many months. Then they took me to another place.'

Strangers were rare in Bahata's home, and one reminiscence led to another. He recalled the Italians coming for the second time, under Mussolini. 'One of those officers picked me up. He kissed me. KISSED me! My parents watched him and said, Oh-oh – he is going to take that boy away – they will take him to their country! But I am still here – STILL here.'

He was chuckling when he unbolted the heavy wooden door and we all stepped out into the moonlight to piss. We fanned out to different spots in the scrub. I stood facing the dark parabola of Mount Semayata. A thousand stars silvered the sky above it. The air was rustling, expectant. Hyenas cackled in the distance. It was our last night before Aksum.

Dawn was the familiar exchange of distant cock-crows, the sniffing of the mules outside our tent and the sun rising behind a mountainous skyline.

Bahata showed us the road. 'You will go down into a valley. You will see a school. You will cross the valley and on the far side see the church of Abba Garima. ABBA GARIMA!'

1 March 1896 was a Sunday and the monthly feast of St George. At dawn, Menelik and Empress Taytu and members of the nobility were in church. A messenger pulled back the curtain and entered the *qene mahalet*. Spotting the emperor, he threw himself in the dust before him: The *farenjis* have attacked!

Menelik dismissed the man. He signalled to Abuna Matteos to continue. He and the empress took communion. They kissed the Abuna's cross. Outside the guns could already be heard. It was a sound, reported the Ethiopian chronicle, like 'the rain of Hamle [July/ August] which falls without stopping'.

The Ethiopian commanders took up their positions. King Tekla Haymanot led his twelve thousand on the right. Ras Alula and Ras Mengesha Yohannis went off to engage the enemy's advance guard. Emperor Menelik and Wagshum Gwangul and the imperial guard were on the hill of Abba Garima.

Empress Taytu meanwhile gathered twelve thousand women from the camp and sent them off to the river with water pitchers. They were to spread out among the troops. Then under a black umbrella she joined her own troops on the slopes of Mount Latsat. With her were Abuna Matteos, the Nereid of Aksum, her eunuch artillery commander, and the carved figure of Mary. Each of them, in their own way, prepared for the Italian assault.

Baratieri's plan was to keep the advantage by drawing an Ethiopian attack. He had ordered his generals to assemble their forces on a series of hills to the east of Adwa. They would still be seven or eight miles short of the Ethiopian positions. But Baratieri knew that once they were spotted, the Ethiopian troops would demand an advance – taking them across difficult, open country.

What decides the outcome of a battle? A million little things, or one big thing? As a historical fact, the victory at Adwa has become part of the pattern of ages. It is a natural extension of that fierce sense of Ethiopian nationhood, of dogged and chauvinistic belief, of a people able to use the natural fortress of their mountains to repel foreigners. But as a battle, a period of twenty-four hours, a series of muddled engagements, it looks less certain. Like most battles it was as much lost by one side as won by the other. And by one mistake above all.

On his left flank, Baratieri had placed Albertone with four native battalions, the staff of the 1st Battery Brigade and the 1st, 2nd, 3rd and 4th Batteries. They were to take up position on the western slopes of the hill of Kidane Mehret. Through the night of 29 February they made good progress. By dawn on 1 March, the advance guard was in place. To their right General Arimondi's brigade was due to arrive on the slopes of Mount Belah. Dabormida was on the right flank and Baratieri himself was with the reserve behind the hills.

But Arimondi had been delayed, and in his absence Albertone became nervous. Consultation with his guides revealed to Albertone that he was actually *not* on the hill of Kidane Mehret. The real Kidane Mehret was some six miles forward. Albertone ordered his men on, and managed to cover the gap. By 5.45 a.m. his advance units were in position again.

For a country in thrall to the cult of Mary, it is appropriate that Ethiopia's greatest-ever victory can be attributed to the Kidane Mehret, Mary's covenant of mercy. According to

Baratieri's orders, Albertone *had* in fact been on the correct hill. It was just that it wasn't called Kidane Mehret. The Italian maps were faulty.

So before the battle had even begun, Albertone was isolated, and right at the gates of the Ethiopian camp. He came under immediate attack from the forces of King Tekla Haymanot, Ras Mikhael and Ras Mengesha. They were soon joined by the Harari forces of Ras Makonnen.

Albertone had placed his men in a rough cruciform. From the centre his batteries began to shell the advancing Ethiopian line. He sent two despatches to Baratieri, each couched in polite reserve. His 1st Battalion was engaged in fierce fighting,

the enemy was approaching in great numbers. He would be pleased to receive reinforcements and grateful if Dabormida on the right could create some sort of diversion. The sun had not yet risen behind the mountains and the heliograph was inoperable. A messenger hurried back across the gorge-cut ground.

The Ethiopians pushed towards them in a long arc. The Italians held their formation. Albertone himself was seen jumping from his horse to embrace the battery captains. Rifle volleys and artillery punctured the Ethiopian advance. The Ethiopians stalled, then started to fall back.

So horrified was Menelik by this initial defeat that he was

said to have favoured a general retreat. It was Empress Taytu who urged them back. 'Courage! Victory is ours!' Unable to refuse a woman, the Ethiopians turned back to face the enemy.

The next Ethiopian assault was much larger. Albertone continued to defend his position. He ordered his reserve, the 8th Battalion, to advance and relieve the batteries. '*Savoia! Savoia!*' they shouted (the cry of their regimental kin when they breached the defences of Rome in 1870 and ensured Italy's unification). The shout encouraged the embattled 7th Battalion. For a moment the Ethiopians were held. Thunderous rifle-fire drove them back. But the Ethiopians could not be turned a second time. They advanced again. At 10.30 Albertone called the retreat. He ordered his batteries to remain behind, 'sacrificing themselves' to cover the withdrawal. Two of the units were Sicilian. For an hour they continued firing until the Ethiopians overran the guns. Out of 130 Sicilians only seven escaped. Albertone himself was captured.

With the left flank destroyed, the Ethiopians managed to engage the centre. On the right, Major-General Dabormida's brigade was soon cut off. Yet of all the Italian forces, it was Dabormida's who had the greatest success. Through a narrow gorge he reached an open valley. High yellow grass covered the valley floor and in the middle stood a single *ficus* tree. On the left were the cliffs around Adi Segala. The Ethiopian camp was still a long way away.

It was 9 a.m., twelve hours after they had left Enticcio, and the Italians stopped for breakfast. General Dabormida was standing talking to some of his officers when one of them was hit in the elbow by a stray round, and from that moment on the fighting was continuous.

Dabormida was known as a brilliant commander. He had the courage and the sense of theatre to carry his men. All morning they held their positions against superior numbers. Shortly after midday he launched an attack. The bugles sounded. He himself rode out in front of his line. *'Savoia! Savoia!'* cried his men. *'Viva il nostro Generale!'*

The first Ethiopians fled. A second bayonet charge and they abandoned their weapons. They ran for the slopes.

'Vittoria! Vittoria! Viva il Re!'

One Captain Menarini recalled that victory: 'Sublime moments which it will never be given to any man to describe true to life – at the memory of which the eyes become dim and the heart beats more rapidly.'

They were hoping for reinforcements to consolidate their advance. Instead Menarini's servant grabbed him by the arm. He pointed *behind* them. 'Sir, here come the enemy!'

It was now clear just how exposed they ·were. Nothing had been heard from Baratieri all day. Captain Menarini gave a picture of Dabormida a little later that afternoon: 'I seem still to see our general walking up and down near the sycamore tree ... he seems preoccupied and nervous ... And in truth we felt that we were approaching *the beginning of the end.*' Even so, Dabormida said: 'I want to try one last general attack.' Again he rode out in front of his men, waving his helmet, leading the charge. Again the Ethiopians were driven back – but this time Dabormida knew their position was untenable. The ground they had gained simply afforded them space to fall back.

Retreat is as intricate a manoeuvre as advance, and Dabormida gave his orders carefully. He rode some way up out of the valley to command Major Rayneri to hold the heights. After that, it is not clear what happened to Dabormida. Months later his brother visited the battlefield and claimed to have discovered his corpse. An old woman said that a *farenj* had asked her for water: 'a chief, a great man, with the spectacles, and the watch and the golden star'.

Several years later in Addis Ababa, a British vice-consul, Augustus Wylde, met an Ethiopian fighter who said that he had seen Dabormida in the midst of the fighting. The Italian general was surrounded. He shot three men with his revolver, then turned to shoot this fighter. He missed, and turned to face some others. The man stood behind a tree and shot the general in the back.

None of those Italian major-generals who had encouraged the attack escaped the battlefield. The reluctant Baratieri survived, and retreated with his remaining forces to Enticcio and then to Asmara.

Azmaris were quick to celebrate the victory:

The corn of Italy that was sown in Tigray
Has been reaped by Abba Dagno* – and he has given it to
    the birds!

I took the last orange from my bag. Hiluf and the others were busy in a *tella bet*. I was on a rock. My boots hung over a low cliff. I pierced the peel with my knife and gave it two quick circumnavigations. The peel came away in quarters. I inserted my thumb in the crown and pulled it in half.

Spread out below were the valleys of the Adwa battlefield – sloping plots and contour-terraces, and the late-morning heat rising from them. If the Italians had reached these fertile valleys first, Menelik's army would have run out of supplies. He

* Dagno was Menelik's 'horse-name'.

would have had to retreat to Abi Addi – and now they'd be speaking Italian in Addis, Ethiopia's gorges would be crossed by elegant bridge-spans and Rome would be full of Ethiopian restaurants. (Or not. Italy was a brand-new state and would have been even more stretched occupying Ethiopia in 1896 than it was in 1936.) As it was, victory sealed Ethiopia yet again, froze its spectacular traditions and earned it another glorious century of isolation.

Just below me a pair of oxen waded through dry pools of soil. The ploughman raised the whip in a brief question-mark and – *craa-ack!* – flicked it over their backs. Far across the valley, a matchbox bus trailed a cloud of dust.

Above it all were the peaks, ancient plugs of magma rising high into the cloudless morning. Griffon vultures spun around their tops. The cliffs were steep and muscled. For hundreds of miles in every direction the earth's surface was raised and buckled into these shapes, then sliced open by seasonal torrents. Nothing better defines the stubborn resistance of the Ethiopians than this broken landscape, these peaks and the tabletop *ambas*. Countless generations have fought on their slopes, hidden in their folds, sown their thinning soil, while those too aware of the world's ceaseless sham lie on their rocky tops contemplating the blue infinity of the sky.

I pulled on my hat. I followed the path around the side of the hill. From the bushes ahead came a metallic *thud-thud*. A road-team was throwing rocks into the back of a truck. Beyond them, far below, I could see the shape of an unfinished road. Yard by yard it came into view. Tippings of soil and rock lay on its rolled surface. I studied its incline, its long modulated curve, its embankments and cuttings. After so long on rough paths, I found its sculpted form thrilling.

The others caught up. We dropped down into Adwa.

We pressed on past the Almeda textile factory and the marble works with its giant dice of white rock. Hiluf was nearing home, but showed no particular eagerness.

There was one more climb. The path took the steep route. It sliced off the corners of the road which had folded itself into coils for the hillside. At the top it straightened out, tapering into the hazy afternoon light, across the plain towards Aksum.

A stall at the summit sold sorghum *tella* and we sat drinking it on the polished roots of a *mirkie* tree. They were building a church, a mud-walled basilica rising inside a frame of timber scaffolding. A collection tin for it stood on the road, with a scarf-wrapped image of the Virgin and Child propped beside it.

We could hear the low groans of trucks as they laboured up the hill. The columns of black exhaust were visible long before the trucks, which cleared the lip of the road at walking pace, then gear-shifted up for the plain. Behind them, on the skyline, were the thumb-shaped peaks of Adwa.

An elderly man left the *tella bet* with us. He emptied his beaker and spat out the husks. He was seventy-six. He was going to visit his cousin in a village near Aksum. His cousin was close to death. He had fought against the Italians, been imprisoned by the Derg and was now dying.

'So much disturbance in this short life,' the man said.

He had long, eager strides. The road didn't move an inch from the straight. As we drew level with the airport, the tarmac began (the first of the whole walk) and we stepped up onto it. The mules were far behind. At a right-angle to the road, the airport's single runway stretched into the distance. A plane was visible at the far end, afloat on a watery grey shimmer.

'Wait,' I said.

We stood with the old man and looked down the runway. It was hard to tell if the plane was moving. But then its fuselage began to bounce in and out of the shimmer. It took a long time to reach us. For the first time, we heard it. Its whine increased as it drew nearer, rising in pitch. We could see the pilot's head behind the screen. Still it remained on the runway, its wheels flexing as they raced towards us. With a roar, it lifted off and cleared the fence. It rushed over our heads. The old man ducked. He straightened up at once, laughed, and let out a long *'Fwheeeeee!'* of joy.

The Crown of King Kaleb

Best-known of all Aksum's antiquities is the collection of granite funerary obelisks. The rulers of Aksum liked to have these columns erected over their graves. As Aksumite power grew, so the columns became higher. The highest one of all stood at about one hundred feet and is thought to have been the largest monolithic structure of the ancient world. It is known as Stele No. 1, but scholars believe that it stood for no more than a few seconds before toppling to the ground, where it now lies. Shortly after this the monarchy became Christian.

The Aksumite empire reached its zenith with the rule of King Kaleb. In the sixth century, he and his vassals controlled land from the banks of the Nile to the Red Sea and beyond. In his four-towered palace stood bronze statues of unicorns. No other Aksumite ruler had such power. His empire was matched only by those of Byzantium and Persia. When word reached him of the persecution of Christians in Himyar in Yemen, he raised an army and drove out the king and spread his rule deep into Arabia.

King Kaleb of Aksum appeared in public on a mobile dais drawn by four elephants. His head-dress was of gold and linen, and it had ribbons of gold. He wore a collar of gold, and bracelets and armlets of gold and a kilt of gold, and across his chest were leather straps studded with pearls. He was guarded by armed members of his own nobility and attended by flute-players and other musicians.

In the year 540, King Kaleb gave up his throne. He sent his crown to Jerusalem to hang over the door of Christ's tomb in the church of the Holy Sepulchre. He left Aksum for a monastery where, a century and a half earlier, Abba Pantelowen had prayed for forty-five years without once sitting down. The monastery is on a steep-sided, cone-shaped hill near the city's airport. In a cell on its narrow summit the great King Kaleb saw out the remainder of his earthly days.

On the edge of Aksum now is Kaleb's tomb. It is said that if you lick a blade of grass and push it through a certain crack in the ashlar and then remove it very gently, you will find on the end of the grass a tiny, perfect pearl.

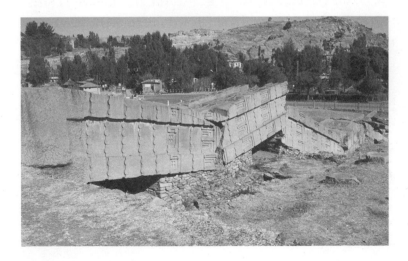

Epilogue

In Aksum, I booked into the Africa Hotel. I paid off Tsegaye and his brother and went with Hiluf to see his wife and seven-month-old daughter. They lived in one room around a courtyard of other single rooms. His wife was squatting by a brazier; the baby was sleeping on the bed. The greetings were warm and simple. Hiluf sat on a stool and undid his boots. A neighbour looked around the door. He began a conversation with Hiluf about a mutual friend, as if Hiluf had just popped out for a couple of hours.

Later that evening I was sitting alone in the bar of the Africa Hotel. A television was showing the news in one corner. Groups of people were scattered among the tables in twos or threes. A barefoot girl was selling nuts. I drank a bottle of Dashen beer. I ate some nuts. I looked at the people and the television. I read and wrote some notes but all the time I was aware of a strange feeling welling inside me. It was a sense of dislocation so intense that before long I couldn't remember how I had got here, or where I was. All power of recall vanished.

When I tried to speak to the waitress, scraps of Tigrinya and Amharic merged with Russian and Armenian. It left behind it a faint nausea. I went to bed, slept nine hours and threw open the shutters. The sun was up. In the courtyard below was a small green square of fruit trees. Firefinches twittered and flitted among the leaves, and a single fat papaya sagged from its stalk.

That morning I wandered around Aksum, and took in its sights. I saw the street-icon of Hayalom, with his carefree grin, and his binoculars and his shorts and gaiters. I paused outside the old Commercial Bank of Ethiopia, scene of the TPLF's first operation. They had only twelve members then, a few old guns and hardly a cent to their name. But they managed to rob the bank. They bundled the cash into grain sacks, loaded them onto donkeys and whipped them back to the hills. There they opened the sacks and found notes worth a total of $82,000.

In the Stele Park, I squinted up at the funerary obelisks. I saw the snake-back form of Stele No. 1, lying in pieces. I descended into the Tomb of the False Door. I blinked in the darkness of the old St Mary of Zion church. I peered through railings at a monk yawning like a caged lion; he was guarding the entrance to the Chapel of the Tablets, in which was housed the Ark of the Covenant.

At midday I left the museum stillness of the town and strode up into the hills. Cattle stumbled among the rocks and above the distant roofs of Aksum was a cloud of black kites. Beneath an acacia I lay back on my folded-up hat. I put my hands behind my head, gazed at the sky and listened to the wind in the leaves.

We'd been lucky. The walk had been lucky. All the things that might have gone wrong hadn't – illness, injury, security. I thought of the luck I'd had in 1982 and how different my life would have been without it. Perhaps it wasn't luck at all. Little was going right for me when I first entered that small circle of Ethiopia enthusiasts. David Hamilton had spent years in Ethiopia under the emperor. His Brixton house was full of Ethiopian maps and pictures and artefacts. Others had told me I was mad to try to go. David was the one who convinced me otherwise. 'You'll never regret it. You *must* go.' It was the beginning of a friendship that grew with my own involvement in the country. David passed me on to Richard Pankhurst, doyen of Ethiopian letters, who was seeing out the worst years of the Derg in an office at the Royal Asiatic Society. He filled my bag with letters for his friends in Addis. 'Do what you can for him,' he wrote. 'Perhaps we have an Ethiopiast of the future?' One of those letters was for Dr Mengesha, and without his *coup de main*, and without Teklu, I would have been on a plane home within days. Then I ran out of money. I was ready to go to Lake Tana but was down to my last £50. Richard's contact list produced Innes Marshall, a vibrant and elderly Scot who'd lived in Ethiopia for years. 'Don't you worry!' she said, pulling out a brick of one-*birr* banknotes. 'You'll need the wee notes for the villages. Pay me back when you're able!' (A year and a half later I deposited £157 into an Edinburgh bank account.)

Each of them, in different ways, lived for the country, believed in its people and loved it as a world in itself. What they saw in me, I now realise, was a rare chance to share that love in the dark days of the Derg. And now where are they? Richard is in Addis, back in his cherished Institute of Ethiopian Studies, continuing to map out the lesser-known territories of the country's history. Innes saw the Derg defeated but died in Addis soon afterwards. David was brutally murdered in London. Dr Mengesha was murdered in Ethiopia. Teklu, born and brought up just a few miles from where I lay, was selling bourbon in a Denver store. And once again I was overcome by the sensations of those initial weeks with him in Addis, the pungent intensity of its streets, the insidious fear, the ecstatic worship, the deep green of its rain-damp hills – the first full shock of Ethiopia.

The following day was the monthly feast of St Mary. I left the Africa Hotel at dawn and met Hiluf on the corner. We set off together for the new church of St Mary of Zion.

'How is it being back?' I asked. 'Good?'

'It's fine.' He was smiling his all-solving smile, but I sensed that he too already missed the open road.

Shreds of mist hung in the eucalyptus. Hundreds of hooded figures were converging on the church, emerging like spectres from the core of the night. Inside people were sitting and dozing, or muttering their own prayers. A priest was fingering his beard and grinning at the floor. A woman, her face veiled, stepped among the refugee bodies as if looking for a missing child. It was one of those moments in Ethiopian services when the whole assembly drifts in a leaderless confusion, when you wonder what it is that draws so many to these sacred chambers.

Then, from the far side, came a deep thud, and every head in that church responded to it with a tiny magnetic movement. It was the first boom of the *kebbero*.